Abuses in the Religious Life
and the Path to Healing

Dom Dysmas de Lassus

Abuses in the Religious Life and the Path to Healing

SOPHIA INSTITUTE PRESS
Manchester, New Hampshire

Contents

Foreword

Now that people have begun to feel able to speak more freely about the question of sexual abuse, instances of spiritual abuse in monastic and religious communities have also come to light. The founding of new communities, or a desire among members of older religious orders to return to a more authentic form of life, has sometimes given rise to unacceptable behavior on the part of superiors or founders. In some cases, this has come about as a result of psychological imbalances in these individuals, but in other cases whole communities are finding themselves in alarming situations, which seem to arise when basic generosity encounters a lack of wisdom. Men and women who had given themselves to God with all the loving enthusiasm of youth have sometimes taken a good number of years to become fully aware of the grip in which they were held and to free themselves from it, most often by leaving their community. The journey of personal, psychological, and spiritual rebuilding is, sadly, a long and painful one.

Rooted in the long tradition of monasticism and in a solid theology of the religious life, Dom Dysmas de Lassus, the Prior of the Grande Chartreuse (and thereby superior general of the Carthusian Order), proposes in this book some diagnostic tools that allow us to assess the potential dangers that can arise from certain spiritual practices or particular ways of governing communities. At the same time, he also gives a very positive account of the sort of balanced approach that leads to growth — both for individual persons and for the community as a whole — all within the boundaries of a proper respect for the human person and the great Catholic tradition. We can only be grateful that such an exceptional book as this has been published. That a Carthusian has chosen to speak

Abuses in the Religious Life and the Path to Healing

out is a rare thing in itself. But in speaking out, Dom Dysmas does not seek to lecture anyone. On the contrary, he recognizes that all religious communities (whether new or old) can encounter tendencies that are aberrant or excessive. Indeed, rooted in the experience of the older religious orders, he teaches us about the proper respect for balance that allows communities to guard against such tendencies. To prevent the discussion from having a flavor that might be too exclusively Carthusian (with the very particular character of that vocation), Dom Dysmas has been careful to ask the advice of an abbot and an abbess living in the Benedictine tradition, as well as of some Dominican theologians, all of whom he has involved in the editing of the text. This fraternal dialogue only serves to underline the authority of what he has to say, since it is not merely the opinion of one person, or of a single tradition.

This book will be of great assistance to various audiences. In the first place, it is addressed to those experiencing any kind of abuse, to try to help them to perceive the reality of the situations in which they find themselves, and to call out the dysfunction that keeps them imprisoned. But in another way, it is addressed to all members of communities, and especially to those holding any sort of position of responsibility, to help them be aware of the various forms of dysfunctionality that can arise in community life, and of the essential elements of balance. It may also serve as a valuable point of reference for canonical or apostolic visitations, allowing the visitors to refer to a reliable text that is the fruit of mature reflection, and upon which communities will be able to continue to reflect after a visitation is concluded.

It may be that some within the Church will feel somewhat weary at the prospect of a text such as this, which seeks to shed light on those dysfunctionalities that fortunately, serious though they are, nevertheless remain fairly rare. Do we really have to air in public, yet again, the worst sorts of pathological behavior, or the most senseless aberrations, instead of spotlighting healthy communities? I think that Dom Dysmas has preemptively addressed this possible criticism, for two reasons.

On the one hand, as must always be the case going forward, a priority has to be given to the voice of victims, to listening carefully to all that they have to say, no matter how difficult it may be to hear, and however great the "damage" that their story might seem to do to the image we may once have had of this or that person who, up until that point, may even have been considered a point of reference for the spiritual or religious life. Publishing this book is one way — not just for the author, but for the whole Church — to say to the victims of spiritual abuse or other aberrant behaviors that they have been heard and taken seriously. They have all too often had to endure long periods characterized by denial or rejection on the part of the very Church authorities in whom they had tried to confide.

But there is also another dimension — an ecclesial dimension — that makes this speaking out necessary. For when one member of the body is sick, the whole body suffers. To all those religious men and women who belong to communities unaffected by these various forms of aberrant behavior, the Carthusian prior — despite the distance from which he himself observes the world — asserts that "nobody can react with indifference if young people, who had placed their trust in the Church and in religious life, have their trust and their whole life destroyed. By the same token, even if we ourselves have not played an active part in this tragedy, we must nevertheless endeavor to bring healing, show sympathy and build up."

To use an image dear to the author, this book has come at precisely the right moment if it is to serve to strengthen the "immune system" of the Church and of its various religious communities, so that these can remain vigilant in seeking to prevent the various forms of aberrant behavior that are always a possibility in our life. In the lucid way in which he seeks to confront this tragedy, he offers us the opportunity to reflect deeply and clearly on the whole question of the religious life.

+Msgr. José Rodriguez Carballo
Secretary of the Congregation for Institutes of
Consecrated Life and Societies of Apostolic Life

Preface

This book is not a work written in isolation. It has arisen out of meetings with a number of people who have suffered abuse in the context of the religious life, and from a series of exchanges that took place over four years. The essential core of the book is the fruit of these exchanges. I thank these people for the trust they have placed in me, and for their support for this work. Their testimonies, generally taken from these private conversations, are quoted anonymously with no attribution; I did not consider it helpful to create aliases. Whenever a quotation is not referenced, it means that it is taken from a testimony.

This book was also born of two years' work on the question of cult-like aberrant behavior in communities.[1] These years provided opportunities for

[1]   Translator's note: *Dérives sectaires* is a term that frustratingly defies easy and consistent translation into English. Recent French law, designed to combat *dérives sectaires* seems to recognize that many groups espousing problematic and extreme ideologies appear to arise from more mainstream, uncontroversial movements (we might think of Islamic extremist groups that, on one level, emerged from mainstream Islam, or some post-Christian sects in the United States, which seem to have emerged from more mainstream Christian churches). The law is intended to punish and discourage problematic behaviors, not individuals adhering to a particular group. The government agency responsible for monitoring these *dérives* (known by the acronym MIVILUDES) defines *dérives sectaires* as "a movement away from the freedom of thought, opinion, or religion that undermines public order, laws or regulations, fundamental rights, security, or the integrity of persons. It is characterized by the use — by an organized group or by an isolated individual, whatever its nature or activity — of pressures or techniques aimed at creating, maintaining, or exploiting in a person a state of psychological

encounters and exchanges that helped broaden our understanding of the question; in a particular way, these exchanges brought to our attention evidence of a surprising congruity of symptoms arising in very different contexts.

I thank those who have accompanied this process of reflection and have contributed to it, perhaps especially Fr. Pavel Syssoev, O.P., but also many others who prefer to remain "behind the scenes."

I thank Msgr. José Rodriguez Carballo, who supported this project as soon as he came to know of it, as well as all those who have supported it ever since the first version was circulated.

I thank most especially Fr. Jean-Marie Gueullette, O.P., whose challenging observations forced me to go deeper in my reflections on the question, and in my attempts to put these reflections into words. The quality of the text owes much to him.

In the Carthusian order, it is customary not to put one's own name to a publication, but to ascribe it simply to *A Carthusian.* I felt, however, that the particular nature of this text called for this custom to be suspended. The subject matter is too serious for my thoughts upon it to remain anonymous; the reader has a right to know who is speaking.

I set about writing this book, first and foremost, out of compassion toward those who have suffered (and who continue to suffer).

May God grant that it may be useful, at least to some people.

Fr. Dysmas de Lassus
Prior of the Grande Chartreuse

---

or physical subjection, depriving them to some degree of their free will, with harmful consequences for the person in question, those associated with them, or for society in general." Thus the term describes the slide into cult- or sect-like behavior. As there is no term in English that is precisely equivalent, this term (and the word *dérive*) are translated by different words on a case by case basis, in order to convey the appropriate sense.

Translator's Acknowledgments

It has been a real pleasure to have the opportunity to read and engage with Dom Dysmas de Lassus's book *Risques et dérives de la vie religieuse* in a close way. It is an important work that has much to offer to the endeavor of promoting healthy and fruitful religious life in today's Church, and in particular to allow religious communities (and the Church at large) to recognize signs of the abusive behavior that is so inimical to the gospel. I am most grateful for his patient and helpful clarifications of a number of passages in the French text.

In translating the text, every effort has been made to adhere as closely as possible to the French original, while at the same time seeking to produce a translation that is faithful to English idioms and modes of expression.

In this work, I have been greatly helped by the invaluable contributions of several of my Benedictine brothers and sisters, whose painstaking reading of the original manuscript and careful comments and suggestions have helped both to eliminate infelicitous renderings and to improve the readability of the translated text. For this assistance — together with the time and intellectual energy that went into it — I am more grateful than I can express. It goes without saying that any remaining errors are my own responsibility, and for these, I ask the reader's pardon and patience.

Yorkshire, March 21, 2023
Solemnity of the Passing of St. Benedict

Abuses in the Religious Life
and the Path to Healing

Introduction

At the end of a speech concerning fifteen diseases that can beset the life of the Roman Curia, Pope Francis wrote:

> I read once that priests are like planes: they only make the news when they crash, even though so many of them are in the air. Many people criticize them, and few pray for them. It is a very poignant, but also very true saying, because it points to the importance and the fragility of our priestly service, and how much damage a single priest who "crashes" can do to the whole body of the Church.[2]

We could apply these words to religious life. Every sort of life with others — the life of the family, of school, business, local community, country, and so on — has its ups and downs. But there is something particularly painful about the failures of religious communities, because in their case the proverb applies: *corruptio optimi pessima*.[3] Communities should help their members find inner freedom in self-giving, love, service, and the fullness of the Spirit; so how is it possible that sometimes the very opposite effect is produced, and they end up offering

---

[2] Francis, Discourse to the Roman Curia, Monday December 22, 2014. http://www.vatican.va/content/francesco/en/speeches/2014/december/documents/papa-francesco_20141222_curia-romana.html.

[3] "The corruption of what is best is the worst corruption of all." In other words, a great good, if it is corrupted, becomes a great evil. Someone with positive qualities will be able to do a lot of good. But if he or she is corrupted, the evil done will be on the same scale as the good that was done previously.

death instead of life? Posing this question is not intended to be subversive, nor does it seek to harm religious life in any way; on the contrary, the intention is rather to protect it from the risks that threaten it.

Plane crashes shock us because of the great loss of life involved, but flying has, for a long time, been a much safer method of transport than driving a car. Traveling one thousand kilometers in a car presents forty-five times as many fatal hazards as traveling the same distance in an airplane. A plane crash seems more dramatic to us, but while remembering the 346 people who died when flight DC-10 crashed at Ermenonville, we should not forget the 13,000 people who died on the roads during that same year. And yet everyone still drives. Air travel has a better track record because each serious accident is followed by a detailed and costly inquiry, so that the precise cause of the accident may be determined with as much certainty as possible. As a result, measures can be devised to ensure that a similar accident does not happen again in the future.

We could say the same about the "accidents" that occur in religious life. The following pages will show that these are no different from the typical accidents that occur in any life lived with others, but they are all the more shocking because they happen among those who profess to follow the gospel way of life. This serves to highlight the contradiction at work here and may invest these "accidents" with more significance. Like air travel, religious life is an extreme case. Professed religious seek to go to the very limits of self-giving, which brings with it a greater risk of going beyond those same limits. Hence, we need to study the accidents that have occurred, so that we can put in place the necessary preventative measures. Have we taken the trouble to study what can cause the religious life to fail and go adrift? The literature on this subject thus far is rather meager, no doubt because people find it hard to imagine that the religious life could present any sort of risk. Still, the question of the various abuses that can arise in religious life has at last come to the surface, no doubt as a result of the issue of sexual abuse. In France, the assemblies of the Monastic Conference of France on this subject, held in 2016 and 2017, represent an indisputable turning point. Since that time, it has been possible to tackle the question openly. The present volume seeks to contribute something to the work of analyzing and preventing these issues by placing ourselves as close as we can to the reality of community life, because a clearly identified risk is far less dangerous than a hidden one. One tragic example of the consequences that can arise if we are tempted to downplay the importance of such questions may help us understand precisely what is at stake.

Ermenonville, March 3, 1974

A Turkish Airlines flight *en route* from Istanbul to London crashes in the forest of Ermenonville, after a stopover at Paris: 346 deaths, no survivors, the most serious air accident ever to take place on French soil. The DC-10 hit the ground at 700 km/h, the aircraft was smashed to smithereens, the passengers unidentifiable. And yet, this was a crash that should never have happened.

It was easy to identify the cause: the cargo door broke away in mid-flight. This flaw had been known about for years. It was even highlighted when the plane was first produced. Less than a year after it first entered into service, the accident the engineers had predicted was only narrowly avoided: the door was torn off, seriously damaging the plane, and it was only thanks to the skill of the pilot that it landed safely. Since there were no victims, the manufacturer of the plane preferred not to acknowledge the extent of the danger, so managing to avoid incurring the usual penalties for such things, and promised to take the necessary action, but in fact only got half-way through. In the end, what allowed the catastrophe to occur was a lie: someone had indicated in the plane's maintenance log that the necessary modifications had been made to the door, but this was not, in fact, the case. This cover-up of the danger ended up being exposed in the most tragic way.

The company that manufactured the plane, and had previously sought to protect its image, now suffered the full consequences of its irresponsibility. Under the weight of the legal trial and the financial penalties associated with it, it collapsed, finally ceasing to exist in 1997.

Seeking Out the Causes

In our own day, the recent revelation that religious life has gone off the rails far too often is playing the same role as did the crash at Ermenonville. It is no longer possible to ignore the dangers presented in the religious life by practices that are either lacking in prudence or are, frankly, deviant. The mental and spiritual lives of real people are at stake. Shouldn't there be the same sort of official report as the one made by those air-safety experts? Must there be a certain number of victims before a known fault in an aircraft is put right? Given that money seems to come before all else, nothing seems to change so long as there are no victims,[4] though, admittedly, in the religious life, it is usually reputation, not money, that is the fundamental criterion.

Today, the solution is gradually appearing due to careful analysis of the situation. We have to get down to the causes of the aberrations we have encountered, to try to understand flawed processes, the risks that may be found, the limits which must not be exceeded, the safety measures we need to put in place, the type of formation that must be guaranteed, any community rules and regulations that need to be put in place or just made more effective.

It may be that looking at questions like these will unsettle some people. But if such scrutiny contributes to the business of making the religious life safer, to the business of avoiding various forms of abuse, then, in the long term, the image of the religious life should end up being enhanced, even if only as a result of having had a good, clear look, from within, at the way religious life itself operates.

In the course of this work, extraordinary patterns came to light. The same processes were seen to be at work in quite different contexts: new communities as well as traditional communities, sometimes communities belonging to large orders, forms of consecrated life, movements — all of the variants of Catholic religious life — were liable to succumb to the same sickness. Outside of Catholicism, the little book *Spiritual Abuse* by Jacques Poujol paints an identical picture in a very different environment, since religious life is largely unknown in Protestantism, and the book is concerned with churches (in the Protestant sense) and parishes.[5] The film *Controlling Behavior and Spiritual Abuse* by Anne and Jean-Claude Duret presents cases emerging from new, non-Christian religious movements.[6] One employee of a large international bank has said that all

---

[4] Boeing hasn't done much better than Douglas; see the story of American Airlines Flight 811. This goes to show that the refusal to face up to risk is quite widespread.

[5] J. Poujol, *Abus spirituel, S'affranchir de l'emprise*, (Paris: Empreinte temps présent, 2015).

[6] J.-C. and A. Duret, *Emprise et abus spirituel*, 52, JCD Production/KTO 2018. Available at www.jcdproductions.fr.

of the problems we have singled out can be found in that professional context too. They are surely also to be found in other large structures, such as political parties. Much independent work carried out in very different environments is coming to the same conclusion. Surprising as it may seem at first, this observation immediately forces us to broaden our scope. The dysfunctionalities that are the subject of this book are not peculiar to the religious life; they are the manifestations of a more fundamental dysfunctionality that exists in human nature itself, which is related to the exercise of leadership.[7] This English word has been chosen deliberately, as it does not quite overlap with the notion of "authority" in French.[8] The *leader* is someone who seems born to lead, someone possessed of personal qualities that draw people along, gather people together, qualities that are a source of fascination. These qualities can make the person possessed of them a great commander, so long as they are held together with other qualities that will make up for the *leader's* natural weaknesses. Such a person can just as easily become capable of exploiting people, if he or she has a significantly egocentric personality, for example.

A Particular Form of Sickness

It turns out, then, that the different forms of controlling behavior and spiritual abuse are not so very different when they crop up in religious life. What is particular about them comes from the tools used, the very tools the religious life places in their hands. Respect for authority, sanctified by vow; the desire for union between all members of the community, the unity that is the legacy of Jesus' Paschal mystery, [as expressed by Him in the Last Discourse, see John 17:21]; the descriptions of union with God in terms of spiritual espousal, so often found in the great mystics; humility, sacrifice, renunciation, conversion, poverty: all of these different dimensions of religious life can be hijacked and diverted from their proper goal, to be put instead at the service of a sickness that has more than a passing resemblance to cancer. Cancer, of course, is not a degenerative disease but, rather, a case of "life" losing control, in a disordered process of multiplication, which ends up as something toxic. "How can these

---

[7] Translator's note: The word *leadership* is in English in the original text.
[8] *Autorité.*

fundamental aspects of religious life become toxic?" That question could sum up the guiding principle underlying these pages.

To this question about the nature of the sickness, we must add another concerning its intensity. Not so long ago, one Christian organization sought to formulate a definition of "sect/cult," to make it easier to detect these groups more effectively. But the definition they came up with gave rise to some dangers since, if used with ill will, it might also have encompassed religious life, especially the life of cloistered religious. Thinking about the nature of things alone is not enough. The difference between an evening breeze, a strong wind, and a cyclone does not arise from the elements that are at play (it is all a question of moving air) but from differences in intensity. Sailors, who need to be able to measure the strength of the wind, have established a scale. The strength of the wind is given a number between one and ten, and every sailor needs to know what his boat (and the competence of his crew) can withstand. When looking at sects and cult-like behavior, this principle has often failed to receive sufficient emphasis. The aim has been to discover the characteristics that *per se* make a group a sect or a cult. But the phenomenon of the sect also makes use of dynamics that, up to a certain point, are perfectly normal and healthy but that begin to be dangerous when their intensity goes beyond certain limits. The absence of any idea of the scale involved makes it very difficult to assess a sectarian tendency, especially since the community in question may well insist that all of the means being used are quite traditional. Perhaps we need a scale that would allow us to distinguish a harmless wind from a storm, rather than a simple definition of what it means to be a sect or a cult.

Vulnerabilities

The extent of the danger is also dependent on the robustness of the system in question; this is not always understood. An experiment conducted by Milgram is directly relevant to the question of aberrant behavior. Milgram sought to investigate the influence of authority on experimental subjects, so he came up with an experiment involving three people: the subject of the experiment; a student who had been supposed to have learned lists of words; and a scientist, who was in charge of the experiment. The subject had to ask the student to recall words; if the student made a mistake, the subject delivered increasingly powerful electric shocks to the student, up to 450 volts, a level clearly indicated as dangerous. Upward of 150 volts, the student would begin to scream and beg to be released. Now, in fact, the student was an actor and was not actually experiencing any electric shocks, but the subject did not know this. Psychologists and psychiatrists who were consulted prior to the experiment ventured that only one subject in a thousand tested (in other words, almost nobody) would turn the voltage up to the full 450 volts. And yet, under the influence of the scientist in charge of the experiment, who demonstrated a certain firmness and self-assurance and simply asked the subject to continue when he or she began to be concerned, 62.5 percent of those who acted as subjects went up to 450 volts. In a modified version of the experiment where there was no scientist present, no subject went up to 450 volts. The results of this experiment are worrying, since they show that if a person is sure of himself, and is invested with the recognized symbols of authority (a white coat, in the case of the scientist), then he can have considerable influence over another person, influence that far exceeds what we might have imagined, influence that can even cause the other person to carry out acts he knows to be wrong but that he believes he has to do because the authority figure is telling him to do so.

This experiment took place in the 1960s, an era when authority was generally more respected than it is today. But if we examine the influence of "political correctness" in our own day (which is merely one kind of uniformity of thought, imposed by a moral authority by debatable means), then we can take no comfort from that: men and women are as susceptible to being influenced today as they ever were, and the mechanism of the abuse of authority has shown its devastating power in the tragic instances of sexual abuse that have occurred. The high value placed upon obedience in religious life makes it especially vulnerable to spiritual abuse, which is less visible and therefore more difficult to detect.

The Immune System

It turns out, then, that it is essential to have some sort of protection against these phenomena; indeed, it is all the more necessary given that, over recent decades, it has become clear that very few of the new communities have managed to avoid these different types of dysfunctionality. We may well ask what has gone wrong, particularly since, as recently as only a few years ago, these very communities were held up as the future of the Church. Known for their fervor, they stand out because of their great fruitfulness and because they are so dynamic, with a capacity for exploring all manner of new opportunities; why, then, have they shown themselves to be so vulnerable to these problems?

Living creatures are constantly being subjected to attack, and they owe their very survival to a defensive system — the immune system — which has the task of identifying and eliminating elements that are dangerous or that cause concern. Human societies also have a form of immune system, which has both preventative and repressive functions, without which these same societies give way to anarchy and the survival of the fittest. Religious life has all the more need of such an immune system, since the elevated goal it proposes makes it all the more susceptible to any number of attacks coming from ambition, a lack of prudence, jealousy, a taste for power, and so on. In cases where significant failures have occurred, what was lacking most often was simply discretion, in the monastic sense of the term.[9] The monastic tradition has always held discretion in high regard, since temptation, disguised as something good, finds exceedingly fertile ground in a way of life that strives for excellence.

Treasure in Earthen Vessels

Anyone who hopes this book will call religious life *per se* into question has completely misunderstood what it is about. It has been written by religious men and women who are very conscious of all they have received from the consecrated life, and who desire only to contribute something that will help it to regain all its proper beauty (perhaps particularly in those areas where it was most at risk of losing that beauty), and to make available to everyone those tools that will enable crashes to be avoided (or, at the very least, serve to minimize their consequences).

All of this emerged, it is true, out of a deep sadness for the suffering of those men and women who had heard the call of God, who had desired (in the vigor of their youth) to give their whole life to Him, making use of the age-old wisdom of religious life, and who were betrayed. Led along dangerous paths,

---

[9]   In the monastic literature, "discretion" signifies the measure suggested by a wisdom that is born of experience. The opposite would be excess.

they have fallen badly, their wings broken, leaving them with an image of God now seriously disfigured. Wounded to a more or less serious extent, they have had to spend years putting themselves back together and not always with success. Scars that remain beyond healing after decades; the suffering of meeting with accusations of malice and with attempts at cover-up from those holding positions of responsibility within the community, and being met, on the part of the Church, with silence, incomprehension, or (what is even more painful) a refusal to see and an attempt to stifle any hint of scandal: none of this can be ignored. We all understand the long fight of the victims of child sexual abuse to have the seriousness of their situation recognized officially. The victims of the religious life also encounter real difficulties in making themselves heard because their suffering is more difficult to detect. It is this harrowing sadness that has triggered the writing of this book, so that a better understanding of the dangers (and of the worldly wisdom that will allow them to be avoided) might contribute to reducing the number of these tragic failures.

Spiritual combat, which is an essential dimension of the religious life, is something we cannot afford to restrict to the personal level only. We know that good and evil are at war within us and that this war will continue until our death. Communities are not exempt from this combat or these falls from grace, since they carry *treasure in earthen vessels* (2 Cor. 4:7). Here, at the community level, the consequences of the evil that dwells within us can also be felt, and these are a constant threat to the beauty that is the ideal to which communities aspire.

To promote an awareness of the risks and sources of abuse; to go to any length to build up or establish an "immune system" that will protect people and communities; to draw what is needful from the accumulated wisdom of centuries of tradition in the religious life, so as to ensure that a demanding school of holiness and love never turns into a kind of slavery of mind and spirit: such were the intentions behind this work.

We would also hope that those who are victims of bad judgment, or of the poor exercise of proper responsibility, will feel that, in the end, their suffering will not have been entirely in vain if it has been able to contribute something to the business of making sure that others do not have to walk the same dark paths that they themselves have had to tread. But we have, also, the responsibility of not allowing ourselves to be satisfied with a compassion that, though sincere, is basically sterile. The dual challenge to those in positions of responsibility can be summarized in two words: "transparency" and "courage." Armed with these principles, those in such positions will be able to make the necessary decisions, difficult though these might be. It is the very credibility of religious life that is at stake.

TRANSPARENCY
COURAGE

1

Passionate Love
Between wisdom and madness

Going to the Full

Going to the full. Couldn't we portray the deepest desire of the religious life like this? Going to the full with our love, with the gift of ourselves for "Him who loved us to the end" (John 13:1).[10] Going with Him to the Cross, to death, to glory too. Going to the full, following the example of the saints, who sometimes seem so uninhibited by what is "reasonable." This is a beautiful idea; it is captivating, and nobody will ever be able to take it away from the religious life. Whatever we might say about it, in all its very different forms, the beating heart of the religious life is to be found precisely here: in rendering love for love. Faced with the limitless immensity of divine love, the heart's desire is to give itself completely.

Such an attitude hardly leads to sagacity but, rather, to madness. There is always the risk that what is prudent will seem too timid, too careful, too human to the young, fired up as they are with enthusiasm. When presented with an idea that is all-encompassing, absolute, uncluttered by subtleties, they tend to gush with enthusiasm and charge forward with great energy. But if the person guiding them lacks discretion, alas, we can foresee that they may end up spinning off the road.

On the other hand, a culture of zero risk would strip the religious life of all its vitality by causing religious to be focused on themselves and their own safety. Can we imagine a totally risk-free mountaineering expedition? Better take the cable car!

[10] This passage was directly translated from the French to maintain original emphasis.

Abuses in the Religious Life and the Path to Healing

How can we set about preserving the vitality and even the seeming madness of love, without this becoming destructive? The various different traditions of religious life that have endured across the centuries have been able to find a proper approach to this risk; they have developed a certain wisdom and a coherent body of doctrine that have been codified in the various rules that exist. At the time of the Second Vatican Council, some forms of this sort of wisdom were criticized for being too archaic and rigid and so were set aside. But after several decades of experience, it is clear that, while this wisdom was certainly in need of some serious purification, abandoning it has, in fact, taken us in the opposite direction from the goal we were aiming at. We see this particularly in the rejection of the letter of the law for the sake of the freedom of the Spirit. The intention was generous: to give the gospel once more all the space it needed, with a greater fidelity to Jesus. But we failed to ensure that the various necessary safeguards were in place. The law that was shown the door came back in through the window, in the shape of seemingly all-powerful authority figures, whose every word was revelation, as if it had been inspired directly by the Spirit. Or at least that is what we were told.

Guiding and channeling the vitality of the religious life without snuffing it out will always be something of a challenge. Should there be a limit to our love for God? No, as St. Bernard says: "How much love should we offer to God? A measureless amount!"[11] On the other hand, there *are* limits to our human nature, to our physical strength, to our health, to our psychological makeup, and it is here that the risks are to be found: love has no limits — no one will ever love too much — but the various tools designed to help our love blossom *do* have limits, and if we go beyond these, then these very tools may end up leading to death rather than life.

From these remarks a first important conclusion can be drawn: love has no limits because it is divine, but expressions of love *do* have limits because they are human.

---

[11] "The reason for loving God is God himself; and the measure of how much love we should offer him is to love him without measure!" Bernard of Clairvaux, *On Loving God (De diligendo Deo)*, Source Chrétiennes (Paris: Éd. du Cerf, 1993), 1, 16, and 22.

A simple example will help us to understand this point. A young man can show his love for his girlfriend by buying her flowers for her birthday. But would this love be better expressed if he were to buy her a whole truckload of flowers, which she would obviously not know what to do with? Or again, would he have expressed it better if he had chosen a bouquet of the rarest flowers at exorbitant cost, so that he was later unable to give her any other presents because he no longer had the money? In these two cases, the means of showing love has been mistaken for the end, but love is not measured by the size or price of gifts. Dostoevsky puts it very well in *The Idiot*. Rogozhin, the merchant, can't stop himself from telling Nastasya how much the presents he bought her cost him in sacks of flour, and this completely destroys the charm of the gift for her. Anyone who loves has to accept that no physical things will ever be able to express his love adequately; such things can only ever be a sign. If the love is real, it will remain forever and will take on the nature of infinity itself. What is infinite cannot be measured.

In the same way, our love for God can be expressed by various types of sacrifice — fasting, for example. But a religious will never be able to intensify his fasting so that it keeps pace with his growing love for God, since here, too, he will run into two constraints: the number of days in the week, and his body's need for food.

So while it is always possible for our love to increase, the same is not true of the ways we show our love. These will always fall short, and the one who loves will always feel some regret about that, but this will diminish over time, since the deeper the love grows, the easier it becomes to sum it up in a few simple words: "I love you, and I am certain of your love, and that is enough for me." With a few necessary adjustments, the same thing could be said of all the virtues — humility, poverty, and so on — and of all the various dimensions of the spiritual life that bind us to God.

The Concepts of Limitation and Risk

The concept of risk is normally linked to the concept of limitation. The sailor who wants to win the race tries to take advantage of the wind, insofar as his boat's limitations allow. If he goes too far, if he doesn't know how to gauge the strength of the wind, if he doesn't have a perfect grasp both of his own limits and those of the boat, he runs the risk of capsizing. We should add: if he is not meticulously prepared, if he has not checked the boat over carefully, he runs the risk of destroying it. Because he wants to give his all, which means pushing things close to the acceptable limit, he must take great care over the preparations for the voyage and display great wisdom in the way he approaches the race. Of course, the simple vacationer who wants to do a bit of windsurfing a few hundred meters from the shore doesn't need to take as many precautions.

Risk is an integral part of human life. Every human relationship implies risk, particularly at the beginning. To eliminate risk would be to eliminate trust, friendship, love, devotion, every situation where we are looking for a response from someone else — a response we can never be certain of, since the person making it is, like us, a free human being. Simone Weil considers risk, as well as security, to be one of the most essential needs of the human soul.

> Risk is a vital need for the soul. The absence of risk produces a sort of boredom that paralyzes, not in the same way as fear does, but almost to the same extent. Moreover, there are situations that, since they involve a vague anxiety with no clearly defined risks, spread these two sources of unease simultaneously.
>
> Risk is a kind of danger that leads to a considered reaction; that is, it doesn't exceed the soul's capabilities so that it ends up being crushed by fear. In certain situations, it can involve taking a gamble. In other situations, when a definite obligation forces someone to confront it, it represents the most powerful of all stimulants.[12]

This can be shown to be just as true for trust and love too.

There Is Something Extreme about the Religious Life

Those who enter religious life should be aware that its extreme nature — the tendency to push things to the limit — entails the same kind of risks as those involved in any sort of sporting experience at the extreme end of the scale.

[12] Simone Weil, "Prélude à une déclaration des devoirs envers l'être humain, 9, *L'enracinement*, in *Œuvres complètes, t. V/2* (Paris: Gallimard, 2013), 137. An English edition is available: *The Need for Roots* (London: Routledge, 2002, 33ff.).

Candidates sometimes lack this awareness, which makes it even more crucial that those in positions of responsibility in the community should possess it.

Anyone who embarks on the religious life is seeking to give herself entirely to God; she is staking her whole life. She submits herself in confidence to another person (or to a number of other people) in order to enter into an experience as yet unknown to her. With respect to chastity and asceticism, for example, she is being drawn into dynamics that are very different to those at work in the world; the common life, lived in obedience, has its own particular laws. The interior work that needs to be done can be just as radical. One postulant said after six weeks: "This is like being cleaned with a pressure washer!" The image derived from his work: he had once been asked to clean some walls with such a washer. Indeed, it is true that an interior life uncovers what had lain hidden beneath the hustle and bustle of ordinary life. The fine line between what is normal and what is abnormal becomes difficult for young religious to discern, and they can end up submitting to the strangest things out of sheer generosity, if they are asked. If the formators are not prudent enough, or are unaware of the risks, more or less serious consequences can ensue. If they brazenly overstep the limits of the religious life, by demanding that their charges submit to them unconditionally and unthinkingly, then we are already on the downward spiral toward sect-like behavior.

To avoid making this sound overly dramatic, we need only observe that we can say the same thing about family life. The guidance given by parents is never perfect; of course, catastrophes are always possible, but we can hardly say that these are the norm. Now, religious life has an essential safeguard: the rule, which sets in place (or should set in place) the necessary limitations. Experience has shown, however, that disasters do happen, and we need to be aware of these.

Furthermore, it can be difficult to see that the extreme caution found in some provisions, though well intentioned, may actually end up destroying the vitality of religious life. Seeking to eliminate risks by levelling things down is like suggesting that the speed at *Le Mans* should be limited to 130 km/h. True, there may be no more crashes, but there won't be a race either.

No situation is risk-free, whether in family life, in the world of business, or in life more generally. Nevertheless, we cannot conclude from this that every sort of risk is normal; some are acceptable, whereas others are rash. We have to take risks with our eyes open and with a proper understanding of the situation.

Abuses in the Religious Life and the Path to Healing

Neither too much, nor too little. Religious life, then, walks along a sort of tightrope — at least if it is not to lose everything that gives it vitality and relish — but for all that, it must not put the religious themselves at risk.

Beyond the Proper Limits: Aberrations

Nobody can survive without such sustaining realities as joy, hope, love, pleasure, and so on. Anyone who is going through a difficult and tense situation at work will be able to bear it so long as, at home, there is an atmosphere of warmth and understanding, which allows all the built-up tension to be off-loaded. But if the situation at home is also tense, if there are no friends to confide in, in short, if there is no safety valve, then anyone in such a situation is going to crack, sooner or later.

Said by a Carthusian

Similarly, in a community that is for the most part healthy, a religious can put up with difficulties, like a cantankerous superior, for instance. With the help of his spiritual life, he will be able to see in this an opportunity to learn patience, self-giving, compassion toward those who are suffering most acutely. It is the very quality of spiritual and fraternal life that makes it possible to shoulder such burdens. But if the superior, in an attempt to shore up his authority, has put a stop to relationships between community members, and if he adds to this a culture of scapegoating, which undermines community life from the inside, then only those who have attained a considerable level of spiritual maturity will be able to bear these things by leaning on the love of God; others will suffer serious harm.

It is impossible, therefore, to single out one factor that causes community behavior to become aberrant; it is always a question of a number of different lines converging. Our discernment needs to take this into account.

Aberrant Behaviors

SECTS AND RELIGIOUS COMMUNITIES

A community can slide into functioning as a sect precisely because of the similarities between the life of a sect and that of a normal religious community (just as there are similarities between a dictatorship and a normal society). In both cases, we have a common life with a respected superior, an ideal that stands in sharp contrast to what is normal in the surrounding culture and thus requires a certain separation from it, an ideal that is attractive, a formation that seeks to involve the whole person, a desire for the radical, which makes us accept the harshness of the life or of formation, a renunciation of certain aspects of well-being, so as to discipline the body for the good of the spirit. This can include an element of poverty, with resources held in common. All these practices are neutral in themselves; it all depends on the way they are used.

In his book, *Les droits de l'homme dénaturé*, Gregor Puppinck gives us an interesting interpretive key:

> Nothing more closely resembles a supernatural deed than a deed that is against nature and yet, while the former will be a human act, the latter will be an inhuman one. The former aims for the greater good, the latter for its own power. We have to make a choice between these two different approaches each and every day, and the choice is often difficult. Adopting an orphan is a supernatural act, which proceeds from a great humanity, whereas voluntarily producing an orphan (by means of a surrogate pregnancy or *in vitro* fertilization) is against nature, and thus inhuman. Judges are wrong to permit surrogate pregnancies on the grounds that they seem to resemble adoption. There are two parallel ways we can go beyond humanity here, but there's only one way to be human. It is the same in every field.[13]

Interesting

Both the surgeon and the knife-wielding assassin use instruments that cause grave injury. The vast difference between these two comes both from intention (since one of these wants to save a life, while the other wants to kill) and from the way in which the instrument — dangerous in itself — is used. Sect-like communities, then, share many of the elements of a healthy community life, which makes it impossible to draw a clear boundary between the two at a merely descriptive level. We have to consider the goal of the life in question: is it to enslave, or to set free?

[13] Gregor Puppinck, *Les droits de l'homme dénaturé* (Paris: Éd. du Cerf, 2018). The quotation is taken from the conclusion, page 285. *Dénaturé* (unnatural) is in the singular because it refers to humankind and not to human rights.

Abuses in the Religious Life and the Path to Healing

A Short Description of Controlling Behavior[14]

The film *Control and Spiritual Abuse*, by Jean-Claude and Anne Duret, gives an excellent presentation of the phenomenon of controlling behavior. In the film, Mélanie, a former member of a spiritual movement from among the new religious groups, describes her journey, a human spiritual quest, which leads her to enter a group, where she is enthusiastically received: "I felt as though I was being welcomed like a VIP. I had the feeling of receiving an unusually warm welcome, which surprised me." In the course of her instruction, she comes to understand that *there is a master, and the master has the answer to everything; the master sees everything.* Her relationship with God, which had always been front and center in her life, became secondary. It was put to her that she was joining an elite group. After several years, once she was deeply committed, the time came when the master began to blow hot and cold. She began to be unsettled by public displays of trust on the one hand and unexpected public reprimands on the other. "I was scared on several occasions." Next came demands of a sexual nature. "One day, the doctor diagnosed me with cancer. I went to ask the master about the meaning of this cancer. From that point onward, it was suggested that I should come up with sexual scenarios, which might be one of the solutions. I accepted the first stages, even if they did violence to me, because I knew I was caught in a bind, and had no choice. I said to myself, 'If I accept this, maybe that will be the end of it, maybe he won't be angry, and I will escape worse things.' But in fact things got more and more intense." In this hellish situation, she became utterly exhausted. "I felt like one of the living dead, a feeling that slowly grew and grew. I couldn't take any more. I was exhausted. I didn't know who I was any more, I was losing everything." Then, one day, when faced with a new demand, she realized that the master simply wanted to turn her into a slave; something clicked, and she woke up and simply said no.

At the beginning, the group and the master were offering a sort of liberation, an opening onto something new. By the end, she recognized that the situation had become a real slavery, even at the level of her thoughts. "Little by little our

---

[14] Translator's note: The term used, *emprise*, has connotations of control as well as the exercise of influence and manipulation.

consciousness had to diminish: the gap between what was decreed for us and our own thinking was just too wide."

A similar dynamic can emerge in a Christian group, although normally it will take a more subtle form. A sort of seduction, a warm welcome, accompanied by excessive compliments, entry into a world where there is an answer for everything, a world that has chosen to be self-contained because it believes itself to be something special. Then, once the honeymoon period is over, stinging criticisms and a denial of everything that gives the person a sense of worth give rise to that little phrase one hears so often from people in this situation: "I don't know who I am anymore." All points of reference to normal life are lost, and life begins to be Hell, because nothing has meaning anymore.

Isabelle Chartier-Siben's Report

And yet, all the practices described above were presented as being traditional. Dr. Isabelle Chartier-Siben — a medical doctor, a psychotherapist, and an expert in dealing with victims — sheds some light on the process.[15]

Virtues That Have Been Diverted from Their True Meaning
Obedience, which should teach us how to love, can be used to enslave someone, even at the level of his thoughts, so that it becomes merely servile submissiveness, even when this is contrary to conscience and involves a person forsaking responsibility for his own actions, as well as any right to his own thoughts. Humility, which should lead us to appreciate the truth about ourselves, can lead instead to a destruction of legitimate self-esteem, which is so necessary in life. Self-giving, an essential motivation for a religious vocation, can be pushed to the point where it becomes a total denial of oneself; this is why people often speak of *psychological murder*.

Praise, so eminently positive a thing in itself, can become a sort of denial when we indiscriminately praise the Lord everywhere, at all times, and for all things. We end up closing our eyes to painful and difficult situations and, failing

---

[15] I. Chartier-Siben is president of the association *C'est-à-dire*, which provides help to victims of physical, psychological, and spiritual abuse.

to ask questions about their causes and remedies, decide instead merely to praise God for uniting the sufferer to the Passion of Christ. Praise can also turn into a sort of magic, if we imagine that God will intervene automatically and change everything for the better.

Forgiveness, an essential cornerstone of any spiritual house, can take on strange forms, with the roles in the situation being reversed:

> The abusive religious leader demands that a Christian should forgive someone who has wronged him, even if the offender (possibly including the leader himself, of course) has shown no remorse. Presented with the manipulator's obvious misconduct, which the believer has noticed and identified for what it is, the manipulator replies that the believer must forgive unconditionally, otherwise God will not forgive him. The manipulator has managed to turn the victim into the guilty party. This is the very limit of perversity![16]

Put more graphically: "I'm going to tread on your toes, and you should then ask me for forgiveness, for having put your feet under mine." The reversal of a sense of guilt that takes place in cases of sexual abuse provides a particularly dramatic illustration of this phenomenon.

Silence, such a precious commodity when it is authentic, can turn into the stifling of speech under a variety of pretexts, such as "not divulging particular graces one has received," or "preserving the community's balance." This can lead to the truth being hushed up when the bishop is passing through, or at the time of a canonical visitation.

The enclosure, established to promote interiority while preserving the very heart of relationships, can be used in order to sever all relations with the outside world, to exclude any influence that could call various aspects of the community's life into question.

Deceptive Obligations

If openness is forced, it can distort the fruitful practice of opening one's heart into a violation of the proper confidentiality that should go with spiritual

---

[16] J. Poujol, *Abus spirituel, S'affranchir de l'emprise*, 41.

companionship (and even of the seal of the confessional) and a total loss of any kind of personal privacy, due to the obligation to tell the superior everything.

Unity, so desired by Jesus, can become "the duty to be loyal," "the vow of confidentiality," which in turn becomes groupthink, which forbids all healthy criticism, and even any sort of personal reflection.

A Forced Confusion

There can be confusion between the internal and external forums, but also of various different ways in which things might be interpreted, as when, for instance, a prayer of deliverance or even an exorcism is carried out whenever resistance is met or questions are asked, on the grounds that these things shatter unity, so they can only come from the devil.

A prayer of deliverance for a religious who has doubts about his vocation at the time of profession is basically spiritual abuse, because the implicit message is very clear: "God wants you to make your profession; it is the demon that is trying to stop you." As a result, the religious in question is not free, because others have made the decision for him, and his profession may even be invalid as a result. There is a danger that such a person will be seriously conflicted as he makes his profession.

(North Dakota / Fr. Tony) H.

Sr. Chantal-Marie Sorlin's Report

Sr. Chantal-Marie Sorlin's report "Sect-like behavior in Catholic communities," which was published by the French Bishops' Conference, as well as in the volume *Vie religieuse et liberté* published by the Conference of Religious of France (CORREF),[17] gives us, in the space of fewer than twenty pages, an insight into the dynamics that are at work wherever this aberrant behavior is to be found. She outlines four stages. *The stage of attraction and seduction, the*

4 stages of sect-like behavior

---

[17] Sr. Chantal-Marie Sorlin is a member of a group analyzing aberrant, sect-like behavior in Catholic communities. See *Les derives sectaires dans des communautés catholiques*, in *Vie religieuse et liberté, approche canonique, pastorale, spirituelle et psychologique*, published by CORREF (The Conference of Religious of France), (Paris: 2018), 7–25. This is re-published in *Documents épiscopat*, 2018, no. 11, published by the general secretariat of the Conference of French Bishops.

Abuses in the Religious Life and the Path to Healing

cult of personality; the stage of isolation, ② cutting off the outside world; the stage of conditioning ③, manipulation; the stage of exploitation ④, the incoherence of life.

All the elements Sr. Chantal-Marie discusses are to be found in the pages of this book, though the various studies were carried out totally independently of each other. This only serves to confirm the conclusion of her study:

> All the forms of aberrant behavior that have been identified in some Catholic communities are indistinguishable from those found in sects more generally. This shows that the line between good and evil is not something that runs between us and the outside world, between our communities and the world, but rather something that runs through our own hearts. Whether they appear in Christian or civil contexts, the aberrant behaviors are the same, because we are all fashioned from the same clay. The three key temptations — power, possessions, and pleasure — are very much universal. But put simply, the existence of such aberrant behaviors is all the more serious when they are found precisely where we would expect, rather, to encounter a witness to God and the fruits of holiness.[18]

THE ONION

In their book *Spiritual Abuse and the Drift into Sect-like Behavior*, Blandine de Dinechin and Xavier Léger quote the report of Sr. Chantal-Marie Sorlin, but they then point out a further problem:

> There is, however, a difficulty with these criteria: put together by researchers on the basis of testimonies of former members, they reveal the tricks used by the majority of sect communities to recruit, manipulate, and cheat people. Now, even if these lists of criteria are of some use to victims, should they wish to review their unhappy experiences, they do not allow us to gauge immediately, from the outside, how dangerous a particular community may be. To find out more, we must experience the community from the inside.[19]

[18] Ibid., *Documents* épiscopat, 23; *Vie religieuse et liberté*, 24
[19] B. de Dinechin and X. Léger, *Abus spirituels et dérives sectaires dans l'Église* (Paris: Mediaspaul, 2019) 27.

They describe this phenomenon in five layers: what we perceive about the community from the outside; what we see when we begin to spend time with the community; what we discover when we enter the community; what we find out after several months; what we discover (eventually) after some years.

A Lived Example

In his book *X-ray of a Sect that was Above all Suspicion*,[20] O. Braconnier tells of his experience with the Family of Nazareth, which goes back to 1965. Several of the elements that have just been mentioned can be found in the following brief story about this Family, which was founded by Fr. Marcel C.

> He was a great priest. From the very beginning, he seemed to me to be someone who knew not only how to charm me, but also how to listen to me, and understand what I was feeling. I was very impressed by his simplicity, his direct way of speaking, his infectious cheerfulness, and the extraordinary facility he had as a storyteller, to such an extent that, at the end of our first meeting, I agreed at once that I should enter the group about which he had just been speaking to me at such length.

> It had all begun in 1961 with a Bible study group that Fr. Marcel C. had founded in a parish in the western suburbs of Paris. Young people had been filled with enthusiasm by his way of making the text seem close to everyday life by means of constantly drawing parallels between the Bible and current events, which compelled them to engage with the text in a real way. After several weeks, the group was thirty strong. The Bible study group then became a fraternity, rooted in the spirituality of Fr. Charles de Foucauld: clinging to Jesus, frequent Communion and Adoration, studying the Bible, and engaging with the poorest in society. Marcel had added the practice of "examination of life," an exercise in openness carried out communally in groups of five little brothers. One of these recalls: "We had a great feeling of freedom: from the outset, we had begun to tackle our problems, problems that we had kept secret from one another despite our close friendship." The author goes on:

---

[20] O. Braconnier, *Radiographie d'une secte au-dessus de tout soupçon* (Paris: Éd. du Cerf, 1995). All of the quotations are taken from this book, pp. 13, 15, 16, 49.

Abuses in the Religious Life and the Path to Healing

At the beginning, I found this quite an ordeal. I was afraid they would tell me to go first, and I would have to confess sins that I thought nobody but me had ever committed. But when I understood that all the little brothers were in the same boat, I started to experience it as something that gave me freedom in every way.

Brotherly affection was expressed openly. They had a tender love for this father, who — they felt — loved them so much, and they had total confidence in him. In 1968, the brothers were joined by some little sisters, and in 1971 the Family of Nazareth was officially recognized by the archbishop of Chambéry. In 1973, the Family had three hundred members. Although they had a period of probation for new members and a formal public commitment to the Family, it was not, canonically, a religious community. Couples were admitted, and it was possible for people to live in their own homes, but generally people lived in groups. "From the 1970s, it was no longer Marcel who was responsible for drawing people in, but a local community that attracted people and recruited them." Until this point, there was apparently nothing but good to report, and it seemed the Family had become a mature movement.

How was it, then, that less than two years later, in the summer of 1974, the community broke off from the Church and became a secret community, behind the façade of a lay organization known as "Vivre au grand air" [Living in the Open], which officially presented itself as a group of friends, before becoming, in 1981, an international society of scientific research, whose members declared themselves to be atheists, with several of them actively demanding to be unbaptized? The society disappeared in 1985. What happened? The discovery of the Charismatic Renewal in 1973 led people to excesses in various areas, excesses that drew the attention of the bishops who had some oversight of the group. Shortly afterward, Marcel began to espouse heterodox theological positions, of which the most notable was the notion that there was no need for a priest to consecrate the bread and the wine; he invited the fraternities to do this themselves. By the end of that year, Marcel announced that the end-times were upon them, and a period of spiritual and practical preparation for the coming tribulations was organized. All of this was very troubling, and several bishops together with Fr. Voillaume expressed their concerns. Marcel interpreted all of this as an attempt to gain a stranglehold over the group, even a persecution. Following an intense preparation, he asked the members of the Family to vote on the nature of their relationship with the Church. They did so, and the vast majority expressed a preference to distance themselves from it. The break became official in 1974. In October of the same year, Marcel claimed that the Catholic Church was a historical sham. During the following years, he tried to gather what remained of the Family, which was of course no longer solely dependent upon him. When his ever-increasing delirium finally went too far and he found himself sidelined, the group dispersed very quickly. And yet everything had begun so well.

In the introduction to his book, the author attempts to analyze what took place, and he identifies two elements: the great talent for charming people that Marcel possessed, coupled with the feeling that the Family was the source of their salvation, created in the mind of the one who had been "saved" an obligation to show boundless gratitude, and thereby a kind of emotional dependence, causing a considerable diminution of their critical faculties. In such a climate, the dependency of the members buttressed the ego (and before long the fantasy) of the one in charge, who would later set in place all the typical ways of clinging to power: using exhortations to be open to control people's thoughts, sidelining those who ask questions, cutting people off from their biological families.[21] This last point seems so important to the author that he writes that being reunited with their family was the clearest sign that those who left really had finished with the group.[22]

> I now think that this group venture, begun in the 1960s and coming to an end some twenty-five years later, could have developed in a positive way, i.e., it could still be a going concern, if the Catholic hierarchy had intervened earlier and with vigor, in order to ensure (*inter alia*) that the proper constitutions of the Family of Nazareth were being respected.

---

[21] A letter from one son to his widowed mother, who had three sons in the Family of Nazareth, shows tremendous violence: "This is the appropriate tone for a woman like you, who has nothing of the mother about her, except the fact that you once had the job of giving birth." Ibid., 213–214.

[22] Ibid., 221.

This would at least have made it possible to limit the fallout, which was considerable on the human level, and at the level of faith.

If the Church, the "expert in humanity," does not in future impose various safeguards, then more communities that enjoy its endorsement or protection will surely suffer dramatic collapses.[23]

It is not absolutely clear that the Church could have prevented the Family of Nazareth from going off the rails, but it is true that a better understanding of the mechanisms at work could have helped limit the fallout, because, at the beginning, the fruits were good.

Abusive Christian Systems

The case described above is certainly not unique; another witness, someone who had left a community that still exists, writes that entire pages "are practically a carbon copy of what we experienced [in our community]." In the case of the Family of Nazareth, it all stemmed from a single person. Jacques Poujol draws a valid distinction between two main sources of spiritual abuse: it can arise from a "manipulative personality," like Marcel C., or from an "abusive system," that is, from a group of people. The two may act together, and indeed an abusive group is often the independent continuation of what was started by a manipulative personality. Poujol adds an important note regarding the group situation: "Caught up in an abusive system, even someone who is not intentionally an abuser may find that in such a group he is not immune from engaging in abusive behavior." He gives an example of a victim, "who is likely to adopt a tyrannical attitude toward children, partners, or friends and family, without being aware of it, for the simple reason that the victim is merely imitating the authoritarian approach to which he or she had previously been subjected."[24] This contagion, which will be addressed in the next chapter, is of great significance in the perpetuation of abuse. Poujol is very pessimistic when assessing how likely it is that a deviant group will be able to change: "An abusive religious system never changes."[25] He is speaking of a Protestant context. In a Catholic context,

[23] Ibid., 218–19.
[24] J. Poujol, Abus spirituel, S'affranchir de l'emprise, 12, 33, 59–60.
[25] Ibid., 69.

the possibility of recourse to higher authorities does offer some possible ways forward, but we can repeat his assertion without hesitation if we make it slightly more nuanced: a religious system never changes on its own.

THE NEED FOR WISDOM

Does what was good become bad? What we have said here may give rise to questions like this. But actually, no method is ever good or bad in itself; everything depends on the intention of the person using it, on the way it is used, and on the particular circumstances. A car is an excellent means of transport. But cars can cause death through circumstances beyond the driver's control: a mechanical failure or the fault of some other driver, for example. They can also cause death through carelessness: there was no intention of causing harm, only the car was being driven dangerously. There again, a car can be the intentional cause of death, if a terrorist decides to use it for that purpose, for instance. However, even if these various cases may differ as regards intention, from the point of view of the victims, the result is the same: death. What became clear in the case of the Family of Nazareth was how the intention slowly changed as soon as Marcel began to be obsessed with controlling the group. From then on, even ordinarily good practices became more and more harmful when, for example, the trust that had been placed in him was used to prevent members from thinking for themselves. Instead of helping them grow by returning their trust, he harnessed the confidence they had placed in him to keep them under his sway.

This is how it is possible to make bad or even destructive use of methods that are quite traditional in religious life, methods that experience has shown to be conducive to progress in the spiritual life, but only on the express condition that they are used with wisdom. And that is where the problem lies.

This observation allows us to contextualize an excuse that can easily mislead. Making use of traditional practices is often presented as a guarantee of safety: "We are in the purest traditions of the religious life; we haven't invented anything for ourselves, we are simply following the great principles that have always been recommended." It can be helpful to remember that traditional practices do not, in themselves, offer any guarantees about the results. Fruitfulness in the religious life does not come from this or that particular practice; it comes, rather, from the wisdom that draws these various methods together harmoniously, in a nuanced and tailor-made fashion. On their own they do not amount to anything, but used appropriately, they serve to support a desire shared by all: to respond to God's love.

The Connectedness of the Virtues

The religious life is not defenseless when faced by the risks we have spoken of. The limitations inherent in the virtues have been expressed in a well-known formula: *in medio stat virtus*. Virtue lies in the middle. That is, between two excesses. This tag is not well liked by extremists, and yet language itself has words that express this middle way. The noble virtue of courage is surrounded by pusillanimity on the left and recklessness on the right. To find oneself in the middle of these two has nothing to do with being mediocre; it is rather a case of walking along a very narrow ridge, with a perilous descent on either side.

Spiritual writers have also emphasized that the various virtues depend on one another: they are interconnected. With his genius for images, St. Dorotheus of Gaza illustrated this mutual dependence in his treatise *On the Structure and Harmony of the Virtues of the Soul.*[26]

> But how is the dwelling place, that is the soul, to be built? We can learn exactly how by observing material dwelling places. Anyone who wants to build one of these must be sure he has all the various component parts. He has to erect it on all four sides, and not simply take care of just one while neglecting the others. Otherwise, he wouldn't get anywhere, but would be wasting his time, and all his efforts would be spent in vain. It is the same with the soul. We must not neglect any part of this spiritual building, but rather construct it in an even and harmonious way.

Speaking of those who seek to develop a single virtue in isolation, he adds:

> They are like a person who constructs a single wall, building it up as high as possible and who, seeing how tall it is, imagines he has achieved

[26] Dorothée de Gaza, *Instructions* XIV in *Œuvres spirituelles*, Sources Chrétiennes (Paris: Éd. du Cerf, 1963). An English edition is available: Dorotheus of Gaza, *Discourses and Sayings*, Cistercian Studies 33 (Cistercian Publications: Kalamazoo, 1977). The three quotations that follow are all taken from this text.

something wonderful, not realizing that a single breath of wind will knock it to the ground, because it stands alone, without the support of the other walls. Nor can we fashion a shelter out of a single wall, since we would be exposed on all the other sides. We must, therefore, not act in this way. Rather, anyone who wants to build his house so that he can shelter inside it must build it up on every side, and make it secure from all directions.

Dorotheus then lists several virtues. Firstly, the foundation, which is faith, then a stone that represents obedience, another that represents patience, another that represents temperance, another that represents compassion, another that represents mortification of the will, another that represents meekness, and so on. He does not forget charity, which is the roof of the house. Then comes humility, the crown and guardian of all the virtues.

But there is still one crucial element, without which all this labor would be in vain:

The house is finished. Is nothing now missing from it? Indeed, there is something that we have forgotten. What? That the one doing the building is skilled at it. Otherwise, what he builds will be wonky, and will someday end up falling down.

Thus, a monk lacking in skill who makes a show of humility in order to satisfy a desire for praise yokes humility with vainglory. This is like laying a stone and then taking it away again.

It would seem, then, that discernment and balance are necessities that together essentially constitute discretion, in the particular sense that the monastic literature has given to this term.

Discretion

This virtue is little appreciated by some leaders of reforms. John of the Cross experienced this, facing the Vicar General, Nicolas Doria, who extolled the virtues of the most rigorous forms of asceticism, and asserted that souls were being lost as a result of what was masquerading as discretion. Nobody could accuse John of the Cross of minimizing the ascetic aspects of the spiritual life, but in his thinking, it always held its proper place, subordinate to love. According to Doria, on the other hand, asceticism should take first place, and the whole balance of the religious life suffered the effects of this. For all that, this situation is not really an example of the particular form of aberrant behavior one finds in sects, but it does show that these risks are nothing new, and Teresa of Avila's reform could have been seriously damaged by it. History has made its judgment, though. Who remembers Doria today?

The boundaries between a normal community life and an aberrant one are not cut and dried, which makes the business of discernment more difficult. On both sides, there is talk of freedom, or respect, or the primacy of the spiritual, of obedience, of a rule, of tradition, and so on. The same language and even the same methods are used, and the more problematic the situation, the more the façade will be carefully maintained, presenting a sort of window dressing that could fool observers for quite some time. The difference will be determined by the imbalances, the excesses, the apparent "absolute" that has shifted from the ends to the means. It will be revealed in its effects on real people. But will those in positions of authority recognize the alarm bells?

2

How Sect-Like Behavior Becomes Established

An abbot who has had experience of several situations where a group has drifted into sect-like behavior, in various different contexts, has reflected deeply on how this happens.[27] When we see a community that has become trapped in a state of affairs and a mindset that lead it to develop some sect-like characteristics, we can't help asking ourselves: "How is it possible? How can brothers (or sisters) who seemed so normal end up living in such a situation, or go on doing so?" "Is it always the superior who goes off the rails, acting like an out-and-out manipulator? But, then, how is it that the community goes along with it?" And so on. We will not seek to resolve all these questions here — after all, no two communities are the same. Rather, I would just like to try to share some points of reference that I have encountered here and there.

The Driven Founder

A fairly typical sequence of events may help us to explain the ways in which a religious community of the traditional model drifted into aberrant, sect-like behavior. In the wake of the Council and the crisis of May 1968, Christians were seriously disoriented. We no longer knew what was true or false, what was good or bad. The Council Fathers had wanted to present Catholic doctrine in a new way, a way that would involve greater dialogue with what was good in human society more generally. All of this meant people had to change their perspective or how they presented things. What had always been presented as the truth was

---

[27] The whole of this chapter is from his pen.

now apparently called into question, or was presented differently, so that we no longer understood where the boundary was between good and evil, and so on. In this atmosphere, people were completely at sea, not knowing who to turn to for support, especially since — while trying to correct overly rigid views, for example — people often fell into the opposite excess, wanting to reinvent everything, to question everything. As a result, all sorts of errors arose, errors that were contrary to those errors that people were seeking to combat. In short, the way our faith was presented became a sort of "construction site." It was around this time that various strong personalities began to appear on the scene. These were men and women who had received a classical formation; they were sure of their own truths and declared themselves to be faithful to what the Church had always taught. These people inspired confidence in many young people who were thirsting for something absolute, for sure certainties and radical ways of living. Out of all this, various more or less religious communities came to be born. The founder would speak with conviction and inspire confidence. If he could demonstrate that he was spiritual, at least in the way he spoke, he would quickly attract many vocations, which could then be organized into an institutional structure.

The founder would often do a lot of good for these young people and their families, and he would be told so. Word spread: "Fr. Such-and-Such is doing a really good thing . . ." It practically became a dogma, and Fr. Such-and-Such gained a reputation for being a sort of reference point in the Church of that time. People would come to see him, to consult him on all manner of subjects, and suddenly the good father begins to take himself too seriously. His radical and demanding way of life inspire confidence in the young people, who join in great numbers in order to take refuge under his wings. The number of people entering the community is seen as an undeniable sign that the Holy Spirit is at work, since "a tree is known by its fruits." People start considering the founder to be a vessel of the Holy Spirit, and they begin to follow him blindly. Those so captivated by his message and his personality recommend him to people they meet. He becomes one of those rare "safe bets" in such troubled times. From now on, his message is considered to be one of the few around that actually bring light, and for those who live with him, he becomes virtually the only way to salvation. A group dynamic is established in which it is no longer possible to think differently from the way the founder thinks. The loop closes. In the end, he is — in a very real way — invested with all authority, and people recognize that the Holy Spirit is with him in a unique way, fitting him to guide the community as a whole, and each individual member, too.

In this process, it is not necessarily the founder who proclaims himself to be the Absolute Master; on the contrary, it may be the community that abdicates its responsibilities and prostrates itself before its founder. True, some founders may have had manipulative personalities, but it is far from clear that this is generally the case. The community can be just as responsible for this if it renounces its good sense, by making the founder the ultimate point of reference for every thought and deed. But it is true that the founder, for his part, would have had to accept what was being asked of him and try to measure up to it. We need to come to a better understanding of the relative responsibilities of founders and communities. The former are not necessarily monsters; it is not necessarily the case that they have sought for themselves a role where they control everything. But neither does this absolve them from the responsibility that is rightly theirs for the way the community degenerates into a sect.

A question arises: if at the outset these founders were not particularly inclined to behave like absolute masters but only became such later on, what warning signs might we look for that could suggest a community or its superior(s) were beginning to behave in ways that could lead them toward becoming a sect?

Group Dynamics and Competition

In all the cases I have come across, a particular group dynamic formed that was rather pleased with the quality of the monastic life as lived in the community or institute: "*we* have vocations; *we* are faithful; *we* have the light," and so on. This dynamic in the community causes the members to outdo one another, to be generous, to be forgetful of themselves for the sake of the community's greater good, not to complain, and so on. All of that is marvelous, of course, and encourages people to strive for holiness. And indeed, some brothers or sisters draw great profit from this competitive atmosphere, but others can end up becoming crushed or exhausted, quite without even realizing what is happening. For a while, they manage to hold out, particularly because they often lack the strength or clarity of thought required to resist what is happening in the group.

Abuses in the Religious Life and the Path to Healing

But one day, something happens that is more than they can cope with, and at that point all kinds of psychological traumas may ensue.

The phenomenon of group dynamics allows us to understand just how subtle is the discernment necessary both for working out what is going on in such a community, and for considering possible intervention. On the one hand, there are some brothers and sisters (not infrequently these are quite a large majority) who seem to thrive in this climate, which spurs them on to grow in holiness — the community is radiant, it is attracting vocations among young people in search of the absolute — but on the other hand, there are some who leave, decrying the idiosyncrasies of the community's leaders, having become aware of the damage these people have inflicted on them. It is very tempting to regard them as "black sheep," people with a score to settle, because "they did not have a vocation."

It takes a little time to realize what may be going on, and to understand that, although some people thrived in this climate, there was, in fact, something seriously wrong with it. People are badly scarred by it, sometimes for the rest of their lives; some resort to attempting suicide (and some have succeeded); others lose their faith completely and find it hard to forgive the superiors who have destroyed them, or to forgive the Church, which allowed them to go through such ordeals, has covered them up, or has been slow to condemn them.

We have to realize that it is hard for those of us outside these communities to imagine what living in the community is really like. On the one hand there are spiritual fruits that seem quite wonderful: religious fervor, vocations, conversion both within the community and outside, and so on. On the other hand, there are some who complain about things that are dysfunctional; it is easy to regard such opinions as unreliable, since they seem to be exaggeratedly serious. We can be afraid that, by intervening, we might "throw out the baby with the bath water," doing more harm than good.

Victim and Accomplice

It is obvious that, in this process, it is the entire system that is defective. The balance of the various forces and relationships means that the whole community joins in this striving for holiness, but it is a holiness that is only achieved by sheer effort. The superior sets the tone, and everyone follows. Nobody dares ask questions regarding the legitimacy of this or that practice. He automatically thinks, "It must be me." And if someone notices that another brother or sister is showing signs of weakness, he is quick to encourage him to redouble his efforts, not to harm the community or its reputation, nor to do damage to the beautiful unity that exists among all the brothers or sisters.

In this way, everyone is both a victim of the environment in the community and complicit in creating it! Everyone is a *victim*, since there is no way to complain about what is going on or to express oneself in any way that differs from the official position. If anyone dares to complain, he is quickly reminded of his own need for personal conversion.

At the same time, everyone is *complicit* because everyone has been shaped by the dynamics of the group or by the manipulative behavior of the superior; he casts judgmental eyes on the smallest infringements of the rules by others, on their weaknesses, or even simply on their basic human needs, and they know exactly how to let them know about it.

The whole art of manipulation consists in the manipulator being able to exercise a grip on victims, such that they participate "freely" in the prevailing atmosphere, which is what makes it so difficult to recognize the truth when it begins to emerge. People have participated in something evil, and that is difficult to accept. They did it in good faith, by trusting in others, and the fruits of this might well have led them to conclude that they were right to do so. Particularly in a closed environment, it can be easier to resist the dawning light than to entertain such questions.

To be sure, we do need to keep in mind that a sort of gradation exists. We often see that at the head of these communities there are two or three people regarded as trustworthy, brothers or sisters who surround the superior and act in practice as a sort of "inner circle." These people are like the superior's eyes and ears. They report everything they pick up on within the community and are then charged with making sure that what the superior decides is carried out. It is clear that, by acting in this way, they share responsibility for the prevailing atmosphere in the community. They have been seduced by the way things operate and gain personal advantage from it (living close to the superior, enjoying his or her confidence, maybe eventually having some authority of their own, and so on). Too often, we observe that, among these three or four, matters that brothers or sisters have shared confidentially are not kept private but are shared. So it is that, "for the good of the community" (as they say), brothers and sisters lose this safe space, where they can ask questions, express disagreement, or address questions that might arise about their own vocations. Everything is passed up to the head and is then shared between the superior and their inner circle.

Independent of this small group, we can often distinguish within the community a small group of people who can see clearly that something is not right but who prefer to turn a blind eye to avoid making life difficult for themselves. Then there is the majority: people who allow themselves to be ensnared, and who, in practice, become unconscious collaborators with the system, but only as a result of manipulation, never intentionally. Last of all are those, probably few in number, who are aware of the manipulative behavior, but do not have the necessary resources to oppose it.

We also ought to consider all those who feel safe in a group that has such clear structures, or those again who live in the relative comfort of being able to abdicate responsibility for their own lives, since someone else has taken this on. Such a warped system can be a sort of gilded cage for some; it may provide a sense of reassurance, which they prefer to the struggles of life, and this may help perpetuate the situation. It also explains why so much clarity of thought, courage, and even some fighting spirit are needed to escape it. Indeed, people hardly ever succeed in escaping without some form of external intervention.

Successors Are Often Like Their Predecessors

There is an issue here: could it be that it is only those who "lack a vocation to the community" who leave, while others are flourishing there and should be allowed to go on doing so? We could quite easily be tempted to say, "Let them live like that if they want to and if it works for them."

But this would be to forget that, when an authority structure functions improperly like this, it provides a model of what governing looks like. Those who come to positions of authority later on, having experienced nothing else, will act in the same way and, indeed, may often become more radical yet, seeking as they do to imitate the founder and be faithful to his or her teaching. Surprising as this response may seem, it is well attested; often, people who have suffered some form of abuse may reproduce the abuse in their own lives.

Two communities were headed by all-powerful abbess figures, one of whom had been forced to resign by higher authorities. The abbesses who succeeded them had never known any other model of government, so they copied the previous abbess's dictatorial way of exercising authority, but without her abilities and skills. When the next election came around, they were not re-elected, which turned into a real crisis for them.

In a system where all authority and discernment come from the head, those further down end up simply following whatever the head says, never learning to discern for themselves where the Spirit is drawing them. In this way, they do not know how to live as children of God.

We are very far, here, from the marvelous chapter 3 of the *Rule of Saint Benedict*, which recommends that, "each time there is something important to decided," the abbot should call together the whole community, and himself set out the matter that is to be decided. Then he is to listen to each of the brothers, to try to see what the Spirit is saying, since the Spirit can speak through any one of them, even the youngest, provided that they speak with the necessary humility and obedience. Then the abbot himself decides, and all commit themselves to obey in an attitude of faith.

St. Benedict is seeking to form sons and daughters. A system of government that is too pyramidal in shape, too authoritarian, where everyone thinks in the same way as the person at the top, is dangerously similar to the Tower of Babel: "Come on! Let us make some bricks, and fire them in the oven ... Come, let us build a city and a tower, whose top will be in the heavens, and we shall make a name for ourselves" (Gen. 11:1–4).[28] The whole group wanted to reach God by means of a single way of thinking, a single will, and a single way of working. But God is a Trinity, which means there is unity in the diversity of the Persons. This means we cannot reach God through uniformity; we reach Him, rather, by learning to respect one another and love one another in our diversity. Is this not perhaps why God scattered those people who wanted to reach Him by dint of uniformity? That is not how we draw near to God; it is not the right way. If we

---

[28] This passage was directly translated from the French to maintain original emphasis.

are to be like God, then we must necessarily learn to love one another amidst the diverseness of people, all of whom are journeying to the same goal.

Perhaps, then, this is something to look for: does the community aim to create a unity from the diversity of different people, or does it try, rather, to create uniformity? The latter will in many ways be very efficient, for sure, and will be highly attractive to young people, but it will not help us to be an image of the Trinitarian God! Couples know this very well; if the marriage is to survive, the spouses have to learn to welcome and respect their differences, all the while placing them at the service of the common good.

The trap of unity-uniformity seems to be one characteristic of those communities that function like sects. It is good for the brothers and sisters to feel that their community is united; it is reassuring, and it seems like a sign that the Holy Spirit is at work. For this reason, they dare not adopt any but the official position, because this would look like excessive pride. If anyone demurs, the others will take on themselves the job of reminding him that he must do nothing to harm the unity of the community. They remind him that people on the outside do not understand the community, that they sometimes "persecute" it, and that this may even include a "persecution by the Church itself." Nobody feels they have the right to weaken the community by taking a view that differs from the general opinion. People sometimes forget that true communion does not preclude a diversity of points of view; rather, it seeks to integrate them into a broader, richer vision.

This all explains why intervention is vital, even if the brothers or sisters seem to be making the best of this way of doing things. It is important that diversity should be able to find expression. Of course, it is no good ending up with a cacophony of views, but any true harmony is able to integrate diversity, recognizing the richness that each person brings. Such an ambiance is a sign of a community in good health.

Outside visitation / Community assessment

A Culture of Lies

We are touching here upon something that is always present in communities that have become sects. It is not that the business of lying is regarded as something desirable in these communities — far from it, since everyone feels totally oriented toward the Lord — but in practice it happens, precisely because of this so-called "perfect turning toward the Lord," which outsiders would never be able to understand. The community begins to protect itself from the gaze of these outsiders; it becomes enclosed in a bubble of self-justification. What goes on out there is filtered, interpreted, judged through the prism of the community's internal discourse, which no longer corresponds to reality. As for what outsiders say about the life of the community, here too — perhaps especially here — careful selection is made of what is on show; things are presented in a way that is quite removed from reality and truth. We can therefore speak of a culture of lies.

> At the time of my first canonical visitation, the superior explained to us that the meeting with the visitor in the parlor was not an opportunity to say bad things about others, but rather to accuse ourselves of our own faults … This stuck with me for the rest of my [religious] life. I didn't dare say a single word against what I saw or what I experienced, until the day I left.

There are certain features of the religious life that can promote the emergence of this culture of lies. The virtue of obedience encourages us to trust in the superior, not to be always arguing, demanding explanations for everything. In the same way, discretion is a religious quality that teaches us not to broadcast what is happening inside the community to the whole world. Here we have elements that a manipulative person can use to his or her own advantage.

> From the first days of the novitiate, they explained to me that our life was beyond anything outsiders could comprehend: it was a mystery, reserved for those who live it from the inside. So when, some years later, a family member said he felt uneasy [about the life], and tried to get me to think about it, I was deaf to what he said. "He just doesn't understand!"

To this, we may add the art of dissimulation and seduction, often practiced on those in positions of authority (the bishop, or the superior general), to make sure they never become aware of what life is really like inside the community. These people become captivated by what they see, to the point where they find it impossible to accept any criticisms against the community. For example, the local superior may make frequent visits to the bishop, giving the impression of being obedient, and yet present things in such a way that the person in authority takes his side. This reveals how expert he is at putting on an act.

> One prioress, who was also the novice mistress, was quite capable of blowing hot and cold, of sulking, or of getting angry whenever the sisters failed to obey her whims. And yet she was as intimidating to those within the community as she was charming to outsiders, among whom she had a reputation for sound judgment. She gained introductions to certain circles and sometimes gave outstanding conferences, which were well received.

The Linchpin

— Be attentive to this reality

In communities like this, one person is usually at the center of everything. To simplify things, let's call this person the "linchpin." Very often, this is the superior, but not always; it may be a brother or sister or, for example, the cellarer; there is an example of one such case where the cellarer had such a hold over the abbess that she was able to get her to dismiss novices one after another. It is also possible that an outsider, who has been welcomed into the community, ends up calling the shots. Outside authorities may not necessarily be made aware of the presence of such a person, or of his impact on the community. His hold on the community grows little by little until, eventually, everything happens in accordance with the judgment of Mr. or Mrs. X. For example: a lay person was employed and welcomed into the heart of one community. By the end, this person accumulated such authority that the superior was unable to say anything of which this person, who by now had become utterly crucial, might disapprove. It all started with the timetable for work but later expanded to include the decisions about community formation sessions, and it eventually came to encompass the community's whole ethos. In another community, it began with the choice of reading in the refectory, then extended to which particular external speakers should be invited, and even to dictating what was taught in chapter. If the linchpin disapproved of anything, a good number of the community would let the superior know, and the superior had to give way! In such situations, nothing inspires more dread than the anger of the linchpin.

This person becomes *the* single point of reference in the community, so much so that people no longer try to conform to some common good but to the linchpin's feelings; whatever happens, the linchpin must never be contradicted! It matters little whether the decision is right or not, whether the analysis is consistent with reality or not; what matters is that the linchpin agrees with it. From now on, what is true or good is no longer the point of reference; this place has been taken by the linchpin's ego. If people are made to live this reality, day in, day out — having no other point of reference than the decrees that emerge from the linchpin, protected by the enclosure — then their mindset becomes deformed; people don't know who they are anymore; they no longer exist in any identifiable way; they become emanations of the linchpin, their own identity dissolving away. According to St. Benedict, people come to the monastery to seek God by following a rule and an abbot (*Rule* 1:2), but where these aberrant behaviors are found, it is not simply that people now live under the watchful eye of the "linchpin"; rather, this person has taken the place of God, and that is a catastrophe!

Let us look at some other examples:

If the linchpin accuses somebody of something (and let's assume the accused person is innocent), his first, instinctive response will be to defend himself, so that the truth can be established. But if the linchpin maintains the false accusation regardless, it can happen that the dynamic at work in the community, once the grip of the linchpin has grown so powerful, is such that the accused person ends up falling to his knees, accusing himself of the very thing for which he had been unjustly rebuked. Over time, the person no longer knows who he is; he becomes convinced that he is utterly wretched, completely useless. He accepts his own ruin, because whatever happens, he tells himself there is still the possibility, at least, that the group will accept him. In any event, the community has hammered into him this thought: "You need to repent."

And if this person is not sufficiently flexible to fit in with what the linchpin wants, he will most likely be rejected, in a situation where his influence upon the community is minimal.

If the superior occupies the role of the linchpin, then the most minor events concerning himself will assume disproportionate significance. The times when he goes out from the community, or returns to it again, will take on colossal importance; the state of the superior's health will be the temperature reading for the whole community, and his moods will determine what should be done.

> When I returned from a long period of absence in another monastery of the congregation, my (blood) sister came to see me. She later said to me: "I wanted to hear about your experiences, but all you talked about was the state of the abbess's soul ... and since we got the same report every time we visited, we decided not to come again. We had lost our sister!"

Often, for the superior, charm is all important; appearances prevail over reality; truth only counts for anything if it can be used to buttress the idea of the superior's greatness or secure his authority and power in the community. To this end, all sorts of justifications may be trotted out. "After everything I have done for you, surely you could ..."; "You are the person closest to me, the one who understands me best ..." After declarations like these, it can prove really difficult to disagree with the superior, because it would entail risking one's special position.

We are touching on something important here: because communities in this sort of situation have lost all contact with reality, they feel an enormous need to justify themselves, whatever the circumstances, using arguments that are actually not arguments at all; perhaps it is really themselves they are seeking to reassure all along. Truth, *per se*, does not need such things. It is self-sufficient. What is, is; there is no need to shore it up with all manner of arguments, plausible to a greater or lesser degree! Perhaps, in this need for self-justification, we have hit on one identifiable feature that might ring alarm bells for an outside observer on a canonical visitation, for example. If a large section of the community is driven by this instinct, is this not a sign that something is amiss? Does truth always hold first place in a community like this? It is a question worth asking.

The Link with Information

Communities like this have been built up within a very rigid system, one which is sometimes at odds with the life as it is lived elsewhere. This, of course, can attract young people. It all seems to be about maintaining this way of living the life at all costs. Access to information will play a key role in this delicate situation, information not so much about what is going on in the world as information about what is going on within the community.

In the majority of these cases, where a community has taken on some of the features of a sect, what we might call "horizontal" communication between brothers or sisters is forbidden. In this way, it is the role of the authorities in the community to decide how much of what is going on in the community will be communicated to everyone, and in what way. When a brother or sister leaves the community or is dismissed, the other members often do not know the deeper reasons behind this, or where the person has gone, or for how long, or what physical and psychological state he was in. In any event, "It was his fault."

Generally, information is withheld; not everything is said, but only those things that will encourage others to arrive at the same judgment as the community's linchpin. In this way, some part of the truth is kept hidden, and everyone ends up believing the lie that has been settled on. The more people lie, the more they become prisoners of the system, trying to hold on to some degree of coherence in it; the whole thing becomes a prison from which there is no escape.

Here is an example: one brother has to go and collect another from the station, and it is agreed with the superior that they will take the opportunity to speak with one another during the journey. This exchange has to be kept quiet from the other brothers. So, rather than saying nothing about the timings, the superior explains to the community that the traveling brothers will certainly be late for supper, as the train is bound to be delayed! A tiny example, we might think, but the result is that the brethren learn they can never trust the explanations they are given. Everything is distorted, depending on what they should be told, or what should be kept from them. They lose contact with truth and reality.

We may observe at this point that the examples given here might seem trivial. If, perchance, some brother or sister should talk about such things outside the community or during a canonical visitation, anybody with any sense would try to help them to see the transgression in perspective. Nobody would see scandal in such things, much less a drift into sect-like behavior! More serious examples exist, but they are not widespread. The art of the manipulator is in avoiding doing anything that might be dangerous for himself, while establishing an atmosphere that makes it easy for him to control everything. The accumulation of these little white lies will end up blunting the consciences of members of the group; they will become acclimatized to such duplicity and end up being drawn into the system. From outside, nobody notices anything serious, nothing concrete that can be reported. And even if, at the time of a canonical visitation, the visitors live in the community, they will still not be able, over those few days, to pick up on just how toxic is the poison of lying that reigns within. They would need to stay for longer.

This is especially true since everything that happens is interpreted spiritually, under the pretext of taking a supernatural perspective, though with no basis in reason, in order to defend whatever matters to the linchpin. If what happens is positive, it is seen as a blessing from God. If, on the other hand, it presents difficulties, people see in it some sort of havoc wreaked by the devil, and a sign that God is testing His friends. This is especially the case when external authorities begin to express doubts and to intervene more directly. This will be perceived as a test permitted by God to encourage generosity of spirit, a call to persevere, as a way of showing the Lord that we love Him. Of course, there ought to be a place in our lives for a spiritual interpretation of what happens to us, so long as we understand that we may need to do some soul-searching when things don't match up to expectation. Faith in the supernatural must not short-circuit our contact with reality. By means of these crude spiritual interpretations, we risk giving significance to events that have none, and, conversely, we may legitimize what is going on at the risk of whitewashing even serious errors, until it becomes impossible to differentiate between what is good and what is evil. In this situation, there is a total confusion of values.

Words are often used in an ambiguous way, to muddy the waters; what is said is kept vague; a sentence is begun, but never finished.... In this way, a superior can complain of being constantly got at, without anyone close to him having any idea what the problem might be.

The very places used for communication may be inappropriate. The superior may use a chance meeting in a corridor to lay a new task on a brother or sister, while chapter is turned into a time of relaxation. Someone may be corrected, without hesitation, in the middle of the Office, or during prayer, and so on. Obviously, this sort of thing can happen from time to time, but when it becomes the standard way of doing things, people become unsettled, feeling exposed to attack from the community authorities at any moment, and they end up being deeply destabilized. Worst of all, perhaps, is when the authorities blow hot and cold, for no apparent reason, showing, by turns, signs of esteem and disdain, displays of confidence and sudden fits of anger. The resulting confusion means people are prepared to accept anything rather than face more of these verbal assaults, which are inescapable because they are so unpredictable.

The Consequences of This Type of Atmosphere

People become incapable of expressing personal thought; they can no longer find the words. Should they try to express an opinion that does not conform to the official line, it won't be long before they are discredited and roundly put in their place. Eventually, there will be a physical reaction in the form of sleepless nights, back pains, or other psychosomatic complaints. More seriously still, there is a risk that these people may end up self-harming (doing violence or deliberately causing injury to themselves), neglecting personal hygiene, or seeking an escape in some crushing job, or escaping into coercive or recalcitrant behavior, perceived by them as the only way to have some sort of independent existence.

This kind of decline will not be experienced by everybody in the community. It may begin with one person — who will be dismissed — then another, and another. At first, outside the community, it will be explained away as some kind of personal failure, a lack of a vocation to this community. But we have to hope that higher authorities (the bishop or superior of the congregation) will quickly take cognizance of these powerful reactions and begin to ask questions.

No human system can be built on a foundation of a lie, of detachment from truth and reality. Sooner or later, cracks will begin to appear, and it is the role of the authorities to notice these and take them seriously. The human harm suffered can be severe. These are people, souls, who were entrusted to the shepherds. And they will have to render an account for them!

3

Charism and Institution

A Fish Rots from the Head

Whichever model is followed in practice — whether a linchpin figure who imposes himself, or a community propelling someone into a leadership role, or a mixture of these two scenarios — the head remains the most important element, carrying others along in its wake and giving direction. For this reason, in what follows we shall mostly be talking about superiors. To be sure, the body does have its own responsibility, but it cannot do anything without the head. A situation where the behavior of a community is beginning to go off the rails presents a particular difficulty, since those external people who are in a position to intervene often know the superiors of the community, and maybe even have quite a close relationship with them. This can make a necessary intervention more difficult at a psychological level. Msgr. Ravel has acknowledged how difficult it is for a bishop to report one of his priests,[29] and it is not difficult to understand why. Would someone who discovered that his blood brother was a pedophile go to report him with joy in his heart? We must not overlook this natural psychological "brake," which can to a great extent take over in situations of abuse. Often — perhaps even usually — a decision-making forum (such as a general chapter, for example) may be slow to take necessary but strong action against a superior who is present there at the chapter. "He is

---

[29] L. Ravel, *Comme un cœur qui écoute, la parole vraie d'un évêque sur les abus sexuels* (Paris: Artège, 2019), 46: "The great pain of a pastor." [Translator's note: Msgr. L. Ravel has been archbishop of Strasbourg since 2017.]

well known, he is a friend, we don't want to hurt him" — although in the end, to spare his suffering we may be letting the whole community suffer instead. We can often see this dynamic at work in discussions: more mention may be made of the suffering of the superior in question, if this difficult decision were to be imposed upon him, than of the present and future suffering of the community.

We need institutions, then, so that decision-making does not depend solely on personal relationships. Otherwise, we risk letting a sort of oligarchy establish itself — an oligarchy that is impossible to oust — and it will be the body that bears the cost.

Why We Need Institutions

Why do we need institutions? Isn't the Holy Spirit enough? The Church needs institutions because "Jesus Christ did not come only to save souls and lead them to Heaven; He came to establish a people."[30] This illuminating remark of Edward D. O'Connor sets us in the context of the Body of Christ, which is not yet fully mature, for "the whole body, nourished and knit together through its joints and ligaments, grows with a growth that is from God" (Col. 2:19).[31] A religious community is a sort of "people" in microcosm.

Paul Ricœur presents an approach that is very suitable for the world of religious. He describes the institution as "a historical community's structured way of living together."[32] In this vision of *living together*, the idea of the institution refers more to a common way of living than to a collection of restrictive rules.

Why should *living together* be structured? Because if nothing governs the relations between different people, the most ancient law — survival of the

---

[30] E. D. O'Connor, "Charisme et Institution," *Nouvelle Revue Théologique*, 1974, vol. 96-1. As a theologian with links to the charismatic movement, the importance of the charismatic dimension does not escape him.

[31] See also: "From [Christ], the whole body, joined and knit together by every joint with which it is supplied, when each part is working properly, makes bodily growth and upbuilds itself in love" (Eph. 4:16).

[32] P. Ricœur, *Soi-même comme un autre* (Paris: Éd. Du Seuil, 1990), 227. An English edition is available: P. Ricoeur, *Oneself as Another* (Chicago: University of Chicago Press, 1992).

fittest — will quickly establish itself. "Between weak and strong, between rich and poor, between master and servant, it is freedom that brings oppression, and the law that sets people free."[33] Nor is it the case that all we need is a system of law to govern all eventualities; we also need the law to be something fixed. As Lacordaire says in another place: "Every changeable law is at the mercy of the strongest people, whatever the form of government."[34]

Now, we can readily find a lack of law, or the presence of laws that are changeable, in communities that have just been founded, or which are undergoing reforms, when superiors change the rules as they see fit. They hold all the power, with all the risks that this entails. This situation is sometimes inevitable at the beginning of a community's life, when everything has yet to find its proper form. And yet a law common to the whole Church does exist — canon law — and it lays down clear principles. Following this common law, which is the fruit of long experience, will allow many abuses to be avoided; just because a community does not yet have a clear canonical existence does not mean that it does not have to conform to the Church's general law in matters that pertain to religious life, especially if such a community will later seek to be incorporated into the Body of the Church. Moreover, once a true community has been established, the superior must be subject to the laws of the community, being herself a member of the community, and having taken a vow of obedience. The institution represents the necessary counter-authority that allows a person in a position of responsibility to avoid the temptation to exceed the bounds of his legitimate authority.

We must also take into consideration how difficult it can be to ensure that we are acting with justice toward everyone in the community. Our natural tendency is to incline toward caring for those we know, and to a significantly lesser extent for others. To make such care sustainable, and to make sure we extend it to everyone, the life of a society must be open to "outsiders, whose face I may

---

[33] H.-D. Lacordaire, *Conférences de Notre-Dame de Paris*, vol. 3, 52nd Conference ("On the twofold labor of man," April 16, 1848). An English edition is available: H.-D. Lacordaire, *God: Conferences Delivered at Notre Dame in Paris* (Welford: Scribner, 1870).

[34] Ibid., 32nd Conference ("On the influence of Catholic society on natural society as regards the principle of law.")

never know,"[35] but that I must nevertheless take into account. They are distant either in terms of space (if they live in another house) or of time (if they haven't yet joined the institute). So it is not possible to have an "I–thou" relationship with them, and yet the care of the body must be extended to them too. It is the institution that allows such care to be extended to the whole body, a care that, with the best will in the world, I will only be able to show to a small number of people. It is also the institution that will guarantee that this solicitude will be able to continue when the initial practitioners have disappeared.

The Fruitful Tension between Institution and Charism

Charism and institution can be compared to the sap of a tree and its fibers. Without the sap, there is no life; without the fibers, there is no tree. The institutional structure of Christianity guarantees its unity, its order, its continuity and its efficacity; the inspiration of the Spirit gives it its life, its dynamism and, in the final analysis, its *raison d'être*.[36]

A body is made up of flesh and bones. A skeleton, on its own, is a symbol of death, but if our body lost its skeleton, it would be nothing more than a small, formless heap, doomed soon to perish. The beauty of a face depends as much on the bone structure as on the flesh.

The Protestant pen of Jean-Louis Leuba writes of the need for the Church to monitor charisms, since the "charismatic ministry" favors (perhaps in a quite surprising way) an "autocratic conception" [of ecclesial life].[37] But we need to go further.

We now need ... to show that, in Christianity, there is something more particular and more sacred going on; here, institution and charism are linked in a way that has no equivalent in secular society. Indeed, it is the

---

[35] P. Ricœur, *Soi-même comme un autre*, 228.

[36] E. D. O'Connor, *Charism and Institution*, 5.

[37] J.-L. Leuba, *L'institution et l'Événement. Les deux modes de l'œuvre de Dieu selon le Nouveau Testament*, (Neuchâtel: Delachaux et Niestlé, 1950), 96, cited in K. Lehmkühler, *Pouvoir de guérir et théologie des ministères, charisme et institution*, Revue d'éthique et de théologie morale 2011/HS (no 266), pp. 109–129.

institutions themselves (such as the Scriptures, the sacraments and the pastoral ministry) that are the privileged vehicles for the most precious charisms in the Church.

For sure, the Bible represents an official document, a public document, settled upon once and for all, destined to remain unchangeable until the end of time. But like any other institution, it is capable of being reduced to a dead letter and a source of death to anyone who reads it with a veiled heart.[38]

At the same time, the Word is living and active because it is animated by the Spirit, without which it is nothing. "We find ourselves, here, in the presence of a close interpenetration of institution and charism, in which each sustains the other."[39] The same is true for the sacraments and (slightly less obviously) for the pastoral ministry. The most spiritual gift there is, that of the Body and Blood of Christ, has been committed to the charge of that most institutional of realities: apostolic succession.

This particular and close bond between institution and charism, which characterizes Christianity, finds its roots (or, better, is prefigured) in the Old Testament, which accustomed the People of God to this spiritual experience of the institution. We only have to examine what the Law represents for Israel, the way the Psalmist sings of it in Psalm 119 (for example), this Law that seems to us so burdensome, and which St. Peter compares to "a yoke ... which neither our fathers nor we have been able to bear" (Acts 15:10). Now, this Law prepared the way for the Incarnation, and Jesus submitted Himself to it: circumcision, the purification of His mother, pilgrimage to the Temple all are mentioned in the Gospel explicitly, but Jesus' entire youth was steeped in the Law.

In the religious life, this tension is lived in a powerful way. Silence in a community, for example, cannot be achieved if there is no rule imposing it, because one person refusing to be subject to silence is enough to disturb the whole community. The rule is necessary to help us in our weakness, as we strive toward a goal we desire but struggle to attain.

---

[38] E. D. O'Connor, *Charisme et Institution*, 11–12, citing 2 Cor. 3:5 toward the end.
[39] Ibid.

Abuses in the Religious Life and the Path to Healing

At the beginning, we need to put effort into keeping silence; but if we are faithful to this practice, little by little, out of our silence something comes to birth within us that attracts us toward silence more and more strongly. This is why it is not permitted for each person to speak whenever he wants, about whatever he wants, to whomsoever he wants, as much as he wants.[40]

On the rule of silence

If it is proportionate, law is at the service of charism, and charism gives law its meaning. We can get this balance wrong in two possible ways. Firstly, through legalism, which strives to apply the law independently of its meaning, being satisfied with the letter without the spirit.[41] The other error has no name. It considers that the spirit does away with the letter, and hence with the law. But which spirit are we talking about? The Holy Spirit, the human spirit (self-will), or the spirit of the Adversary? The Athonite monks who, in the name of the freedom of the spirit, experimented with idiorhythmic monasteries, where everyone constructed his own rule, quickly abandoned the experiment, on account of the decadence that resulted.

The institution both holds the religious life in check and protects it; therein lies its paradox. There is something burdensome about it, which the charismatic leader will protest against, since it prevents him from manipulating people and situations as he might wish. It can also restrict desirable developments, not so much in and of itself perhaps, but because it can easily be used by those who dislike change. For the institution does not exist in isolation; it draws its very existence from the people who compose it. But it also protects the existence of religious life from our fickle whims, knowing that the spirit is willing, but the flesh is weak (Matt. 14:38). None of this is news to us.

Objectivity and Affectivity

Some people criticize the institution for being cold and impersonal. But this, too, can be an advantage, helping us to avoid unfortunate confusion. If a pilot

---

[40] *Carthusian Statues*, 14.1–2. (Online at www.chartreux.org). See Isaac of Nineveh, *De perfectione religiosa*, C. 65, ed. Bedjan, 450.

[41] This is also known as Pharisaism, which is perhaps a little unkind to the Pharisees, not all of whom were legalists.

has demonstrated that he is incapable of flying a plane properly in bad weather, there is no way that we would seek to keep him in his post, *so as not to hurt him;* the lives of the 150 passengers are more important than any consideration of the potential disappointment of the pilot. And yet, in monasteries where there are regular elections, we may sometimes observe a tendency to re-elect an abbot, an abbess, or a prioress, *so as not to hurt him,* even though his government of the community is unsatisfactory. Incidentally, the abbot or abbess may take advantage of this, even unconsciously. A typical example of this confusion is the reaction of one nun of otherwise sound judgment, when a prioress was not re-elected: *she must be disappointed not to have the affection of her sisters.* This remark confuses everything. A vote to elect a prioress is not a sign of affection for her (or the lack of it), but a recognition that she is competent to govern a community wisely.

The same sort of confusion can occur in votes at the different stages of religious life. The community — and thus every monk or nun — has a responsibility to decide whether a candidate is capable of committing to this way of life. They must think of the good of the candidate and of the community; the point of the vote is not to determine whether a candidate is likeable or not. Thus, the community needs to be properly informed, sufficiently in advance of the vote, so that people can reflect and pray about it, rather than simply allow their vote to be determined by emotion.

Something to keep in mind if we are voting to dismiss someone. Have we had sufficient time, reflection & information to make this decision?

4

The Common Life

"How good and how pleasant it is for brothers to dwell together in unity" (Ps. 13:1).[42]

This verse from the Psalms could serve as a kind of charter for the common life. However, the reality usually turns out to be less idyllic, since living together with others in a religious community is not something that happens automatically, any more than it does in a marriage. Here — as in other contexts — human weaknesses will show themselves, but certain boundaries have been laid down by age-old wisdom, to make it possible to live a life in common, conformed as much as possible to the gospel.

"Anyone who does not love the brother, whom he can see, cannot love God, whom he cannot see" (1 John 4:20).[43] A path has been traced out for us here, for learning to love God "not in word or speech but in deed and in truth" (1 John 3:18). The common life is a school of charity, of patience, of self-giving, of service, of humility, of forgiveness, of listening, of sensitivity ... the full list would be lengthy. But none of this is automatic, and we could apply to the common life that saying of the Lord: "Narrow is the gate and hard the way that leads to life" (Matt. 7:14).[44]

It is hardly surprising, then, if the common life is also a place where things of a very different sort also spring up: all kinds of friction, selfishness, vanity,

---

[42] This passage was directly translated from the French to maintain original emphasis.

[43] This passage was directly translated from the French to maintain original emphasis.

[44] This passage was directly translated from the French to maintain original emphasis.

57

over-sensitivity, rivalry, anger, grudges ... here, too, the full list would be a long one. Why would we be surprised by this? A religious life, after all, is still a human life, and those who come to the monastery do not do so because they are already saints but in order to become saints. The monastic fathers clearly saw the desert as a place of combat against evil, following in the footsteps of Christ who was tempted there. All the various forms of religious life recognize this.

If any sort of life together is to be possible, we need a structure and a system of rules. St. Pachomius, the founder of cenobitic monasticism, learned this through bitter experience. Filled with charity, he had established a community of which he was the servant. He thought that his brethren's desire to follow the Lord would be as strong as his own. Alas ... in the end, he had to acknowledge that, at a certain point, they had abandoned all their ideals and had become self-serving in a spirit that was entirely worldly. He expelled them all and started again from scratch, this time establishing a system of rules.

The creativity of the religious life is manifested in various structures, which are often dependent on the culture from which they emerged. The *Rule of Saint Benedict* remains close in spirit to the ideals of Roman society, and the abbot has something of the *paterfamilias* about him. Monasticism has tended to retain a fairly monarchical structure, whereas the mendicant orders have tended to need more flexibility. Every form of secular government has had its equivalent in the religious life. It is very important to be aware of this diversity if we are to avoid reducing the common life (and its system of government) to a single model.

All these different forms have existed at some point, and all the deviant forms, too, from tyranny to anarchy. But evil is far less inventive than good, and experience shows that it is oft repeated.

Authority as Service

Authority is a service, without which no society can exist in the long term. It is a demanding service that carries risks for the one who undertakes it, due to the temptation of power. St. Benedict reminds the abbot numerous times that he will have to give an account to his Master, since he, too, is under another's authority. True authority is at the service of life, peace, and communion. It finds joy in each person being able to put the riches he has to offer into the life of the community, as well as into his own personal life. It knows how to listen, understand, sympathize, and console. It also knows how to encourage, how to move people forward, and how to help them give the best of themselves. Sometimes it needs to reprove and correct, to attempt to restore proper order whenever our natural inclination toward the easy option gets the upper hand.

There are several places in the *Rule of St. Benedict* where we find eloquent examples of an approach, peculiar to the abbot, that requires the ability to marry firmness with kindness; these are particularly to be found in those parts regarding situations where he needs to impose some sort of sanction on a monk. This is a typical act of authority, in which the whole of the superior's power is apparent. But in its immense wisdom, the *Rule* always makes clear both the sanction — which is necessary for making the monk aware of his mistake and ensuring proper order is respected in the life of the community — and also the need for kindness, and a solicitude toward the person or persons involved. Indeed, if the sanction has the effect of crushing the monk, depriving him of any hope of escaping from the impasse in which he has placed himself, no good will come of it. Having established a penal code, which defines the different sorts of sanctions that can be imposed on an errant monk, the *Rule* insists (in chapter 27) that the abbot must take "extreme care" to watch over those who have failed in some way. This solicitude does not prevent him from imposing a sanction, but it does forbid him from humiliating people or pushing them to the point of despair.

> The abbot must take care of brothers who have failed in some way with every solicitude, for "it is not the healthy who need the doctor, but the sick" (Matt. 9:12). For this reason, he must, like a wise physician, make use of all the means at his disposal. He should send in *senpectae*, that is, wise seniors — who will, with discretion, console the brother who is in any sort of trouble, and encourage him to make humble satisfaction; they will support him, lest he should be overwhelmed by excessive sadness. As the Apostle says, "charity toward him must be intensified (2 Cor. 2:7–8), and all should pray for him.[45]

---

[45] *Rule of St. Benedict* (RB), chapter 27, vv. 1–4. Translated here directly from the French. Many English translations are available. A commonly used edition is: Timothy Fry, O.S.B. (ed.), *RB 1980: The Rule of St. Benedict in Latin and English with notes*. (Collegeville: Liturgical Press, 1981).

Abuses in the Religious Life and the Path to Healing

The wisdom of this teaching is manifested in the fact that the abbot knows that he is not alone in bearing responsibility for the brother who has committed some fault. To be sure, it is up to him to take any necessary decisions, but he is also to call on the whole community to ask their prayers, as well as on a small number of monks (other than himself) who will support the struggling brother discreetly. In communities, a public fault, especially if followed by some sort of sanction, often gives rise to an excommunication far more drastic than those forms of excommunication pronounced by the Church's *magisterium*. The guilty party is regarded as an outcast and condemned to the most crushing solitude. In this regard, while the *Rule* recognizes that a temporary exclusion may be necessary in some cases, it also establishes a framework allowing us to prevent a sanction from becoming fatal and lays down that such a sanction can only be initiated by the abbot.

Abbots, priors, and superiors are thus all at the service of life: spiritual life, human life, community life. The example of Christ, who came "not to be served but to serve" (Matt. 20:28), is their help and their guide.

But there is more to be said about this, since religious authority cannot be understood apart from the Incarnation.

Both Authority and Obedience Spring from the Incarnation

Religious life, following in the footsteps of Christ, arises entirely out of the Incarnation. When the Word became flesh, this union did not only concern His own personal humanity. St. Augustine speaks of the *totus Christus*, the entire Christ. We can shed light on this expression by saying that the entire Christ is both Himself and us, the head and the members. Jesus expressed this powerfully when He spoke of the Last Judgment: "I was hungry and you gave me food, I was thirsty and you gave me drink, I was a stranger and you welcomed me" (Matt. 25:35). All monastic hospitality finds its source in this saying, and all the services of the active congregations draw their inspiration from it. Indeed, we must not downplay these words, which are, after all, in the first person: *I was hungry.*

When we show love to someone in a concrete way, it is Christ who is the recipient. The foundation of this truth [of the faith] is Christ, who has "made this person His own." It is an extension of the Incarnation, upon which the Fathers — especially Cyril of Alexandria — insisted so much. Christ has made the whole of humanity "his own," not just in some moral way, but in a real way, at the level of being. St. Augustine too sees things in this way, which is testimony to his marvelous meditation — a true "key to living" — in his commentary on Psalm 86, where we see people of all generations crying out, and then passing away, leaving their place to the generations that follow after them, who will in the same way cry out, then pass away. This continuous cry of the human race, he says, is really the cry of Christ, whose Passion continues until the end of the world. This explains that saying of Pope Benedict (which would otherwise be rather surprising): "Not a tear is lost."[46]

This is how we know that all the love and care given to the sick is in reality given to Christ. We are not saying here that the sick person doesn't matter (given it is Christ that I am caring for in him), because if the actual sick person does not receive care and love, neither will Christ. So the sick must be loved and cherished for their own sake, but this love and charity, while being entirely for the sick person, at the same time touches Christ, all in a single movement, without our even needing to advert to it. How immense is the goodness of God, who in this way gives us the opportunity to serve Christ just as concretely as did Mary, Joseph, and the contemporaries of Jesus. What Christian would not envy Mary of Bethany, with her marvelous gesture of drying with her hair the perfume she had just poured out over Jesus' feet? The infirmarian who helps a sick brother to wash, if he does it with love and sensitivity, is being offered this same opportunity.

Religious authority and obedience have their foundation in the Incarnation. Their source is to be found in the life of Nazareth and was expressed in a few short words by St. Luke: "He lived under their authority" (Luke 2:51).[47] Having come in the flesh to experience our humanity and take it to Himself, Christ entered into human nature totally. As a child, He was obedient to His parents. And yet the evangelist shows that His understanding of the mystery was more developed

---

[46] A Carthusian, unpublished letter.

[47] This passage was directly translated from the French to maintain original emphasis.

than theirs: "They did not understand what he was saying to them. He went down with them to Nazareth and lived under their authority" (Luke 2:50–51).[48] Jesus discerns, through the words of His parents, that for Him, at this moment, to be *in His Father's house* is to be under their authority, even if they do not understand this crucial aspect of His mystery. The submissiveness of the incarnate Word brings into the world an obedience that will put right the disobedience of Adam and Eve. It will be accomplished on the Cross — *"It is accomplished"* — but it begins already in Nazareth. And just as the obedience of Jesus is made manifest in His Passion, through His submitting to events that are all too terribly human in nature, so, in Nazareth, the depth of His obedience finds expression in His living under the authority of His parents, people who are fully human, with all the limitations that implies. Far from being an obstacle, these limitations are essential; otherwise, would the life of Jesus in any sense be fully our life?

Just as the infirmarian serves Christ in a concrete way in the suffering humanity of the sick, so a religious follows Christ in freely submitting to a limited human authority, marked by sin,[49] and thus capable of making mistakes. These limitations are not in any sense just an unfortunate "bump in the road"; they are an integral part of religious obedience.

It has become dangerous these days to rely too heavily on the formula (which is classical, but difficult to understand properly) that has it that the superior *holds the place of God*. This does not mean that, in virtue of their responsibility, superiors somehow share in the divine prerogative, and that their word is truth, but rather that, in relation to the religious in their care, superiors hold the place that Mary and Joseph held in relation to Jesus. But let us hope that superiors do not forget that they are much less worthy than Mary and Joseph to hold this place.

For the Superior, the One Who Obeys Holds the Place of Christ

This theological vision of obedience has a further consequence. The superior must exercise his authority over the brethren as over the children of God. This means that when we say that the superior *holds the place of God for us*, this formula has

---

[48] This passage was directly translated from the French to maintain original emphasis.

[49] For the religious, but also for Jesus, since St. Joseph was, like us, a repentant sinner.

itself to be completed by another one: for the superior, *the one who obeys holds the place of Christ.* And this for the same reason. Just as the infirmarian can serve Christ in the sick under his care whom he has responsibility for, if this is done with love, so the superior can serve Christ in those in his charge, provided this is done with love and respect. Otherwise, it is Christ who is mistreated.

If the infirmarian meets Christ in the sick being cared for, the sick, too, can meet Christ in the infirmarian who cares for them. This way in which the sick and the infirmarian make Christ present to one another we find implicit in a beautiful text of Guigo:

> Thus we exhort the sick to fix their attention on the sufferings of Christ, and those caring for them to fix their attention on His mercies. In this way, the former will gain strength to bear their sufferings, and the latter will become all the more ready to provide support. And while, ever keeping close to Christ, the former reflect on the service they receive, the latter will not neglect them, for they both await from the same Lord the same reward for what they do; the former for their suffering, the latter for their compassion.[50]

We could borrow this text and apply it to the authority relationship: it is for the religious to meditate on the obedience of Christ; it is for the superior to meditate on His mercy. The former will thus be the more ready to obey, the latter will pay more attention to ruling with justice. If everyone remembers that it is out of love for Christ that the former submit themselves to authority and the latter make demands of people, there will be no negligence from the former or obduracy from the latter; rather, each will await from the same Lord the reward for the duty he has fulfilled, the former with docility, the latter with sensitivity.

THE EXAMPLE OF THE HOLY FAMILY

The authority that the superior has received is thus not simply a kind of delegated power, which would only touch on the externals of what must be accomplished.

---

[50] Guigo, the fifth prior of the Grande Chartreuse, put together the first rule, which carried the title of *Customs.* Guigues, *Coutumes,* 38.2, Sources Chrétiennes, (Paris: Éd. du Cerf, 1984), 241–242.

Abuses in the Religious Life and the Path to Healing

As well as the concrete mission of bringing the community to life, he has also received that more mysterious authority of allowing his brethren to be obedient to Christ in their everyday lives. The limitations of his character, his wisdom, or his competence are not altogether an obstacle to this mystery, as St. Teresa of Avila explained with humor to her brothers, in her reply to a spiritual challenge:

Allowing his brethren to be obedient to Christ

> To every knight of the Virgin who offers once each day, with firm resolve, to submit his life to a superior who is foolish, full of vices, a ferocious eater and weak of character, she gives, the same day the offer is made, half of his merits for that day.[51]

In order to catch the right tone, it is worthwhile to ponder the extraordinary picture offered to us in the Holy Family. If Mary asks Jesus to go to bed, He goes to bed, and if Joseph asks Him to cut a plank of wood, He cuts it. There is something astounding about the submissiveness of the incarnate Word. But it also implies that Mary and Joseph treat Jesus according to His dignity as Son of God. It would be absurd (or even heretical) to imagine a Jesus who obeyed unthinkingly, without discernment, because this would imply a separation between His human will and His divinity. Jesus has a human will that is distinct from His divine will;[52] each of the two natures remains intact in the Incarnation, but they belong to the same person and cannot be in opposition to each other. The same goes for His human intellect and His divine intellect.

A religious superior gives orders to a child of God, understood in the strongest sense. Better: a superior gives orders insofar as the religious is a child of God, since it is the vow of obedience addressed to God that gives the superior authority over him. This calls for a deep respect for his freedom and dignity.

> Let the prior, whose office requires no small degree of self-denial, apply to himself these words of Guigo: "Your Lord has deputed you to be the servant of your sons; let your intention be that they do, not what pleases you, but what profits them. It is for you to adapt yourself to what

---

[51] Teresa of Avila, *Œuvres complètes*, "Réponse à un défi" (Paris: DDB, 1964), 1058.

[52] To suggest the opposite would be monothelitism, a heresy against which Maximum the Confessor fought strenuously, winning the palm of martyrdom as a result. Monothelitism asserts that Christ has only one will.

is beneficial to them, not to bend them to your will; for they have been entrusted to your care, not for you to preside over, but so that you may be of use to them."[53]

He also has the daunting duty of presenting himself to his brethren in a manner that does not make it too difficult for them to see his authority as a presence of Christ, the Master. His own human sinfulness is an obstacle to this mission, and only a real humility will allow this opaqueness to regain its transparency, since he must realize that it is not him whom the members of the community are obeying, and that in this sense he is a bit "like a donkey carrying a reliquary on its back."[54]

" a donkey carrying a reliquary on his back "

The Star-Shaped Structure[55]

But human beings are human beings, and it is always possible for things to slide, so that power is no longer at the service of others but rather seeks to be served.[56] The more sparkling the superior's personality, the more the community will be lost in admiration, and the greater the temptation will be. Little by little, the structure of the community is subtly altered, in order to change its fundamental purpose, until its role is now to be at the service of authority, and to maintain that authority. While naked authoritarianism is easily recognized due to its

---

[53] *Carthusian Statutes*, 23.24, quoting Guigo: "Do not make your lords — that is, the sons of your Lord, to whose services you have been destined by their Father, the Lord your God — do what you want, but rather what is of benefit for them. For you must bend to what is of benefit to them, rather than bending them to your own will. Indeed, they have been committed to you, not so that you can order them about, but so that you can be of use to them." Guigo I, *Meditations*, Sources Chrétiennes (Paris: Éd. du Cerf, 1983), 225. An English edition is available: Guigo I, *The Meditations of Guigo I, Prior of the Charterhouse*, Cistercian Studies 155 (Cistercian Publications: Kalamazoo, 1995).

[54] A French proverb.

[55] The first French edition spoke of a "pyramid structure." Experience has demonstrated that people understood this expression as referring to a power structure, whereas the author had intended to speak of a relational structure. For this reason, he has decided to alter this term to "star-shaped structure."

[56] Authority and service must not be seen in opposition to each other. Authority must not abdicate its role in order to become service; it has rather to exercise this role rightly, and with a pure intention. Every sort of social group needs authority.

bruising effect on people's feelings, this sliding away from the community's true purpose is much more likely to go unnoticed. And yet it is clearly shown up by the fact that everything begins and ends with the "head."

In the older orders or congregations, with a well-tried structure and a long history, corrective elements have long been in place; these do not offer total protection from the possibility of a rogue leader, but the problem will generally be limited to a single community and will not affect the totality of the body. It is difficult to imagine the whole Order of St. Benedict going off the rails, but, on the other hand, this has happened in individual abbeys. In these cases, however, the institution that is in the process of going off course has recourse to remedy, particularly through canonical visitations or chapters.

The risk is higher in situations where communities are being founded or reformed, when the superior is also the author of the constitutions (still in the process of being written), and he may feel free to alter them at whim. In this way, all power is in the hands of the superior — legislative, executive, and judiciary. All decision-making comes from the superior, including decisions about the direction the community should take. Since he is regarded as the repository of the community's charism, there is a real danger that he will remain the community's sole point of reference. The superior's qualities in this way become a trap, firstly for himself, and then for the spellbound community.

PROHIBITING INTERACTIONS BETWEEN MEMBERS OF THE COMMUNITY

When everything begins and ends with the head, we have a pyramidal structure, which is a power structure. In its turn, the pyramid structure normally rests on a relational structure, which is star shaped. One abbot, who has had direct experience of situations where the behavior of communities has gone in such a wrong direction, said: "Each time, I noticed that all the relationships in the community were vertical, never horizontal; people could communicate with the superior(s) of the community, but there was never any communication of substance with other community members."

He is not the only one to have noticed this phenomenon, which always surprises people who see it from the outside. Try to imagine a family where the children were forbidden to speak to one another and could only have any sort of personal relationship with their parents. Wouldn't this be patently absurd?

And yet this is precisely what occurs in communities where communication between members is forbidden. Why?

The structure of a normal community is like a web. There is a link between each member and the head, but this is complemented by many links between the members themselves.

If the superior is anxious to do what he wants, he has to silence all opposing voices. Except in the case of the headstrong, it will be difficult for a single monk to oppose his superior, if he sees that nobody else seems to be challenging what is going on. It will be easy to convince him that he is misjudging or exaggerating the situation. The danger lies in his discovering that someone else — or indeed several others — thinks like him, which might strengthen his conviction that his perspective might be right after all.

To avoid this risk, all the superior need do is sever all the lateral links in the structure, thus ensuring that there are no true personal relationships between the members of the community and no conversation on important subjects. Now that the religious have meaningful contact with the superior alone, there is no risk that they will stray from the line that he seeks to hold. Sometimes intermediaries can spring up, but in reality, they are only go-betweens. In this way, since there is nobody else to talk with, anyone who has doubts about the way the community is working will be unable to get the confirmation he would need, to turn his intuition (which may well be vague) into conviction. He will remain in doubt, and will take things no further. In an enclosed community, the members may thus exist in a state of real isolation.

A diagram will help us to understand how pernicious this structure is. On the left, we have the normal web-structure. On the right is the star-shaped structure: all of the lateral links have been severed. Thus any relationship between one

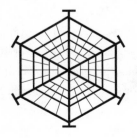 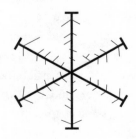

member of the community and another necessarily passes through the person in the center, who can thus control everything. In fact, only the skeleton of the original web-structure remains. This skeleton is important, just as our skeleton is essential for our life, but when the skeleton is all that remains, there is no longer any life.

What sort of spiritual discourse can be used to make such an unbelievable state of affairs acceptable to the members of a community? There is a great deal of variety in the methods employed, and these make use of many different aspects of the religious life: an insistence upon silence, on discretion; seemingly spiritual and mystical reasons may be advanced, such as the perfect communion of the elect or of the Trinity, a respect for the other's interior life, and so on. All of this can be invoked, with a bit of imagination. Anyone looking closely, however, will be able to easily discern the real reason for it, simply by observing what comes of it, which is the suppression of something so natural and necessary as real personal communication between the members of the community. If everything comes from the head, the body becomes entirely passive, and personalities (especially the more vibrant ones) will quickly suffocate — or be suffocated. *This from a Carthusian*

From the perspective of the power figure who has given in to the temptation of wanting to be in control of everything, the reaction is quite logical: *Divide and conquer;* it is an ancient method. Solzhenitsyn, in *The Gulag Archipelago*, demonstrates the tactic the Bolsheviks used, once they were in power, to get rid of their former allies, the Socialist Revolutionaries: they moved them around. Not wanting to take the risk of mounting a real persecution, they simply shifted the leaders of the movement around from town to town. In a world where there was no Internet, people arriving in a town unknown to them suddenly found themselves with no connections, and by the time they had built up a network of acquaintances, they were moved to another place. The method is different, but the goal is the same: to avoid relationships between people who could oppose us.

In a community, the principal counterbalance to the power of the superior is the community itself. The abbot or the prior does not just do whatever he wants. There is the rule, and there is the community. At the congregational level, there are councils and chapters. The superior is also obedient, and submits to the reality of life in the community, and this is a good thing. If there are free exchanges between the members of the community, and if there is a real possibility for people to express their views, it is not possible for the community to have something that only appears to be unity but is in reality a façade; the unity will either be real or non-existent.

Thought Control

Whether it is deliberate or not, the star-shaped structure is essentially a structure of control. The superior controls everything, since everything is under his authority. Having no other point of reference than him, the members have no means of reaching any judgment than that of the superior, at least if they have always lived inside such a structure.

This situation can lead to a shocking restriction: that of access to books. The library is closed, and what can come into the community is subject to drastic filtering. Is it to protect the community members from the risks presented by any work that is foreign to the internal way of thinking — even if it is only the risk of it becoming apparent that the superior is not as great as people say he is?

Naturally, reasons are advanced that, at first glance, seem to be quite acceptable. *We have our own spirituality. If you go drawing refreshment from other sources, you will never enter into your own vocation at depth. You mustn't wander about. It's enough for you to plough one furrow. The Desert Fathers had no desire for books.* Austerity, flight from the world, simplicity ... Given that these are all Carthusian practices, we should set the record straight here. There is a certain restriction in the first years of the novitiate, so that the newly arrived novice doesn't go wandering in every direction. But after this period, there is free access to the library for everyone.

To be sure, it is normal for religious to be invited to show a certain reserve with respect to certain types of reading that are of little interest to their vocation. Our consecrated life belongs to God, and we must mistrust our curiosity. The question becomes still more serious when it is a question of access to the Internet. Setting limits can thus prove to be useful or necessary, but there is one criterion that allows us to understand the meaning and the relevance of this sort of restriction: if the goal of the restriction is to protect someone's vocation, and it flows naturally out of the community's way of life, it is normal; but if its goal is rather to protect the exclusive influence of a sort of uniform thinking, then things are grave indeed. The restriction can also be a question of the nature of the content. Restricting access to the superabundant and often unnecessary information that is such a feature of our time can be justified. But if it is a question of books on spirituality or theology, or documents of the Magisterium, and so on, then it ceases to be acceptable.

<h2>PRIDE AND ISOLATION</h2>

Why establish such defensive structures, isolating the members of the community from one another and the outside world? There is no single answer. A taste for power and a concern to maintain it are not necessarily the most important factors. On a visit to the Grande Chartreuse, Msgr. Carballo, the Secretary of the Roman Congregation for Institutes of Consecrated Life and Societies of Apostolic Life,[57] said something that, at first glance, might seem surprising: *The drift into sect-like thinking begins when a community or an institute considers itself better than all the rest.* This remark, made by someone who is aware of so many cases of aberrant communities, certainly gives food for thought. Indeed, because of its feeling of superiority, such a community or institute will quickly become separated from the rest of the body.

"From before the creation of the world, it pleased God to call our religious family to be holy and immaculate in His presence." The striking thing about this phrase is that it is a quotation. It defines perfectly the vocation of redeemed human nature—that is, the Church Triumphant. It is true for the whole Body, and it will be true for each member, as a member of that Body. A single religious family cannot appropriate it for itself; that would be an illicit claim. Whatever the precise words used, the sentiment remains the same: a feeling of superiority or even exclusivity, which could be formulated in phrases such as "we are the best," or even, "we are the real religious." Ordinarily, this will come with a certain mistrust of other religious, who will ultimately be treated as decadent. This feeling of being out of the ordinary (and above it, of course) isolates the

---

[57] Editor's note: With the promulgation of *Praedicate evangelium* by Francis in 2022, most bodies that were formerly titled "Congregation" were renamed to "Dicastery." This book preserves "Congregation" for the sake of simplicity; but note well that many of these curial bodies have retained their previous prerogatives under new names.

group, which becomes self-referential. All thought comes from within the community, and uniquely so. The group's thinking becomes the reference point for truth and religious practice. We often find here in an implicit form (or even explicitly formulated) the idea of some sort of divine mission, whose goal is to save the religious life or the Church, as well as a certainty that this group alone has managed to preserve truth or wisdom; it is like Noah's Ark, in the midst of universal perdition. If the Church seeks to point out dysfunctional elements, the community is no longer able to hear it and might even end up refusing obedience to the Church for the sake of obedience to the founder and to that "charism" of which the group considers itself to be the sole repository.

To illustrate what we have just said, here is an analysis, written by a religious, concerning the crisis that his congregation went through:

> Due to the human charisma of the founder and to the dynamism that he inspired in the members of the community, the congregation lived for a long time in the midst of a sort of Messianic omnipotence, at a time when many congregations in the Church were living in disobedience to the Council. The idea of being among the faithful children was exhilarating. At a time when relativism was everywhere, and people were ruled by uniform thinking, a good number of young people felt attracted by this almost heroic mission. Saving the Church: what an honor, what an enthralling mission!
>
> To protect ourselves from the enemies of the Church, we needed to live totally cut off from the world. Enemies were everywhere, even within the Church. Only those who praised our way of doing things and our way of life were worthy of consideration. That said, you must not think this isolation was a physical cutting off from the world. Our separation was at the level of the intellect and the emotions, and it was all the stronger and deeper because of this. It guided our every thought and deed.

Uniform Thinking

This collective pride gives rise to uniform thinking — if, indeed, it is not a consequence of it, since these two support each other. A group that believes itself to be the only survivor of catastrophe will believe that its own way of thinking is the only one that is true and right, the only one that is faithful to the charism, or even to the faith,[58] and any notion that departs from this will be automatically regarded as coming from the Adversary, or whatever name you prefer. Worldly thinking, as opposed to the way of thinking proper to the chosen of God; psychological thinking, as opposed to spiritual or mystical thinking; thinking that is carnal, deviant, mediocre, modernist (if we are talking about a traditionalist group) or traditionalist (if the group considers itself to be modern), is diabolical: the list is long and depends very much on the context.

Not everyone within the community reacts in the same way. Sometimes it is the whole community or congregation that takes a stand. Sometimes only the head is really responsible for this; the rest follow only because they receive nothing but the information (or formation) that the superior wants to give them. As for the clearheaded members of the community, they will have been driven underground long since.

The single word "group" in fact covers two smaller sub-groups: those who offer explicit adherence and share actively in the work of maintaining the status quo, and those who might think differently were they free to do so, only the context in which they find themselves never offers them this liberty. One witness speaks of this problem:

> Even those who suffer from psychological frailties or emotional dependences are capable of acting and reacting, provided they know what is true and what is false; what is just and what is unjust; what is virtuous and what is sinful. But when it is claimed that blind and absolute confidence and obedience are the highest virtues, when any doubt is considered to come from the demon and to be sinful, when any sort of questioning is considered to come from pride and the Old Adam, when any independent discernment is considered a consequence of original sin, then people are totally disempowered.

---

[58] The distinction depends on the "Messianic" context of the community in question. If the community thinks it has a mission to save its order or congregation, then it will feel that it is the only one that is faithful to the charism. If it thinks its mission is to save the Church, it will think it is the only one true to the Christian faith. This can be expressed in statements such as "The bishops have lost the faith."

A Culture of Exceptions

If we confuse the superior with the rule, it can quite easily follow that everything must surely be allowed for the superior. The star-shaped structure that places him at the center of everything, the collective pride that serves to reinforce the feeling of being separate from the masses, the being accustomed to an authority figure who presents as the ultimate point of reference: all of these place the superior in quite an anomalous situation. If we are above every rule (because in a sense we have become the rule), where will we find the strength of will necessary submit to things that might be unpleasant? Food, enclosure, silence, comfort — everything becomes an occasion for exceptions to be made. This phenomenon does not only necessarily relate to the superior; in practice, the exceptions permitted for the superior are quickly extended to his close collaborators.

There is nothing extraordinary about the tendency superiors may have to make exceptions for themselves. The *Carthusian Statutes* give an explicit warning about this to the procurator:

> The procurator — and also all the other officers of the house — must be careful not to abuse his office by allowing himself dispensations or unnecessary things that he would be unwilling to concede to others.[59]

But we move to another level if the exception becomes the rule. Besides the fact that the superior loses all ability to set an example, a progressive sliding creates a distorted relationship to money, or indeed to sexuality. A recent scandal incriminated one abbot who, together with one of the brethren, had become accustomed to luxuries, such as weekends in big hotels (costing €30,000), all the while diverting funds that had been intended for the poor. Examples like this one, mercifully rare though they are, show that religious are not necessarily immune to the seductive power of money and pleasure. Examples where a superior has the use of a personal bank account (which is at best questionable) are noticeably more frequent. We really need to be vigilant about this, for in cases where aberrant behavior becomes established in communities, problems related to money nearly always spring up.

---

[59] *Carthusian Statutes*, 26.8.

This culture of exceptions does not directly harm the members of the community, but it does create a creeping malaise and a sense of injustice. If on the one hand the superior imposes restrictions in the name of poverty and on the other hand has a personal bank account, which he uses at will, with no accountability to anyone, then the others in the community no longer have the support of a good example and may be scandalized. Those who are weakest will feel their own commitment called into question.

Signs of honor can thus become excessive. The monastic life sees the abbot as holding the place of Christ in the heart of the community, and this can translate into signs of respect, or a special table in the refectory. But when this involves secret use of money, and being offered more refined meals than the other monks receive, is this still the devotion to the representative of Christ, as described by the *Rule?*

If the superior does not live like his brethren, this has an effect on an essential dimension of the religious life. A certain hypocrisy can even be established. In one new community (which, incidentally, has not survived), the religious were forced to live in the harshest conditions, sleeping in dormitories in a poorly-heated building, and having no form of private life, while the founder was leading a pleasant existence, living alone in a separate building, where he had the benefit of all necessary comforts — and maybe a few more besides. But out of humility, he used to celebrate Mass barefoot.

The prophets thoroughly castigate those shepherds that do not take care of the flock:

> Woe to the shepherds of Israel who are shepherds for themselves! Is it not on account of the sheep that you are shepherds? But you, on the contrary, drink their milk, you dress in their wool, you butcher the fattened sheep, you are not shepherds for the flock. (Ezek. 34:2–3)[60]

A modern version of this text might include (alongside money, which has already been mentioned): immoderate use of the Internet, being free to engage in all manner of unnecessary or even worldly relations with people outside the

---

[60] This passage was directly translated from the French to maintain original emphasis.

community, comfort in manner of life or when traveling, habitually missing Mass or common Office, and so on.

The weariness that comes from bearing the burdens of responsibility can justify some exceptions, and indeed everything is a question of moderation, which should be discussed with another person: perhaps a spiritual father, or similar. But we must not forget that the ministry of example holds a very important place in the mission of superiors. The *Carthusian Statutes* advise a prior who is no longer able to give an example to ask to be relieved of his responsibility:

> A prior who is prevented by age or infirmity from taking care of his flock and from giving an example of regular observance, will humbly acknowledge this, and, without waiting for the general chapter, will ask the Reverend Father for mercy.[61]

A culture of exceptions can, in practice, be supported by a culture that inclines toward the extraordinary. In a community that feels as though it has reinvented everything, the extraordinary is to be found everywhere: the personality and history of the founder, the circumstances of the foundation, and even the basic elements of the community life. Priests for the community are not ordained by the local bishop but by the nuncio, by a cardinal from the Curia, or even by the pope, if possible. The community itself is a part of what is exceptional.

> We were told quite clearly that we were part of an elite group. This community was part of the renewal of the monastic life, it was the community that Jesus had wanted to found for His return in glory.[62]

> And God had called us — us! So it was up to us to save the Church! The salvation of the world rested upon our shoulders.[63]

Taken a bit further, this can give rise to perverse consequences. The members of the community will tend to accept, without asking too many questions, dubious behavior, which gives away the fact that power is being wielded over

[61] *Carthusian Statutes,* 23.23. *Mercy* in this context means being relieved of his responsibility. The "Reverend Father" is the Prior of the Grande Chartreuse.
[62] M.-L. Janssens, in the film *Emprise et abuse spirituel*
[63] X. Leger in the same film.

the community or individuals within it, for nothing in the house is ordinary; and this can go so far as to include those situations that the Holy Father has called "sexual slavery." Even if the victim's conscience reacts and names the evil for what it is, the context makes him think that it is surely not normal, but people in the community have grown so used to being outside the norms that they submit, from force of habit. Nothing inside the house is as it is in the world; normal reasoning does not apply, and in the end they all take up the same refrain: *It's normal for us.*[64]

When the Charism Becomes Institutionalized: A Trap

At the time of the last council, there was much criticism of a certain fossiliza-tion that, it was felt, could threaten religious life, if it was reduced to fulfilling the rule. A real rediscovery of the action of the Holy Spirit was the driving force behind a great movement, which sought to shake up a Church that had fallen into slumber and teach people once more how to love in a way that was more according to the Spirit. It was a period rich in works of various kinds, reflections, and the emergence of new things. It would be an exaggeration to suggest that all of this was golden, but the real richness that was there cannot be denied. Many Christians — religious or not — were able to learn how do-cility to the Holy Spirit is able to breathe life into a rule, a law that, taken on its own, risks being dead.

This new approach led to a greater spotlight falling upon the creativity of the reformers and founders. This was nothing new in itself, as charismatic personalities have always been at the origin of new bursts of energy in the reli-gious life. The peculiarity of the post-conciliar period consisted in a mistrust of institutions, with the implicit or explicit idea that the institutional dimension was in opposition to the charismatic dimension. From this grew the tendency to build everything upon the charism, upon flexibility, upon the word of the one in charge, whatever name this person might go under. A light structure presents a number of advantages: agility, creativity, and an ability to respond. One word from the head, and the whole body follows.

---

[64] This refrain is typical of sexual predators, who use it to numb the conscience of a victim who is beginning to ask questions about the morality of their relationship.

But in the wings a twofold process is slowly established, whose consequences are not immediately understood. On the one hand, if the charism rests entirely in the hands of the one who is in charge, if he transmits to the community the word of the Holy Spirit, then it becomes more and more unthinkable to contradict him, as this would be resisting God. Presenting a text of the superior general, one secretary wrote to his congregation: *Here are some words of the Holy Spirit as they are today, spoken through the mouth of X, and for each person a defining truth.* These lines are seriously over the top. If the words of X are a defining truth for everyone, then it becomes impossible to entertain any critical opinion.

On the other hand, once it has been laid down that the community's entire dynamism needs to be charismatic, and that everything charismatic comes from the head, people begin anxiously looking toward the horizon: what will happen when the key person disappears? Even if it is not adverted to consciously, it becomes more and more evident that the institution is necessary for establishing a life in the long term, and then we witness a strange kind of inversion.

In the beginning, we followed the one in charge because he was the dwelling place of the Holy Spirit, the first to become obedient [to His promptings]. Wasn't this what drew us to follow him? Now different people are in charge — whether because the reformer or founder is no longer in place, or because others have found their way into positions of responsibility as the institute developed. If the charismatic model is not to be altered, then it must be perpetuated, and since charismatic people do not always spring up when and where we might want them to, those chosen to shoulder responsibilities in the community may end up being invested by the community *ipso facto* with the label "charismatic." The charism has become an institution. We have moved from one model to another. "That particular person is at the head of the community because the Holy Spirit dwells within her" has become "The Holy Spirit dwells within that particular person because she is at the head of the community."

Now, this is not totally false; there is such a thing as "grace of state"; when someone receives a responsibility in a proper way, God gives that person the graces necessary for exercising her responsibility. But this canonization (we might say "prophetization," if the word actually existed) of the superior, just because she is the superior, is still nonsensical, since the consequence is that every element necessary for establishing absolute authority is set in place. There is a risk that the freedom of the Spirit will give way to a form of tyranny.

This process is helped along by confusion at the level of terminology. The term "charism" can take on quite different meanings, depending on context. Its first meaning is personal and, in a Christian context, refers to a special grace of the Holy Spirit received by someone, for a certain fruitfulness within the Body of the Church. When applied to a religious community, the same term refers to what we might call the community's own grace, the particular way in which it seeks to reflect one of the aspects of the life of Christ or, better, the particular way by which a community invites its members to enter into union with one of the dimensions of the life of Christ. Now, in the first sense, a charism is a gift that is particular and non-transferable, whereas the charism of a community can be maintained for centuries, particularly if it is expressed in a set of constitutions. A confusion between these two distinct meanings can lead us to think that, unless there is a charismatic person at the top, the community may lose its charism. This can lead to a situation in which a charismatic person is artificially produced by the institution, to make certain that the community's charism will be maintained. There is no need to stress how absurd this is; we don't give orders to the Holy Spirit. As for the community's charism, there is no need for concern; it can always be kept alive through others who have understood the meaning of the initial impulse provided by the founder of the movement, if these others are capable of pursuing that initial impulse with creative fidelity. The community thus enters into the process of "tradition" in the broadest sense of the word, which really means "a handing-on": one generation giving to the next what it has itself received, lived, and adapted, so that the life can continue.

But this requires a certain amount of humility and demands of us that we accept the possibility of losing something. The fire that was there at the founding (or re-founding) of the community wanes a little, and the risk of routine becomes apparent.[65] It is the cost of continuity but also the price of success. An institution that attracts others to it will draw in mediocre elements along with quality ones. Continual enthusiasm is an illusion, and even the early Church — close

---

[65] What is being said here does not only apply to new communities but to any situation where a renewal is brought about by an exceptional person.

as it was to the Lord — soon became acquainted with lukewarmness. St. Paul and St. John (among others) both complain of this. "I have written a letter to the Church; but Diotrephes, who seems to like pre-eminence, will not receive us" (3 John 9).[66]

The Cult of Unity

UNITY: UNIFORMITY OR HARMONY?

Religious have always sought to realize on earth a version of the unity so fervently desired by Christ (see John 17), without waiting for the Body of Christ to be brought to perfection. There is surely no need to emphasize that the verse of the Psalms quoted at the beginning of the chapter only covers part of the reality, since living together and being united is above all a journey of conversion that needs to be constantly begun again. We are so different from each other! How can we unite — and not just seem to unite — a group of people so disparate? Dom Guillaume Jedrzejczak, the former abbot of Mont des Cats, once said in a talk: "We tend to think that monasteries are places of uniformity, whereas in fact they are probably the places where we can find the highest density of original characters per square meter on the planet!"[67]

A unity that is manufactured on the principle of a single mold in which everyone is formed can only end up doing violence to people because anything that doesn't fit into the mold will have to be cut away, time and time again. This approach is immediately doomed to failure; it can only ever result in a superficial semblance of unity because it considers differences to be a threat to unity.

Another way would be to begin from the opposite premise and to change one of the words in the question above. The adjective *disparate* sheds a rather negative light on the notion of difference; perhaps it would be better to ask: *How can we unite — really, and not in appearance only — a group that contains such a rich mixture of different sorts of people?* The key to unity is to be found in the way we look at difference. When building the house of God, do we want a wall made up entirely of identical cinder blocks, or do we want a wall made up entirely

---

[66] This passage was directly translated from the French to maintain original emphasis. Cf. Phil. 1:15; 2 Tim. 4:10–16.
[67] Talk given at the Grande Chartreuse, September 2018.

of different stones? True, fitting them together will take a lot of expertise, but will not the beauty of that wall be incomparably greater? The first wall is only a unity-uniformity. The second is a unity-harmony. The principal characteristic of uniformity is the notable lack of any difference; harmony, on the other hand, makes intelligent use of those differences that exist, so as to create a better unity. The ideas of polyphony and symphony come from this principle.

This richer unity forms around a central core that assembles, and this is true of every sort of human society. In a religious community, unity coalesces around the community's own way of life, first and foremost in its essential core (the search for God or the following of Christ), then in some elements that are perhaps less fundamental but nonetheless specific to this particular community. Someone who simply cannot abide the common life will never be able to be a Trappist, and someone who cannot bear solitude will never be able to be a Carthusian. Every form of religious life contains some key elements, on which it is essential that everyone agrees. Vocational discernment turns precisely on these elements. St. Benedict gives us an example: *Si revera Deum quærit*. "If he truly seeks God."[68] If this is not the case, then the young man or woman in question has no place in the monastic life, and he must be told this. It is not a reproach or a criticism; the person is simply knocking at the wrong door. And if we try to turn him into a Benedictine at all costs, then we are leaving ourselves open to serious problems. There is thus a central core, consisting of a few non-negotiable elements, and it is these that define the vocation and are found in all the houses of the institute.

Around this central core is a whole ring of elements that give a community a certain "feel," and it is this that will cause a particular individual to join this abbey, rather than another. These are less important things usually — more on the cultural side of things, we might say — but they make it easier for people to integrate into the community.

Beyond this, there is great freedom, which means that one soul doesn't resemble another any more than one face looks like another. We can live in

---

[68] *RB*, chapter 58, "The Discipline of Receiving Brothers." "The novice should be observed carefully, to see whether he truly seeks God, and whether he is obedient for the work of God, for obedience and for trials."

unity and have quite different preferences in the realms of spirituality, liturgy, politics, or food; that is all part of life. If we don't make distinctions in these areas, how will we avoid confusing what is essential with what is purely incidental, or interpreting as a threat to unity something that really just reflects a healthy diversity?

Nevertheless, the common life — including marriage — does require that certain activities are carried out together; perhaps liturgy is the most typical example. In a community, one person may have a preference for the vernacular, while another prefers Latin, but it cannot be the case that, at the same Mass, one makes the responses in the vernacular and the other in Latin. The unity of the liturgy requires us to be ready to embrace a certain restraint (or, better, many acts of restraint). There is an essential distinction here. If the liturgy is in French, the lover of Latin is not being asked to renounce his preference; he is simply being asked not to insist on it at this precise moment. In practice, everyone has to renounce something, which makes the liturgy a place where we can be purified of every sort of egoism, and which forces us to put our own subjective preferences second, so that we can discover again what is really essential: the praise of God, which is more a question of the heart than of precise form. One person wants to sing more quickly, another less; one person wants more silence, another less; one person wants something livelier, another something more meditative, and so on. True love shows itself by the ways we let go of things out of love for God and for one another. True unity follows the same path but with the distinction mentioned above, and it is worth emphasizing this: we need to set aside the desire to *impose* our preference, not the preference itself. It is quite legitimate for there to be a range of different preferences; it is when everyone is determined to impose his own preferences on everyone else that chaos ensues.

The model of unity-uniformity generally seeks to trim back all the different preferences in a community until they end up being identical, so that, in this way, conflicts may be avoided. Unity-harmony, on the other hand, will set to work instead upon our natural inclination to impose our preferences on others; it will work on our listening, our receptivity, our discernment, the attention we give to others, our respect for the others in the community, and even the relativizing of our preferences—which, after all, are only one way of living the life and not necessarily the definitive way.

Abuses in the Religious Life and the Path to Healing

The Tyranny of Uniformity

Unity-uniformity tends to produce tyranny, because it involves everything being standardized: the same way of thinking, the same preferences, the same enthusiasm for the same people, the same dislikes: everything is covered. In a community marked by this vision of unity, a brother who does not fit the mold ends up choosing to keep silence whenever his opinions differ from those of others in community meetings. He is told by his superior: *We feel you don't agree; you must show that you do agree.* The command is clear, but unbelievable: you *must* be in agreement, otherwise you will destroy the unity. If agreeing is a duty, people are no longer allowed to have any personal thoughts; it even becomes forbidden to think for oneself. Everyone *must* fit into the mold, and everything that does not correspond to the group's way of thinking must be ditched.

This way of understanding unity can surreptitiously become a means of control, so that nothing escapes. It does great harm to what is most personal to people, in order to give the impression that everyone is of one mind. A healthy response would be: *We hear that you don't agree, and we're keen to know why.* And this must be accompanied by a genuine desire to understand the reasons behind this divergent opinion.

In the Christian context, the arguments used most typically to maintain this sort of forced unity appeal to feelings of guilt. If someone is often told, "By disagreeing with us you are destroying the beautiful unity we have," the person ends up feeling guilty before Christ, who, after all, prayed that "they may all be one" (John 17:21). A sort of intimidation can be added to this. *It is the prince of lies that is making you say these things, the one who sows division everywhere. If it were the Holy Spirit, you would be united with us.* A certain degree of spiritual maturity is needed to dismantle the underlying fallacy here; a novice will never be able to avoid the trap that plays on the tacit identification of difference with division, and on the implied claim that the Holy Spirit is on *our* side (plural), not *your* side (singular).

A bit of humor can't do any harm. The idea that everyone *could* agree in a community should really make us grin. Whatever question the superior might put to the community, it is a safe bet that there will be at least some who will not agree. Often enough, superiors know they will be treated to the full range of possible responses. Of course, this is not particularly comfortable, and they can't just do what they want — but isn't this precisely the point? An unconditional submission to a unity without divisions allows the superior to do whatever he likes. This is not so dramatic if it only concerns material things, but if he ends up doing what he wants with people, then he is entering the realm of manipulation.

Vow of Unity, or Vow of Trust

Can a vow of unity or a vow of trust mean anything? The very question leaves us perplexed. Any religious vow has to be related to Christ. In the case of vows of chastity or poverty, the link is clear. The vow of obedience calls for deeper reflection. Is this why the more ancient formulas of monastic profession make no mention of chastity and poverty? Stability, obedience, and conversion of behavior:[69] these are the three vows explicitly laid down in the time of St. Benedict. The vow of *tending* toward continual prayer, as it exists today in some contemplative communities, is one particular expression of the vow of *conversatio morum* and an expression of *sequela Christi*,[70] since Christ was constantly united to His Father. *To tend* is the essential term here, since it must be possible for a vow to be fulfilled, with the help of grace. Now continual prayer is a special grace, which is not necessarily accorded to all who desire it.

But a vow of trust? If it is trust in God we are talking about, that is understandable. God deserves this absolutely, of course. But if we are speaking about the superiors, what sort of trust are we talking about? It is quite possible to have a superior in whom we cannot place our trust (at least regarding certain things), but that in no way absolves us of our duty to obey him when he commands something that is in accordance with the constitutions. Jesus said: "Practice and observe whatever they tell you, but not what they do; for they preach, but do not practice" (Matt. 23:3). Jesus could submit to the prescriptions of the law, as St. Matthew recounts concerning the half shekel (see Matt. 17:24–27), but

---

[69] Translator's note: this is the translation the author gives (in French) of the Latin term *conversatio morum*, which is now usually understood not as referring to the notion of conversion specifically, but to a fidelity to the monastic way of life, which of course includes (but is perhaps not limited to) the notion of conversion. It was previously known as *conversio morum*.

[70] The *following of Christ* is a traditional expression of the meaning of the religious life.

He did not submit to the religious authorities or show confidence in them; it would be absurd even to suggest it. He expressed His disagreement with them quite sharply, but this did not prevent Him from respecting them in the domain that was properly theirs.

In practice, a vow of trust is as good as giving up our own discernment and our own conscience, which is never permitted and, quite clearly, can never be demanded. Obedience is possible since it concerns acts. Trust concerns the inner depths of a person and can never be forced; such a thing is simply impossible. Faced with someone who does not practice what he preaches, for example, trust will always remain partial.

However we approach the question, such a vow seems to lack any serious foundation; in fact, it resembles, rather, a straying from the vow of obedience and consists in asking for unconditional obedience. More prosaically, it is a bit like what any totalitarian regime seeks to impose: the outlawing of all criticism and the gagging of dissidents.

We are also left perplexed by the notion of a vow of unity. At least — people may say to us — it is somehow linked to Christ, who so fervently desired unity among His disciples. But what is the substance of such a vow? If we were speaking of a vow of *tending* toward unity, then that might have some sort of acceptable meaning, as long as it was clearly specified what kind of unity was meant. If it means submission to everything the superior says, or a commitment never to criticize, then we are in the same situation as above.

The unity of the community does not solely depend on people making such a vow. Can anyone make a vow of unity of Christians? That is clearly meaningless. To make a vow to strive for such unity with all our strength? Yes, potentially. This shows the sticking point of this sort of vow. Confidence depends on another person; unity depends on other people. I can't make a vow on their behalf. In the case of obedience, the request comes from someone in authority, but the act of obedience belongs to the one who obeys.

Finally, let us observe that even if we are speaking not about a vow but a promise, or of a sort of "ethos," with all kinds of nuance, the problem remains the same. This impressive mechanism and, in particular, the brilliant spiritual justification it is often endowed with, ends up robbing community members of any sort of personal thought. The prisoner has become his own jailer, since he condemns himself. In the Maoist regime, this was known as "self-criticism." The case of father Marcial Maciel is very revealing. In 1956, when he understood that what he was up to was about to be revealed, he established a private vow, particular to the Legionaries of Christ, which he called the *vow of charity* (!!!).

> This vow consists in an official commitment, contracted with God: Firstly, never to say, in any way, whether in speech, in writing, or by visible gestures, anything at all that could discredit the person of the superior or his authority. Secondly, to warn the superior without delay, as soon as it is discovered that any member of the institute has offended against this vow, as set out here.[71]

It is difficult to say which is the more appalling: that a superior could decree such a thing, or that an institute could accept it and submit to it for fifty years, seemingly without understanding what clearly lay behind this vow. This illustrates the capacity for blindness that can exist in an atmosphere where there is veneration and unconditional submission.

THE FORBIDDING OF ALL CRITICISM

The forbidding of all criticism aimed at superiors has a very strong whiff of the sect about it, and a potential candidate would be strongly advised not to join any community that would request such a thing. Our unease increases still further if we observe that, in a community where this principle is at work, it is nevertheless quite permissible for the superior(s) to criticize (even publicly or in chapter), in a very cutting way, other members of the community, other communities, the Church, and even the entire world. Moreover, this contradictory behavior is a clear sign that things are not working as they should, because such behavior is often found in a sect-like environment: the master knows everything, and

---

[71] X. Leger. *Le statut* épistémologique *des concepts d'emprise, de manipulation mentale et de secte*. Mémoire de fin d'études, Master Enseignement, option philosophie, Université Catholique de Lyon, 2013/2014, 59. Online. A note reads: "This vow had already existed for a number of years in the Legionaries, but unofficially. The Jesuit father Lucio Rodrigo, the rector of the University of Comillas, had already reported the grotesque effects of this to the Vatican in November 1950." (See lavoluntaddenosaber.com, document number 60).

thus cannot be criticized, but public criticism will be one of the means he uses to establish his dominance.

Forbidding all criticism has no religious or theological value. It has nothing to do with obedience, or with respect for the superior, or with unity. It is even opposed to one essential element of the religious life: conversion. If nobody can say anything to the superiors anymore, how will these ever become aware of things that may need changing? In the *Carthusian Statutes*, the following recommendation can be found:

> If, in the reading of these Statutes, it is noticed that there is some point that is not being observed sufficiently, all will examine together and with care how this can and ought to be remedied. If the fault is the responsibility of the prior, then the vicar, or one of the older monks of wiser judgment, can and must ask him privately to correct the fault.[72]

It must not be concluded from what we have said thus far that all criticism is good. Criticism itself must be submitted to discernment, as regarding its substance (since the criticism may or may not be pertinent), but also as regarding the intention behind it, since it might be objective and healthy, or (on the other hand) it might stem from the passions, and even be slanderous. It is not enough, then, that the community and the superiors should be capable of hearing a criticism; there needs also to be a system that allows constructive criticisms to be at the service of the community's life.

Unity: A Fragile Beauty

"May they all be one, Father, as you are in me, and I am in you. May they be one in us" (John 17:21).[73]

We are not going to abandon the search for unity just because there may be pitfalls along the way. In searching for unity, we need to know how to distinguish what is essential from what is not, so that we can welcome differences as an enrichment and not as a threat. We also need to know how to be self-effacing without ceasing to exist. To be self-effacing is to leave some room for others; it

---

[72] *Carthusian Statutes*, 35.4.
[73] This passage was directly translated from the French to maintain original emphasis.

is an opportunity to see beyond ourselves, to learn how to recognize the other, so that we are prepared to meet the One who is completely Other. Has someone else been chosen for a responsibility for which I was suitably skilled? That's fine; I didn't enter religious life to show off my skills. But it would be unhealthy to try to persuade myself that I am rubbish at whatever it is, if it is not true. To be self-effacing is to leave room for others, to accord them the right to think differently, without this destroying our relationship as brethren; it is wanting to avoid imposing our point of view in areas where diversity is not only legitimate but even desirable. This can be a matter of small things, like not dominating at times of community recreation, but rather knowing how to listen and understand, even if we do not agree. At a deeper level, this attitude springs from an ability to rejoice in the good of others; this is a great virtue, though an inconspicuous one, and an undoubtable sign of spiritual maturity. Being focused on whatever matter is in hand will involve believing that the other person is as intelligent and cultured as I am (or possibly even more so), and knowing that that is perfectly all right; both of us are children of God. The kingdom of God is not made up of clones, and even if we are all created in the image of God, these images are all different because the Spirit does not like to repeat Himself.

True unity demands that we are true to our word and that we agree to go on searching for this challenging unity that allows us to live out our personal differences in a way that does not cause division. This journey will never be over, since differences can always be the cause of a certain degree of pain, especially if one is a superior.

Example, Trust, and Communion

The priors play a key role in the spiritual decline or progress of the houses of the order; let them carry out the service of setting an example to others, being the first to put into practice what they teach. No word ought to come from their mouth that Christ would have refused to make His own. They will give themselves over fully to prayer, to silence, and to the life of the cell; in this way, they will be deserving of the trust of their brothers, with whom they will create a real communion in love.[74]

[74] *Carthusian Statutes*, 35.6.

Abuses in the Religious Life and the Path to Healing

The triptych presented by this text warrants emphasis: the *service of setting an example*, which will *be deserving of trust* and will end in *a real communion of love*. The link between these three elements explains one aspect of the mechanisms that lead the behavior of a community to become aberrant. If a good example is no longer given, then trust, which is no longer deserved, must be demanded, and a communion, which is no longer natural, is imposed. These elements follow one another logically, but not necessarily chronologically. Aberrant behavior does not necessarily begin with the absence of good example; it can often begin elsewhere, often where there is a taste for power. On the other hand, when it comes to trying to resolve situations where things have gone off course, this order must be respected. Without good example, there will be no real trust; without real trust, there will be no true communion.

We have marked out the way, then. Let superiors set an example, beginning with the example of recognizing their own weaknesses and limitations. For they will fall into another kind of trap if they feel they simply have to present a perfect façade, which will do nothing to help others in the community live with their own difficulties. Let them encourage trust by showing trust themselves, by trying to recognize the value of each person in those areas where they have qualities that can be useful to everyone else. Out of this, a true communion in love will be born or strengthened, and this may require everyone to deny themselves to some degree. This is truly following Christ, who denied Himself to the point of death, and who came, not to do His own will, but the will of Him who sent Him (see John 6:38).

5

The Relationship with the Outside World

Separation from the World

The religious life entails a certain separation from the world, and this is rooted in the saying of Jesus:

> If you were of the world, the world would love its own; but because you are not of the world, but I chose you out of the world, therefore the world hates you. (John 15:19)

The vocation to the contemplative life, following the ideal of the desert, which was so characteristic of the beginnings of monasticism, pushes this separation to quite an extreme; and the hermit life places an even greater accent on this feature. In this chapter, where we try to provide some norms *vis a vis* separation from the world, the contemplative life can serve as a reference point of the more extreme limits. But we must keep in mind that what is quite normal for a monastery may not be normal at all for the apostolic life. There is thus scope for considerable variation in this area, but there are some principles of discernment that are valid for all.

It is precisely because noise from the world can so easily perturb our inner life and our dialogue with God that the monastic life is structured so as to allow us to avoid it as far as possible. The rules concerning this point bear within them a spiritual dimension, which is the one thing that justifies them and allows them to be properly understood.

> Rigorous observance of enclosure would, however, be merely pharisaic, were it not the outward expression of that purity of heart, to which alone

is attached the promise of seeing God. To attain this, great self-denial is required, especially of the natural curiosity that people feel about human affairs. We should not allow our minds to wander through the world in search of news and gossip; on the contrary, our part is to remain hidden in the shelter of the Lord's face.[75]

This text, which comes from a demanding rule for the enclosed contemplative life, nevertheless contains an observation that is valid for everyone: there is a danger in unbridled curiosity and searching after novelties. If we are to avoid encouraging our spirit's natural tendency to go wandering, it is reasonable to have some restriction in communications, particularly in our own day, when there are so many more means of communication than ever before. What is the sense of maintaining a physical enclosure if there is effectively a permanent tunnel that allows us to leave the enclosure at any moment by means of an Internet connection or a mobile phone? Can a religious who has consecrated his life to God spend hours each day chatting on social media, to the detriment of the time that might be given over to prayer? We need some boundaries; after all, is there anyone who can claim to be able to resist all temptations?

The restrictions set out by the rule may be quite normal; we just need to understand under what conditions they are normal. Healthy precautions can slide toward quite different outcomes when boundary vigilance becomes an iron curtain intended to defend the community against any sort of external influence. There is too great a similarity, at least outwardly, between a case where these rules are applied in accordance with norms and cases where the rules are applied in an aberrant way to allow us to distinguish them at that level. For example, in both cases, there will be some limit to communication with the family. The boundary between these two zones cannot be measured by the number of letters that are permitted. Where, then, is it to be found?

Criteria of a Healthy Separation

The first criterion must be looked for in the motivation behind those rules concerning separation from the world. The principal motivation must be to protect

[75] *Carthusian Statutes*, 6.4.

what is essential to someone's vocation. The quotation from the *Carthusian Statutes* given above provides an example of this. The solitary life demands quite a rigorous separation, without which the idea of the "desert" would lose its meaning. Any limitation in communications (whether by means of mail, telephone, Internet, visits) has the aim of protecting that interior silence that is essential for the contemplative life. If the same rules were applied to a different kind of institute, this could give rise to an abnormal situation, to the extent that the rules were not consistent with the different charism of that institute. Rules, then, must flow naturally from the form of religious life that is proper to the institute in question.

Accordingly, any rules must be linked, one way or another, to Christ, or to the particular aspect of Christ's life that the proper charism of the institute is seeking to follow. For contemplatives, they will of course be linked to the forty days of Christ in the desert, or His hidden life in Nazareth. For an apostolic vocation, they will be linked to His preaching ministry. Can we imagine Jesus whiling away the evenings playing video games while the crowds were like "sheep without a shepherd" (Mark 6:34)?[76]

A second criterion, linked to the first, will relate to whatever is being forbidden. A certain limiting of communications with the outside world is usual in the context of monasticism and follows from choosing the contemplative life, but the situation is altogether different if it stops being a question of limiting how much communication there is and becomes simply a restriction of communication full-stop, which in no way arises from the particular vocation in question but answers to another motivation entirely. A restriction that seeks to protect a vocation, as a consequence of a choice of a particular way of life, is normal; a restriction that seeks to ensure that people on the outside do not find out what is going on within the community is certainly not.

In a setting where speaking and writing are permitted, there should be freedom of expression. During a family visit or when writing a letter, a religious should be able to speak freely about any subject, including his doubts if he so wishes, so long as he does so with propriety. When a regime of secrecy creeps

---

[76] "He was filled with compassion towards them, since they were like sheep without a shepherd, so he began to teach them at length."

into relationships permitted in a particular way of life, we should begin asking questions. Why the secrecy?

Secrecy

To this question, we can add another: how far does this secrecy extend? If it extends to anyone at all who comes from outside — family, friends, confessor, etc. — is it not perhaps the case that what is being established is a sort of isolation, which has little to do with protecting the interior life?

If a regime of secrecy becomes incorporated into a star-shaped structure, where only one way of thinking is allowed, then many of the key elements of the sort of aberrant community behavior we have been thinking about are in place, since, in this situation, any members of the community who might have doubts are no longer able to face these together with someone else, whether from inside the community (due to the effect of the star-shaped structure) or from outside (due to the regime of secrecy). Is this not an attempt to eliminate any risk of dissidence, just as every totalitarian regime has tried to do?

In practice, this type of aberrant behavior often manifests itself in a ban on speaking to people from outside the community, particularly family members or confessors, about anything related to the community life and the personal lives of community members. Since it is impossible to give the real reasons for such a ban, motives that are more acceptable are advanced: the need to avoid washing dirty linen in public, or to keep family secrets because "other people wouldn't understand us," or even that slightly enigmatic word of Jesus: "Do not give what is holy to dogs; do not cast your pearls before swine" (Matt. 7:6).[77]

There can be an element of truth in these precautions, which makes it quite difficult to discern the point beyond which a sensible piece of advice becomes a gag. There is no harm in showing a modicum of discretion concerning the quirks of the brethren or community gossip. But if a member of the community is experiencing real difficulties, then to forbid him to speak with people from outside the community really amounts to shutting him in with his difficulties and depriving him of any hope of finding the light.

---

[77] This passage was directly translated from the French to maintain original emphasis.

Reading People's Mail

It used to be quite common for superiors to open and read all incoming and outgoing mail, and this practice has not totally disappeared. And yet, it is no longer possible to ignore the fact that it constitutes a form of restricting freedom of expression, as well as an intrusion into a person's private life; both these things are nowadays considered to be typical of sects, and rightly so. The practice itself has become unacceptable, and even reprehensible, in the eyes of French law. Here too, we have to ask the same question: Why? What is the motivation behind such a custom? The fact that it was once quite common is not a good enough reason. We cannot remain detached from time and culture, ignoring developments that make what used to be quite common a few centuries ago impossible now. Today, religious men and women who are subjected to this sort of treatment feel as though they have gone back to elementary school. Past cases of this sort of abuse are too numerous for us to ignore them.

When a regime of secrecy has been established, examining the mail is a way of checking whether it is being respected. All of this gives rise to an atmosphere of suspicion and paves the way for abuses in the realm of openness and transparency. Trusting people is always a risky business, but trust engenders trust, and if we want community members to be adults, we have to treat them like adults.

The Image Presented to the World

A regime of secrecy inevitably leads to a certain dishonesty in the way the community presents itself to the outside world. There is a clear contradiction between the suggestion that "people wouldn't understand us" and the published material used to attract vocations: brochures, books, videos, or websites. Either the presentation is honest and complete (in which case, why the regime of secrecy?), or we are not being told everything, and something is being kept from us. It is only once the fish has taken the bait that it discovers it has been duped.

This can lead to a practice that should not surprise us. It can happen that candidates are not allowed to read the community's rule until they commit themselves to the community, sometimes after a period of several years. They are only aware of selected passages. How can people make a commitment in such circumstances? And once again, why the refusal? One sister who asked the question received this explanation: "Because the rule is so sublime that we can't understand it before we make our profession, i.e., before we have been properly initiated. Otherwise, we would be overwhelmed by its sublime nature, and as a result utterly discouraged when confronted with our own nothingness." This explanation simply doesn't hold water. Profession is not an initiation; it is a commitment to live according to a rule,[78] and consequently it is not possible to make any commitment without knowing the rule. Vows made under these conditions could easily be declared invalid. Canon law states clearly:

> One who enters the institute induced by force, grave fear, or malice, or the one whom a superior, induced in the same way, has received, is admitted to the novitiate invalidly.[79]

To conceal the community's rule of life from a candidate before he makes a commitment could be considered a *dolus*.[80] Who would agree to sign a contract he had not been allowed to read?

Limits Imposed on External Confessors

The relationship with confessors from outside the community deserves special consideration. In an enclosed community, it is not possible to speak to whomsoever one chooses, and for women's communities, confessors are chosen both by the bishop and the superior.[81] When this choice is being made, the question remains: *Will he understand the spirit of the religious life?* This is an understandable question, but it needs to be considered in a broader context. Anyone who has made any progress in the spiritual life can ask the same question: *Will this confessor understand me?*

---

[78] This is not all that profession is, but it certainly involves this.

[79] *Code of Canon Law*, can. 643, §1, 4 (online at https://www.vatican.va/archive/cod-iuris-canonici/cic_index_en.html).

[80] A juridical term, which covers the whole range of deceptive tactics that can lead to a contract being agreed, when in practice it would not have been, if one of the parties to the contract had not been subjected to such tactics.

[81] Although the practice varies from community to community.

Apart from the ambiguity of the question (which, after all, might be taken to mean: *Will he tell me everything I want to hear?*), we have to admit that this sort of situation is almost inevitable, and the grace of God is strong enough to make use of imperfect tools.

A more difficult question concerns whether the confessor will keep to his proper limits and not try to direct too much from outside. There is no point in hiding the fact that it is always possible for people to get things wrong in this area, and that discernment is needed. We have a right to expect two qualities in those who hear confessions in religious communities: a respect for the religious life (contemplative or not), and a certain discretion. A confessor seeking to reform the community could cause a great deal of chaos. His mission is not an easy one, since though he may be well aware of existing difficulties, it is not his job to resolve them and, what is more, in practice his understanding is limited to what he is actually told in confession. He will need to take great care not to favor one party over another and to be aware that some people may try to manipulate him in this way.

That being said, there must be complete freedom of speech within confession. It is possible to establish some kind of policy: religious do not normally need to speak to the confessor at length on a weekly basis; a penitent should speak to the confessor about matters concerning his own soul and not at all of what is going on in the community, except insofar as it affects him personally. We have to recognize that discernment with regard to this last point is far from easy. But it would be completely unacceptable to ban any sort of exchange with the confessor, limiting his words to the formula of absolution. Nobody has the right to interfere with the sacrament to that extent.

The *Carthusian Statutes* summarize these thoughts in a single sentence:

> [The brothers] of course enjoy complete freedom to go to see their confessor or director; but they will not speak to him except insofar as is necessary for the good of their soul.[82]

Freedom and moderation are therefore both indicated here in a balanced way.

---

[82] *Carthusian Statutes*, 14.8.

Abuses in the Religious Life and the Path to Healing

Further:

Any member of the order can, for the peace of his conscience, both validly and licitly confess to any priest who has legitimate faculties.[83]

Conversely, this testimony of a former member of one Christian movement demonstrates what an abnormal restriction looks like, even if it is apparently justified by "spiritual" reasons:

For us, Confession had to be — or so we were taught — an act of Love for God, and for the priest who represented Him. We were to make a gift of our sins to God, through the priest, but not to share confidences. We were not allowed to be open with him about just any subject, or ask him any questions.... To do so was considered seeking human support instead of that supernatural relationship. No spiritual direction. The maturity (or immaturity) of the local superior had to suffice here. No outside perspectives were allowed and thus there was no openness to other points of view!

There is great variation between communities when it comes to their relationship with the outside world. The formula *in medio stat virtus*[84] applies perfectly here, so long as we bear in mind that the location of this "middle" will not be the same for everyone. But we are all in danger of falling into either of two extremes: on the one hand, a systematic lack of trust, and on the other, a trustfulness that lacks discernment.

---

[83] *Carthusian Statutes*, 62.2.
[84] Virtue lies in the middle.

6

Obedience (and Particularly the Third Degree of Obedience)

Obedience: Foundation of the Religious Life

St. Benedict

Listen carefully, my son, to the master's instructions, and attend to them with the ear of your heart. This is the advice from a father who loves you; welcome it, and faithfully put it into practice. The labor of obedience will bring you back to him from whom you had drifted through the sloth of disobedience. This message of mine is for you, then, if you are ready to give up your own will, once and for all, and armed with the strong and noble weapons of obedience to do battle for the true King, Christ the Lord.[85]

Thus begins the *Rule of St. Benedict*. Countless texts confirm that obedience is something fundamental to the religious life. In its wisdom, the Church has established religious vows of chastity, poverty, and obedience,[86] but before the Middle Ages, the ancient formulae of profession made no mention either of chastity or of poverty. Since the *Rule of St. Benedict* does not give the text of the profession formula, here is an example that was in use at Cluny:

I, brother N., promise monastic stability, *conversatio morum*, and obedience according to the *Rule of St. Benedict*, before God and His saints, in

---

[85] *RB*, Prologue 1–3.
[86] *Code of Canon Law*, can. 573, §2.

this monastery, built in honor of the blessed apostles Peter and Paul, in presence of Dom N., abbot.[87]

GOD, THE RULE, AND THE ABBOT

Notice, first, that the brother does not promise to obey *the abbot* since the intention looks beyond particular individuals: the abbot can change, obedience remains. Moreover, obedience is not only owed to the abbot, but to others too: the prior, other superiors, and so on. All of this is specified by the *Rule*, hence the notion of *obedience according to the Rule*, which removes the danger of an idealized master-figure, who would make himself the focus of all obedience. The abbot is mentioned as a witness, who ratifies the act of profession in the name of the Church. The obedience that the brother owes to him is fixed by the *Rule* and thus has defined limits. This crucial point derives from the profession itself.

Nor does the brother promise to obey God. Of course, some profession formulae say that he does make such a promise, but there is a meaning behind the absence of this notion in the ancient formulae. It is the duty of every Christian to obey God; this comes from faith itself, and religious life does not add anything special to this. What is particular about the religious life comes from the promise to show this willingness to obey God through obedience to a human intermediary. Essentially, the obedience of consecrated religious is addressed to God Himself but in such a way that it takes flesh in something concrete, which gives it a particular depth, a firm rootedness in real life that allows the religious to take his identification with Christ further.

Thus, the balanced nature of monastic obedience comes from three elements, as the different parts of the profession formula make clear: *According to the Rule, before God, in the presence of the abbot.* From the outset, this formula helps us to steer clear of a misinterpretation of the nature of obedience. A religious who gives himself to God desires to live obedience to the full, by being conformed to Christ, but here it is clearly indicated that he must not seek to do this by submitting himself without condition or reserve to a human being, which a younger person might easily be inclined to do. This false absolute might steer such a person away from the very depth of Christ's obedience. What is absolute

---

[87] Cons. Clun. Lib. II, cap. 27. J.P. Migne, *Patrologia Latina* 149:713B.

cannot be found in something concrete — this would be to turn the concrete form into an idol; it is rather to be found in the heart's being totally available, always ready to undergo a renunciation if it should be required in the ordinary run of the religious life.

In reality, these three dimensions are mixed together. We could emphasize the ambiguity that is present in those passages of the Prologue of the *Rule of Saint Benedict* that are not taken from the *Rule of the Master*, that is, those verses at the beginning and the end. Which master are we talking about? God? The *Rule*? The abbot? It is not clear that we can draw a neat distinction. By obeying his abbot, the monk shows his obedience to God:

> They carry out the superior's order as promptly as if the command came from God Himself. The Lord says of men like this: No sooner did he hear than he obeyed me.[88]

> For obedience given to the superior is given to God, for he said: "Whoever listens to you, listens to me."[89]

Obedience to God is mediated in two ways: by the *Rule* and the abbot, and these are related to one another in a complex way, since even the abbot must submit to the *Rule*: he may not command anything that is beyond its scope, but he does have a role in interpreting the *Rule*. Neither the human being nor the law has the absolute authority here. The *Rule of St. Benedict* leaves the abbot quite a lot of room for maneuver, but it reminds him that he must always act in accordance with the rule:

> Nevertheless, just as it is proper for disciples to obey their master, so it is fitting that the master, on his part, should settle everything with foresight and fairness. Accordingly, in every instance, all are to follow the teaching of the rule, and no one shall rashly deviate from it. In the monastery no one is to follow his own heart's desire, nor shall anyone presume to contend with his abbot defiantly, or outside the monastery. Should anyone presume to do so, let him be subjected to the discipline

---

[88] *RB* 5:4.
[89] *RB* 5:15.

of the rule. Moreover, the abbot himself must fear God and keep the rule in everything he does; he can be sure beyond any doubt that he will have to give an account of all his judgments to God, the most just of judges.[90]

The *Rule* is insistent about the responsibility to be borne by the abbot, who will have to "give an account." Here are a couple of the relevant passages:

Let the abbot always remember that at the fearful judgment of God, not only his teaching but also his disciples' obedience will come under scrutiny.[91]

Whatever the number of brothers he has in his care, let him realize that on judgment day he will surely have to submit a reckoning to the Lord for all their souls — and indeed for his own as well. In this way, while always fearful of the future examination of the shepherd about the sheep entrusted to him and careful about the state of others' accounts, he becomes concerned also about his own, and while helping others to amend by his warnings, he achieves the amendment of his own faults.[92]

As for the *Rule*, it is not simply an absolute that the abbot has merely to apply. This understanding creates a balance, which allows the monastic life to preserve its essential principles while being able to adapt to the real situations. The *Rule* is a critical authority over the abbot's power, and the abbot interprets the *Rule*. He is subject to the *Rule*, like any monk — all the more because he is abbot — but he is not subject to it as a slave, as he has considerable freedom to interpret the *Rule* in accordance with the circumstances of the community. This admirable balance allows us to avoid two opposite pitfalls, both of which end up according an absolute value to something human: on the one hand, the despotic power of a superior who is all-powerful, because his role has been unduly canonized; on the other hand, a strict and literal adherence to law, without regard to the reality of the human person. There is no "trick" that enables

[90] *RB* 3:6–11.
[91] *RB* 2:6.
[92] *RB* 2:38–40.

us to discover God's will; this always comes from listening to the heart with a discernment in which all must participate.

THE ROLE OF EXAMPLE

Thus everything comes back to God. If the *Rule* makes the abbot into the vicar of Christ, then just like any other representative, in his words and in his deeds, in what he asks of his monks, he will have to demonstrate that he is behaving as a credible image of his Master. Hence the prime importance of setting an example.

> Furthermore, anyone who receives the name of abbot is to lead his disciples by a twofold teaching: he must point out to them all that is good and holy more by example than by words, proposing the commandments of the Lord to receptive disciples with words, but demonstrating God's instructions to the stubborn and the dull by a living example. Again, if he teaches his disciples that something is not to be done, then, neither must he do it, lest after preaching to others, he himself be found reprobate and God may someday call to him in his sin: How is it that you repeat my just commands and mouth my covenant when you hate discipline and toss my words behind you?[93]

SEEKING COUNSEL

Nor is the abbot the sole repository of wisdom; the *Rule* makes this clear in simple words:

> As often as anything important is to be done in the monastery, the abbot shall call the whole community together and himself explain what the business is; and after hearing the advice of the brothers, let him ponder it and follow what he judges the wiser course. The reason why we have said all should be called for counsel is that the Lord often reveals what is better to the younger.[94]

Again, the last line here forbids any identification of the word of God with the word of the abbot. God speaks to whomever He wants; in this passage, the role

---

[93] *RB* 2:11–14; the quotation at the end is Ps. 49:16–17.
[94] *RB* 3:1–3.

of the abbot is to discern what, out of all that has been said, people should hold on to. Then all should subject themselves to this with good will.

MUTUAL OBEDIENCE

Finally, obedience is not limited to a hierarchical relationship. The spiritual intention behind obedience — conformity with Christ — invites us to live it even in fraternal relationships.

> Obedience is a blessing to be shown by all, not only to the abbot but also to one another as brothers, since we know that it is by this way of obedience that we go to God.[95]

These few texts quoted here should be enough to shatter all the dysfunctional manifestations of authority that were covered in chapter 3. We ought to quote everything that is said [in the *Rule of St. Benedict*] concerning the abbot. I advise any superiors who have lived in an abusive environment to meditate on these texts.[96] We could quote rules other than St. Benedict's, each of them having its own nuances, but the balance between God, the rule, and the superior remains the same throughout them all, since it is fundamental for the religious life. This does not mean that there cannot be, for example, a fundamental difference between the Benedictine and Augustinian models of religious community. For Benedict, the common life is a school of the Lord's Service, where we place ourselves under the direction of a master; for Augustine, on the other hand, the community is constituted above all by the communion between the brothers. But this, too, needs a superior.

ST. BRUNO

In his letter to his Carthusian brothers, St. Bruno writes for *conversi:*

> I rejoice since, though you have no knowledge of letters, almighty God writes with His finger upon your hearts, not only love, but a knowledge of His holy law. Indeed, you show by means of your works what you love, and what you know. For you practice true obedience with all possible

---

[95] *RB* 71:1–2. See also 72:6.
[96] Moreover, such meditation is profitable not only for them!

care and zeal, and this is fulfilling the will of God, the key and the seal of all spiritual observances. [Such obedience] never exists without great humility and extraordinary patience, and it is always accompanied by a chaste love for the Lord, and an authentic charity. From this, it is clear that you are reaping with wisdom the sweet and life-giving fruit of the divine Scriptures. Remain then, my brothers, in the state you have attained.[97]

It is noteworthy that this passage never mentions the superior explicitly, though his presence is implied. The presence of the superior is necessary, and goes without saying, but it is in no sense the center of it all.

The Limits of Obedience

We need to understand properly the classical formula that states that the superior holds the place of God for us, since this formula has led to many excesses, supported in part by expressions such as *blind obedience, perinde ac cadaver,* "like a corpse."[98] Experience shows that, since it is so easy to misinterpret expressions such as these in a way that leads to aberrant behavior, it is perhaps better to avoid them in the current climate.

It is to God alone that we owe total and unconditional obedience, whether intellectual or moral, since He is absolute Goodness and absolute Truth.

All obedience to a human being, in any setting, is limited by this primary truth. As Peter and the apostles said before the Sanhedrin: "We must obey God rather than men" (Acts 5:29).[99] There can be, then, a duty to disobey. Whatever

---

[97] Bruno, "Lettre à la communauté de Chartreuse, 3," in *Lettres des premiers chartreux*, Sources Chrétiennes (Paris: Éd. du Cerf, 1962), 85. An English translation is online at www.chartreux.org.

[98] On the interpretation of these formulae, see the illuminating article by H. Donneaud, "Les enjeux théologiques de l'obéissance dans la vie consacrée," in *Vies consacrées*, 88 (2016-4), 33–42. In summary: To obey "like a corpse" is not to stop reflecting or willing things, but in a much deeper way to offer no resistance to a command, and to submit oneself to it entirely with the will and the intellect, despite a clear awareness of one's own shortcomings.

[99] In Acts 4:19, Peter and John had said: "You must judge for yourselves whether it is right to listen to you rather than to God."

might be being asked, the person obeying must make a judgment concerning what is being asked of him: is this in keeping with the law of God or not?

Obedience is not something automatic; it involves the intellect of the one who is obeying. This is a characteristic of any human act.

The *Code of Canon Law* outlines briefly two other limits of religious obedience:

> The evangelical counsel of obedience, undertaken in a spirit of faith and love in the following of Christ obedient unto death, requires the submission of the will to legitimate superiors, who stand in the place of God, when they command according to the proper constitutions.[100]

On the one hand, obedience requires submission of the will, and always concerns an act. This means that the superior can ask one of his subjects to do something, but he cannot ask the subject to think something. The abbot can ask a monk to bring the chairs back inside because he thinks that it is going to rain tomorrow; he cannot ask him to think that it is going to rain tomorrow. By the vow of obedience, we promise the submission of our will, but not of our intellect. True, the intellect necessarily cooperates in the process (more on this later), but there are limits to this cooperation. In any case, submission of the intellect can never be the proper object of a superior's command.

On the other hand, superiors themselves owe obedience to the authorities over them and to the constitutions of the order. They can only give orders that are in accordance with their rule: a Dominican prior cannot order one of the brethren to become a hermit.

Finally, there is a further limit, mentioned in Paul VI's Apostolic Exhortation *Evangelica testificatio*: a serious and certain evil removes the obligation to obey. Nevertheless, the Exhortation continues, warning against imagining too readily that one is in this situation:

> Apart from an order manifestly contrary to the laws of God or the constitutions of the institute, or one involving a serious and certain evil — in which case there is no obligation to obey — the superior's decisions concern a field in which the calculation of the greater good can vary

---

[100] *Code of Canon Law*, can. 601.

according to the point of view. To conclude from the fact that a directive seems objectively less good that it is unlawful and contrary to conscience would mean an unrealistic disregard of the obscurity and ambivalence of many human realities. Besides, refusal to obey often involves a serious loss for the common good. A religious should not easily conclude that there is a contradiction between the judgment of his conscience and that of his superior. This exceptional situation will sometimes involve true interior suffering, after the pattern of Christ Himself, "who learned obedience through suffering" (Heb. 5:8).[101]

So, when we say that the superior holds the place of God for us, this needs to be understood within a particular context of which both superiors and religious in general should be aware. The religious should see in the superior's command an invitation from God to put into practice his vow of obedience, which does not in any way mean that he ought simply to carry out the command unthinkingly. Fr. Berceville, O.P., put it very clearly in the film *Emprise et abus spirituel*:

> Clearly, what the superior says to me from day to day is not the Word of God. God can speak to me through what the superior says, but this means that I must interpret, and exercise judgment; I never lose my responsibility to discern what God is saying to me through the medium of the superior's words.[102]

"Through the medium." This little expression puts things in their proper perspective. True: God can speak to us through human errors, but these are not thereby sanctified; they remain errors, and those who commit them will bear responsibility for them.

Can We Speak of "Blind Obedience"?

This expression should be avoided altogether, since it is often understood as designating an obedience that is shown without reflection or responsibility,

---

[101] Paul VI, Apostolic Exhortation *Evangelica testificatio*, June 29, 1971, no. 28. This is taken up by no. 27 of the CICLSAL Instruction *Faciem tuam, Domine, requiram: on the service of authority and obedience* (May 11, 2008).

[102] J.-C. and A. Duret, *Emprise et abus spirituel*, 2019.

and that is contrary to the mind of the Church. And yet we must respond to a possible objection, which might remind us that St. Francis de Sales speaks of such obedience in his twelfth Spiritual Conference to the Visitation Sisters. This is true — he does — but the meaning there is totally different.

> There are three conditions for blind obedience: the first is that it never pays attention to the superior as a person, but only to his authority; the second is that it doesn't pry into the reasons or motivations superiors might have to give this or that command — it is enough to know that a command has been given; the third is that it doesn't ask questions about how what is commanded is to be achieved — it is certain that God, by whose inspiration the command was given, will surely grant the power to carry it out, and then it gets to work. Rather than ask how to do it, [blind obedience] simply gets on with it.[103]

There it is; that seems to justify the usual meaning we give to the expression "blind obedience." Certainly. But the next paragraph offers us an essential clarification:

> Let us now return to the first condition of this loving obedience, which is one facet of religious obedience. It is a blind obedience, which sets about doing with love all that is asked of it, in all simplicity, regardless of whether the command was well or badly given, provided that the one giving the command has the authority to do so, and that the command serves to unite our spirit to God; for the truly obedient person never does anything without this. Many have been seriously mistaken about this condition of obedience, believing that it meant indiscriminately doing whatever might be commanded, even if it should be against the commandments of God and His Holy Church; in this, they have gone badly astray, for, just as superiors have no power to give any command to do what is against God's commandments, so subordinates, by the

---

[103] Francis de Sales, *Spiritual Conferences,* Conference 12: On the Virtue of Obedience. An English translation is available online at https://www.oblates.org/spiritual-conferences.

same token, have no obligation to obey. Indeed, were they to obey, they would be committing a mortal sin.

Concerning the first condition, he will repeat later on: "People say that such obedience is blind, since it obeys all superiors equally, without 'looking at their face' — by which I mean, 'without considering who they are in themselves.'" A religious owes obedience to a superior, whether the superior is good or bad, gentle or cantankerous. Anyone who obeyed only because he considered his superior to be faithful to the religious life, but felt he was dispensed from this obedience if the superior were to fall short in this regard, would have failed to understand the meaning of a vow of obedience. It would remain a purely natural kind of obedience. Even if the superior gives a poor example, a religious owes him obedience when he commands something according to the rule, not on account of the superior, but as an offering to God.

The second and third conditions require us not to ask about motives, reasons and means.

But as for the content of what is commanded, Francis de Sales uses a *provided that* in his text, and the meaning of this is clear: anyone who obeys must make a judgment about what is being asked; he cannot simply do "whatever," just because an order has been received. Sometimes, he may even have a duty to disobey. This kind of situation ought to be pretty rare, but the superior's authority does not make his word into God's Word, and those in his charge need to hold on to the integrity of their conscience. An example will speak more eloquently than a long discourse.

Let us suppose that a superior asks a monk in a delicate situation to give an answer that is a lie. It is not permissible for the monk to obey, since his superior has no right to ask him to lie. The monk's conscience will allow him to make a judgment concerning the situation since, in this particular case, he cannot trust his superior's discernment.

Should he agree to reply with the lie, as he has been asked, knowing that it is indeed a lie, there is a twofold fault: the monk is responsible for the lie he has told, but his responsibility is clearly lessened by the fact that he was not entirely free, due to the superior's command. The superior, who does not have this excuse, carries all the responsibility for the lie that has been told, as well as that of having coerced the monk's conscience and having led him into the way of sin by means of his command. This is much more serious than if he had lied himself, especially if it causes scandal in the soul of the monk, who runs the risk of losing confidence in the superior.

This is nothing more than common teaching, and we would be wrong to think this might revolutionize the practice of obedience since, in the world of the religious life, the superior knows the law of God and of the Church, and the type of situation we have just described is (or should be) rare. Still, it is important to know that it can occur, and it can give rise to painful situations.

Even under obedience, a religious remains a free human being, responsible for his own actions because, for God, only a free and informed "yes" has any meaning. The angel gave a detailed explanation to the Virgin Mary of what was expected of her. Any interpretation that turns obedience into an automatic process, occurring without discernment, is neither human nor religious.

ACTS OF HUMAN PERSONS AND HUMAN ACTS

St. Thomas Aquinas helps us to understand this by drawing a distinction between the *act of a human person* and a *human act.*

> Of actions performed by human beings those alone are properly called "human," which are proper to a human being as a human being. Now a human being differs from irrational animals in this, that he is master of his actions. So those actions alone are properly called human, of which a human being is master. Now a human being is master of his actions through his reason and will; hence, too, the free will is defined as "a faculty of the will and of reason." Therefore those actions are properly called human that proceed from a deliberate will. And if any other actions are found in a human person, they can be called actions "of a human person," but not properly "human" actions, since they are not proper to the human being as a human being.[104]

The act of a human person that lacks a deliberate will and/or freedom can be objectively good, but it is not a human act; it is not what God expects of a

---

[104] Thomas Aquinas, *Summa theologiæ* IaIae, q. 1, a. 1.

human person. An unreflective obedience is thus not religious obedience, since it is not really human; it is merely the obedience of an automaton. Advocating this sort of obedience clearly belongs to aberrant, sect-like behavior.

THE WILL OF THE SUPERIOR IS NOT THE WILL OF GOD

If we may hope that religious superiors rarely command things that are opposed to the divine law, there is another situation — rather more common — which occasioned an illuminating response from St. Francis de Sales. A sister wrote to him, objecting:

> I can see clearly that what people want me to do proceeds from a human will and inclination, and hence God has not inspired my mother or my sister to make me do such a thing, since it has come about by a movement of their natural or habitual inclination, or even as a result of a passion.

St. Francis de Sales's answer:

> No, doubtless God did not inspire that, but you should of course still do it.[105]

We should take note that he says *No, doubtless* ... St. Francis de Sales doesn't dispute the idea that the superior's command does not come from God if she has spoken at the prompting of the passions; she is thus responsible for this word, which may well be a sin for her (anger, envy, etc.). And yet, by obeying it, it is indeed God that the sister obeys, since He is not asking that she should imagine He has inspired this word in the superior: He is asking that she should obey out of love, on account of the vow of obedience. Thus, fulfilling the vow can transfigure any task that is in accordance with divine law.

The vow of obedience is ordered to the perfection of the sister and not to that of the superior. What God is asking of her is not the same as what the superior has asked; He is asking instead that she obey what the superior has asked. This clarification is so important that it should be chiseled over the entrance to the novices' quarters. The value of an act of obedience lies in submission to God,

---

[105] *Spiritual Conferences,* Conference 16: On the Subject of Condescension.

through the concrete mediation of the superior, but this mediation in no way transforms the superior's every whim into the will of God. St. Francis de Sales concludes:

> No, doubtless God did not inspire that, but you should of course still do it. Neglecting to do so would be contrary to your determination to do the will of God in all things, and as a result, would be opposed to the care you should have for your own perfection. So we must submit ourselves to doing whatever is asked of us, in order to do God's will, provided that it is not contrary to His will as it is shown to us in the way I mentioned above.[106]

The will of God is to be found not in the material content of what is commanded but rather in submission, which requires discernment if it is to be human. Thus, obedience can take on its full meaning, since its value lies not in the importance of the act but in the love that inspires it. A trifling thing done with great love unites us to God as effectively as a great act; this means that every passing hour is an opportunity for holiness.

If this is not clear, it can lead to great perplexity or foolishness. If a sister is asked to sweep the cloister, though the community later in the afternoon is going to do a job that will make it dirty again, the sister is right to conclude that there is no sense in it, and she should remind the superior, who may have forgotten. If the superior repeats the command, then the business of discerning is easy, since sweeping the cloister never did anyone any harm. The sister can see that she is being offered a beautiful opportunity to express her love to the Lord in the concrete reality of an everyday task. If she sweeps the cloister, it is not out of good sense (which is conspicuous by its absence), nor to please the superior (beware of this subtle slide, which transforms religious obedience into

---

[106] Francis de Sales, *Spiritual Conferences*, Conference 15: On the Will of God. "The way I mentioned above" includes: the Commandments (of God), his own counsels, the commandments of the Church, and inspirations received. On the subject of "counsels," he gives a further clarification: "The counsels we must put into practice are our rules; I mean, all [the counsels] are contained within them."

a merely human act); no, it is because one day in the past, she promised the Lord she would obey, so it is out of love for Him. And this is enough to give a full and perfectly human meaning to an act that, with a clear conscience, has been considered and willed, not for its usefulness but because of its deeper meaning. Whenever we do useful or interesting things, there can be a lot of "human" mixed in with our obedience. In the example I have chosen, the sister can do the sweeping joyfully, saying to the Lord: *I am doing this for you and you alone.* Only an intelligent obedience can reach this point; a blind or automatic obedience cannot, because fulfilling a command, pure and simple, is enough for it.

But if the sister, not having really understood the true object of her obedience, should ask herself if it can really be God's will that the cloister should be swept in the morning to be dirtied in the evening, no answer will be forthcoming, since the will is not about the sweeping; it is about her. This sort of questioning, which was unknown among religious of former times, has become quite commonplace, not only in religious life but also in a certain understanding of spiritual direction, fostered by a prophetic outlook that suggests that the director is inspired by God. So the question has shifted from the personal and relational level to the objective level of the thing to be done. "Lord, what do you want me to do?" becomes "Lord, what is it that you want to be done?" The "I" has disappeared. The frame of reference is no longer the loving relationship with God, the most important goal of religious obedience, but the concrete reality: the cloister and the sweeping. All manner of complications will come from this. How can I explain that God should want the cloister to be clean in the morning when it is going to be dirtied in the evening? Is He stupid, or is He making fun of me? Happily, the answer is easy: we just have to know what it is. God never asked that; it was the superior who asked it, and we had better leave her with the responsibility for her decision and her words. God's expectation is that the sister should be obedient in general; it is not confined to this particular question of the sweeping.

Understanding this properly makes the sister's life a good deal easier; she won't drive herself mad, wondering whether God wants her to use a broom or a mop. Dear sister, God has given you the gift of intelligence; it is up to you to make use of it! St. Teresa of Avila once remarked humorously (and perhaps a little testily): "My God, what have we come to? As though we weren't stupid enough by nature, we want to become stupid by grace too!"[107]

For the superior's part, if he becomes accustomed to considering his every word or decision to be inspired by the Holy Spirit, his governing of the community will become more and more arbitrary. An example that may make us smile can help us to understand this. The founder of a community claimed that he received everything from the Holy Spirit, down to the melodies of the chants that he imposed on the community. Since it is difficult to suggest that the Holy Spirit is not a top-flight composer, they all submitted themselves to his ditties. Of course, there is nothing particularly serious in that, but the tragedy is that this instinct will operate in the same way, whatever the seriousness of the matter at hand. The Holy Spirit has spoken, case closed. In this way, the most arbitrary things can be justified.

Moreover, anyone who has held a position of responsibility knows well, if he has a modicum of sense, that the superior does not know the will of God but, on the contrary, needs to seek it out even more diligently than the rest. How many insoluble problems he has to confront! How useful it would be if all that was needed for God to speak was for the superior to say something! Mostly, superiors feel their way forward, they are tentative, they take advice, and, since at some point there has to be a decision, they eventually decide, but with no certainty about their own docility to the Holy Spirit and with no guarantee that their decision will be in accord with the will of God. Being a superior is not an easy job.

We should note, too, that in Catholic theology, we never mistake the words of a human being for the word of the Holy Spirit (expressing Himself directly through the person's mouth), even in the case of Sacred Scripture. The spirit of prophecy is subject to the prophets; it is they who speak according to what they have understood, received, and interpreted from the inspiration that came from God. The Holy Spirit did not dictate what they saw fit to write. On this point, it is sufficient to look up a good treatise on fundamental theology or an introduction to Sacred Scripture on the subject of inspiration.[108] If this is true

---

[107] *Les fioretti de sainte Thérèse d'Avila*, sayings translated and presented by J. Gicquel, O.C.D. (Paris: Éd. du Cerf, 1977), 90.

[108] See, for example, W. Harington, *Nouvelle introduction à la Bible* (Paris: Éd. Du Seuil, 1971), which has a good chapter on the subject.

of the inspired authors, how much truer it is of superiors, who do not have the benefit of the charism of inspiration.

So we must exercise great care when we say or hear that the superior holds the place of God, in a certain sense. A little anecdote can serve to illustrate just how significant this subtle slide has become in Christian culture. Despite being well aware of the concerns just expressed, the author of these lines had written in a previous version of the text that *a religious sees in the words of the superior a word that God is addressing to him.* Someone who read the manuscript pointed out that this particular form of words was open to criticism.

> An expression like this puts the focus on the content of this word, with all the errors it may give rise to, or the dilemmas of conscience when we think the abbot is mistaken. But in Benedictine obedience, what is at stake is not the content of the obedience, obedience to a command that is thought to be an expression of God's will; what is essential is the interior attitude. The monks obey their abbot as they would obey God, that is: obedience is an experience of their relationship with Christ being fleshed out. They must have toward the abbot the same feelings they have toward Christ; the essential thing is that they obey joyfully.
>
> The abbot carries this name, "not because he has taken it to himself in an act of usurpation, but because it has been bestowed upon him for the honor and love of Christ."

The observation was perfectly correct. This small slip in the first version shows how easy it is to slide into this way of thinking, even unconsciously. Moreover, as precious a text as it is, St. Ignatius's famous letter on obedience leaves a little to be desired in places when dealing with this topic.[109] There is no shortage of phrases that, taken in isolation, would equate the will of the superior with the will of God. It is crucial to read the letter in its entirety, without forgetting the restrictions it sets out concerning the third degree of obedience, which we will now address.

---

[109] Ignatius of Loyola, "Lettre aux pères et frères du Portugal du 26 mars 1553" in S. Ignace, *Lettres*, ed. G. Dumeige (Paris: DDB, 1959), 296–306. An English translation of this letter (Letter 25) is available online at https://library.georgetown.edu/woodstock/ignatius-letters/letter25.

Abuses in the Religious Life and the Path to Healing

Third Degree of Obedience

THE SUBMISSION OF JUDGMENT

If we submit our will by means of our vow of obedience, it nevertheless remains the case that our intellect cannot simply be set aside. In his letter on obedience, Ignatius of Loyola distinguishes with great clarity between the various degrees of obedience. Material obedience to whatever is commanded — the first degree — takes up a mere four lines, before the text goes on immediately to consider the second degree — submission of the will — which receives a slightly longer treatment. But he places all his insistence upon the third degree — the submission of judgment[110] — and it is worth considering first why this is necessary.

If a superior asks one of the community to repaint the whole house, and to do it in pure white, whereas the person asked to do it thinks that it would be better to do it in off-white, then the latter will clearly be able to submit to what the superior is asking without abandoning his own preference, but this situation presents a difficulty that St. Ignatius emphasizes: "Without great violence, it is not possible for the will constantly to submit itself in matters that the judgment condemns."[111] It is difficult, if not impossible, to go on giving oneself totally for any length of time when one is divided in this way. Obviously, each person naturally believes his own idea is better than the next person's and that there are objective reasons (so he thinks!) to confirm this. The third degree of obedience asks us to accept that it is possible that the superior's idea may be just as good as (or even better than) mine and to adhere to that in a real way, by putting my own point of view in the proper perspective. This degree has an essential connection with humility.

But we need to add some essential clarifications here.

The intellect is not as supple as the will; it is directed by truth. It can never be right for us to allow our intellect to diverge from truth.

Submission of the intellect is desirable in particular situations, where opinions differ, perhaps. Painting with pure white or off-white is simply a question of preference and has nothing to do with truth, in the proper sense of the word.

---

[110] Or of reason, i.e., intelligence.

[111] Ignatius of Loyola, *Lettre aux pères et frères du Portugal du 26 mars 1553*, 296–306.

It follows that the monk's excessive attachment to his own preferences in this area is clearly an imperfection.

But this doesn't apply in all circumstances. If the superior asks for the tractor to be filled with cooking oil, a monk who knows anything about engines will not be able to set aside his own understanding. He knows perfectly well that if he does this, it will cause serious damage to the engine. Moreover, he can't assume that this is the superior's intention, so he has to let the superior know. If the superior persists in thinking that it is in fact a very neat solution and that the engine won't suffer as a result, the monk will find himself in a difficult situation. He will have to judge whether the evil, here, is grave or not.[112]

St. Ignatius is quite clear about those areas where it may be appropriate to submit intellectually:

> Although this faculty of the spirit does not enjoy, in its operation, the freedom that the will enjoys, and naturally consents to whatever it finds to be true, nevertheless in many situations, where the evidence for the truth, as it perceives it, is not necessarily compelling, it can follow one or other of the options, according to the movement of the will. It is in these tricky situations that anyone who professes a vow of obedience should submit himself to his superior's opinion.[113]

There are clearly defined limits within which submission of the intellect is possible: we are really talking about situations where the evidence of the known truth is not compelling. This principle gives considerable freedom: only those situations where there is no major reason to prefer one point of view over another invite the religious to submit his intellect, too. In all other cases, the rights of conscience are to be maintained.

For his part, Francis de Sales takes pains to explain that he only asks for blind obedience (as he explains it) for things of little importance. If the matter at hand is planting cabbages, and the superior wants them to be planted in a stupid way, the consequences are sufficiently unimportant for obedience to prevail here. If it is a question of planting fifteen hectares of cabbages, and the detriment to

---

[112] Cf. Paul VI, Apostolic Exhortation *Evangelica testificatio,* quoted above.

[113] Ignatius of Loyola, *Lettre aux pères et frères du Portugal du 26 mars 1553,* 296–306.

the community could be more significant, then the sister has a duty to warn the superior of her mistake. Ignatius of Loyola has this to say about it, too:

> All the same, if an idea, different from that of the superior, should come to mind, and if, after consulting our Lord about it in prayer, it seems to you something you ought to make known, then you should do so.[114]

He adds that in all this, we need to maintain a spirit of detachment.

So long as we are only considering questions whose import is at a purely material level, we do not encounter too many difficulties. But once it becomes a matter of what is good for people, the responsibility of individual members of the community becomes more important, and they can no longer justify doing just anything on the grounds that the superior asked them to do so.

In any event, we need to emphasize strongly that the submission of the intellect is limited to situations concerning things a religious ought to do. Obedience in no way allows a superior to lay down what a religious must think. Our intellect must be submitted to Christ through the Church, and while the superior can teach this submission to the Church, he must not go beyond this. It is not the superior who holds authority in matters of faith or morals, since he is himself subject to this obedience to the Church, in the same way all religious are. And since he can only give orders that are in line with the constitutions,[115] it is clear that he cannot give any such command in the realms of politics, philosophy, and so on. Of course, he must ensure that the religious in his care receive the proper formation, but this is not a matter of obedience: the understanding must be convinced; it cannot be forced. Neither can the superior give commands in spiritual matters; these questions will be treated in greater detail in relation to spiritual abuse.

It has always been difficult to arrive at a correct understanding of the role of submission of the intellect in religious obedience. Nevertheless, if we do not have this understanding, there may be significant consequences. From the point of view of the subject, someone who totally rejects the principle of this form of submission generally ends up saying: *I obey so long as I agree with the command.*

---

[114] Ibid.
[115] See the text from the *Code of Canon Law* quoted above.

Or as it was once humorously expressed in a small cartoon, where a young nun was shown kneeling before her prioress, saying: *I'm taking a vow of obedience… provided the superior is kind, and I agree with what she proposes, after negotiation.*

THE DEGREES OF EXERCISING AUTHORITY

St. Ignatius of Loyola's *Letter on Obedience* remains a key text, in particular because of the clear distinction that it established between the different degrees of obedience. Having a good understanding of these different degrees and their characteristic features will allow us to preserve true religious obedience, with all of its demands, without falling into excesses.

And yet we may be left feeling uneasy once we have read the text. All of the demands made seem to be on the part of the person who is obeying, with none for the person who is giving the orders. With St. Benedict we had become used to more of a balance; after all, though he gives the abbot the fullness of authority, he still reminds him several times that he will have to render an account to God for the way in which he carries out his responsibilities, and in particular for the way in which he exercises his authority. A large proportion of the abuses that have occurred in this area have perhaps arisen because people did not take the trouble to define with sufficient care the different degrees in the exercise of religious authority. We sometimes see superiors demanding a very developed form of obedience, for which they advance religious motives, whereas they exercise their authority in a way that is extreme to the point of being inhuman. They will be quick to emphasize that a religious must obey as Christ obeyed, unto death, but seemingly without realizing that anyone who gives a command must do so with the love of the Father, who is not first and foremost someone who issues demands but someone who gives: gives life to creation and gives His Son to redeem us.

A REVEALING TEST

A small example will be enough to help us understand the matter. The novice master has given an order to one of the novices, who has not carried out the order, or has not carried it out quickly enough, or has perhaps done so in a way that owes too much to his personal interpretation. The novice master gives him a sharp telling off. Let us try to understand what is going on.

Abuses in the Religious Life and the Path to Healing

THE FIRST DEGREE

If the novice master is angry because the novice has not obeyed, this must mean that he does not accept that his authority should be called into question in this way. His anxiety seems to be centered on himself, his role, his authority. What does any of that have to do with the religious life? Basically, nothing. An army officer who had given a soldier an order that the soldier didn't then carry out could have the same reaction, for exactly the same reasons. This reaction demonstrates that the novice master is exercising his authority in the first degree. I've given the order, now you have to obey because I am the superior. This is how things work in civil society, and this is how the first degree of obedience works; it is about the simple carrying out of the order. Whether in terms of obedience or authority, there is nothing about this first degree that is particular to the religious life. Clearly, this does not mean that it is bad, as this sort of authority is necessary in any kind of human society. But shouldn't the religious life impart a very particular character to authority?

THE SECOND DEGREE

If the novice master has a real sense of what religious obedience is, he will know that the essential thing about it is that it is not practiced in relation to him (the novice master) but in relation to God. If he experiences his authority at this level, then, rather than anger, his reaction ought to be one of sadness or compassion for the novice, not for himself.[116] We can imagine that, if the novice master has this sort of approach, the correction offered to the novice will have a very different tone. Nevertheless, the key thing is not the nature of the correction but the inner attitude and intention.

Now we need to recognize that living out obedience in a supernatural way is much easier than living out authority in such a way, and that for a simple reason: obedience costs us, whereas authority can be something pleasurable. Nobody likes to obey, many people like to give orders, and some people elevate this pleasure to the status of a real passion: the taste for power; a close relation of pride, and something very much appreciated by the devil, who made it into

---

[116] Presuming, naturally, that the situation was sufficiently serious to justify such a response; sometimes we just have to smile about trivial things, of course.

one of the three temptations of Christ. It can do a great deal of harm to members of the community but even more harm to a superior who is afflicted by it.

The distinction between the first and second degree of authority is at the level of intention. In the first degree, the intention is simply that the thing should be done, with no regard for the interior state of the one who has to carry out the order. In the second degree, the dimension of service comes more to the fore, with a concern for the person's well-being. Any sort of boss might have this kind of concern, even if only at a purely natural level. Religious life gives this degree a particular character, which comes from Christ's washing the apostles' feet. The superior's intention will really be "religious" in nature if he is concerned to lead the one obeying to his proper goal, if he exercises his authority to allow the subordinate to fulfill his obedience to God. This intention puts both people here on the same path, at the same level, which makes the term "superior" seem a bit unfortunate.

A THIRD DEGREE?

Can we identify a third degree? It ought to be linked to the third degree of obedience, through submission of one's own intellect to divine wisdom. A superior often has to give a certain direction, because this is part of the mission any superior receives. But he knows just how weak his own wisdom is, and that the one to whom he gives an order may well be closer to God than he is himself. Perhaps we could say that this third degree is characterized by the fear of God, in the broad sense of the expression: a reverential fear of one standing in the presence of the all-powerful and infinitely wise God, who confers on such weak creatures the mission of leading others. Of course, the superior must not be paralyzed by this fear, but it should help him to hold on to the awareness that he, too, has taken a vow of obedience, and so when he gives a command, his desire ought to be to obey, in everything he says or commands, that higher wisdom that he must seek in prayer.

BETWEEN VIRTUE AND VICE

The degrees of authority and the degrees of obedience have one aspect in common: they represent progress in self-denial. But there is another aspect that clearly distinguishes them from one another: there are also negative degrees, in that authority can become a vice, but this is not really the case with obedience. From the first degree, which is neutral (coming, as it does, from the requirements of any life with others), the superior can descend to a way of exercising authority that is more and more centered on himself: the pleasure of giving orders, of dominating, of bending other people to his will. This becomes the center of everything, and God no longer has any place in the way he does things. On the other hand, the superior can also ascend toward an ever-greater detachment from himself and learn to exercise his authority out of love for those in his charge (which would constitute the second degree) and out of love for God (which would constitute the third degree).

In civil society, where the same positive and negative degrees exist, things are normally obvious; a tyrant appears precisely as a tyrant. But alas, religious life offers authority a sort of disguise, which allows what is a vice to pass for a virtue in the eyes of other people, but even more in the eyes of the superior himself. The evil form of false mysticism that has come to light so horrifically in the realm of sexual behavior has also besieged the realm of authority. In the case of sexual abuse, this "mysticism" can cloak the most carnal kinds of love, claiming that it is a gift of God that is so elevated in love that it is above — i.e., dispensed from — all morality. In the case of abuse of authority, this "mysticism" claims to represent the greatest love that has ever existed, that of Christ in His Passion, and justifies itself by referring to Gethsemane and the Cross. This perversion is the more subtle, but it is no less remarkable, since this "mysticism" makes use of the Cross to justify the harm that it inflicts. The damage done to people is grave because it twists people's image of God.

Moreover, when authority is exercised poorly, it makes it more difficult for people to obey. A saint may be able to draw spiritual profit, but the average religious runs the risk of experiencing feelings of frustration or resentment, which will not do him any good.

Are there signs that the direction of things is wrong? We mentioned one above. At a more fundamental level, the safest criterion is obedience. There is a parallel between the degrees of obedience and the (positive) degrees of exercise of authority: they cause us to turn away from ourselves more and more, so that we can turn toward God. Self-denial comes to the fore because the love of God takes us over to an ever-greater extent. The negative degrees of exercise of authority follow a path that leads in the opposite direction: evil passions grow there, and the love of God is replaced by a sort of disguise that is really only a caricature. The clearest sign is an attachment to power. We can observe very great differences in [people's relationship to power]. Some have only a single desire — to be set free from it; others live in fear of being deprived of it, or do not respond well when [it is taken from them].

Owing to the parallel we mentioned above, self-denial out of love and in obedience is the surest sign of the quality of the exercise of authority that, if it is to be just, calls for a great deal of renunciation. A small, concrete exercise (which is thus easy to understand) will consist in the superior renouncing his own will whenever he can. Imagine that a book has to be chosen for the refectory. The abbot may prefer one book, but the prior suggests another. From time to time, it will be very profitable for the abbot to renounce his own will, consciously and deliberately, bending himself to another's choices, whether the "other" in question is an individual member of the community or, perhaps especially, if it is the community as a whole.

Reflection on Providence

The nature of obedience, as something that allows us to encounter God's plan through a very imperfect person, is not limited to particular, given situations: it affects our whole life. Indeed, in life, nobody can do whatever he likes. Religious have taken a vow of obedience, but whether he likes it or not, everybody has to be obedient in a whole host of circumstances he would never have chosen for himself. These circumstances are not the result of blind chance, since

> by his providence God protects and governs all things which he has made. ... The witness of Scripture is unanimous that the solicitude of divine providence is real and immediate; God cares for all, from the least things to the great events of the world and its history. The sacred books powerfully affirm God's absolute sovereignty over the course of events.[117]

Jesus tells us as much when He speaks of the sparrows: "Not one of them will fall to the ground without your Father's will" (Matt. 10:29). The *Catechism*

---

[117] *Catechism of the Catholic Church* (CCC), nos. 302–303.

of the Catholic Church gives a very good summary of this in nos. 300–314. A concrete example will help us untangle the relationship between providence and religious obedience.

Hector is driving calmly on a small country road. Anatole is driving the opposite way; he has had too much to drink and recklessly overtakes a truck on the blind summit of a hill. The two vehicles collide and Hector, seriously injured, is left paraplegic. Can we say that God willed this accident? The answer is not as simple as it might seem.

Directly, no. God did not ask Anatole to get drunk and commit a serious act of recklessness that might cause Hector's death as well as his own. To think this would make a mockery of human freedom. Any notion that "it was pre-ordained" is basically replacing God's loving providence with a kind of fatalism, which reduces our life to a play.[118]

> God is in no way, directly or indirectly, the cause of moral evil. He per-mits it, however, because he respects the freedom of his creatures and, mysteriously, knows how to derive good from it.[119]

God, then, does not will the evil act, but He permits it to happen. In a sense, this would also be true of a good act, since God has given us the freedom to be the real cause of both good and evil acts:

> God grants his creatures not only their existence, but also the dignity of acting on their own, of being causes and principles for each other, and thus of co-operating in the accomplishment of his plan.[120]

This will save Hector from rebelling against God: *What did I do to God that He should treat me this way?* No, God did not do this, but He did respect Anatole's freedom, even when Anatole used it badly. He does this with us constantly.

But we can't just stop there, otherwise how would we maintain that prov-idence takes care *of the smallest things?* God would seem to be keeping His

---

[118] "C'était écrit."
[119] *CCC*, no. 311, which adds references: Augustine, *De libero arbitrio* I, 1, 2: PL 32:1221–1223; Aquinas, *Summa theologiae* IaIIae, q. 79, a. 1.
[120] Ibid., no. 306.

distance and getting Himself off the hook by saying to Hector: *Sorry, it had nothing to do with me,* which might provoke another rebellion.

What happened to Hector was not willed by God, but He permitted it, and for Him this permission is not an act of powerlessness but is a free choice of His providence. God was not absent when the accident happened; He was just as present to Hector as He was to Anatole. Sometimes, He intervenes more directly, as in the attempted assassination of St. John Paul II. Astonished that none of the pope's vital organs were affected, the surgeon said: "One man pulled the trigger, another guided the bullet." These particular interventions of the Lord or of our guardian angels remain the exception, and they are not really a part of ordinary life, except perhaps in a dimension invisible to us. They didn't prevent John Paul II (or Hector) from being injured. Our condition as free human beings is part of divine providence.

A question arises, then: if God neither willed the thing nor did it Himself, why did He not prevent it, why did He allow it to happen? Giving an answer to this profound question is well beyond the scope of this book, so let us stick, instead, with a specific situation: Hector has some interior work to do on this, so that he can understand that God never abandoned him, never turned His face away, not for one moment during the accident, the details of which He is infinitely better acquainted with than we are. That God was present with Hector during every moment of the trauma will allow Hector to discover God's presence and love for him in this moment of his life and in everything that follows. If God permitted it, He must have been able to draw good out of it for Hector.

> For the all-powerful God ... because He is supremely good, would never allow any evil to exist in His works, were He not powerful enough and good enough Himself to draw good out of evil.[121]

This begins with everything we have not chosen: our parents; the historical, cultural, and familial context in which we are born, with all its flaws; our handicaps (we all have them), whether physical, intellectual, or emotional. In all of that, there is so much that is not good, and yet God allows a child to be born into circumstances that are imperfect and potentially even harmful. But He remains

---

[121] Augustine, *Enchiridon*, 11, 3, quoted by *CCC* no. 311.

present to all people in all circumstances, to transform this path, strewn with imperfections great and small, into a path that leads to Him, absolute Goodness, with no shadow of evil. Even our poor choices, all those no's that place us in opposition to Him, and which were obviously never willed by Him: all of this He respects, out of His infinite regard for our freedom, and He accompanies them by following us along the path we have chosen, for even if He has not directly willed the path we have chosen, He has directly willed our condition as free human beings.

So Anatole's sin, the evil he has inflicted upon Hector, can become a path to sanctity for Hector; for Anatole too, for that matter, if he will commit to a way of repentance. Such is the transformation to which providence subjects all of life's events: "God causes all things to work together for the good of those who love him" (Rom. 8:28).[122]

Such is the dynamic that allows a religious to accept obediently from the hand of God all that is asked of him, within the limitations previously discussed. With the eyes of faith, a religious knows that the Lord is present in it all, and that He expects from him that intelligent obedience that, with discernment, is addressed to God through the superior. And in the many small things of no moral consequence, which make up so much of everyday life, God expects a religious to be faithful to the vow professed, to obey, giving concrete meaning to this vow.

There is a distinction between the freedom and the responsibility of the superior who gives commands and the freedom of the religious, whom the Lord expects to show his or her love by fulfilling wherever possible the vow of obedience; this distinction allows us on the one hand to avoid an undue sacralization of what the superior wants or says and, on the other hand, to avoid reducing religious obedience to something merely human, as if saying: "I obey if I agree" or, in other words, "I only obey myself."

When the Limits of Obedience Are Exceeded

When we depart from the proper limits of obedience, as just discussed, what ought to be a great benefit can become a great evil.

---

[122] This passage was directly translated from the French to maintain original emphasis.

WHEN THE EVIL IS CLEAR-CUT

We have already looked at the first case: if a superior asks something that is against divine law, a religious has no obligation to obey and would even be committing a sin if he or she were to do as asked.

If the superior asks the bursar to cover up financial fraud, the situation is clear, even if the decision to be made is much less clear. The situation is clear since the bursar, who has a moral compass, will understand that he must not obey this order. But if he refuses to obey, he knows that he will have to bear the consequences, in particular the displeasure of the superior, who may show this quite openly. If he decides to obey the superior against the promptings of conscience, he will likely have to anesthetize the conscience, saying that the matter is really not all that serious, that others do it, or that if he doesn't do it here and now, someone else will later on in any event. This last argument is perhaps the most compelling. Is it worth making life any more complicated if in the end it will make no difference?

Such situations are hopefully rare in a religious setting, but they can crop up. We seriously fail in showing people proper respect if we don't keep up with pension contributions,[123] or we make people work without a contract or insurance. People thus exploited can find themselves on the streets when they choose to leave the community.

This situation can arise as a result of tiny things, like the superior asking his secretary to tell a caller that he is out. Clearly, this is nothing particularly serious, and we might say that the person ringing will understand. And yet, if the secretary has a delicate conscience, it may be a cause of distress. But does the secretary have the right to correct his superior? It is difficult. In any case, even if the situation is clear, the decision is much less so.

WHEN THE EVIL IS NOT CLEAR-CUT

Things get more difficult by degrees when it is a question of prudential judgment. Here is a situation that occurred in a monastery some years ago. A monk who was a former doctor was the infirmarian. An old monk with a weak heart had

---

[123] We mustn't forget that a religious may leave the community one day and find himself dependent on an old age pension.

been prescribed an injection by the community's doctor to help his condition. The prior asked the monk to administer the injection, but he thought to himself: *The dose is far too strong; it will kill him.* He went to speak to the superior, who telephoned the doctor, who replied that the monk's anxieties were absurd, and that there was no problem. So the prior upheld the request. Caught in a dilemma, the monk asked various people for advice, but he received different opinions. In the end, he decided to give the injection that evening, and the old monk died in the night. Whether the injection was a causal factor or just a coincidence, it is clear that the event was very hard for the monk to bear.

We can imagine that the prior apologized to him, but what would have happened if the monk had refused to give the injection, if a nurse had come to do it, and the old monk suffered no ill effects? Would the superior have accepted it in the same way? And yet, as regards the monk's conscience, there was no difference, since he never argued that the monk was certain to die, only that the risk was significant.

The difficulty for the monk arises from the fact that the situation was much less clear than the previous cases, and the wide range of opinions he received shows this. Lying or committing financial fraud is clearly contrary to moral norms. But in this case, the big question for him is: "Am I right to think there is a risk that this injection could be fatal, given that the doctor said the exact opposite?" He finds himself caught between two bad solutions: disobeying the prior, or disobeying his conscience. He is going to feel bad whichever solution he opts for, and this is why the prior wronged him by imposing the dilemma upon him when there were other possible ways forward, in particular the more usual solution of asking for a professional nurse.

When the Very Principle of Discernment Is Affected

The examples we have examined up to now could just as well crop up in life outside a religious community. But religious life presents a particular risk, on account of the value given to obedience (by vow), a value that resides not in the deed but in the person. By our vow of obedience, we wish to be conformed to the image of Christ, who was perfectly obedient. Now Christ learned obedience from what He suffered. As we reflect on the total offering of ourselves to God, might we arrive at the conclusion that, if this offering is to be totally effective, a religious must renounce not only his own will but also his intellect? Some people have come to this conclusion, using various ancient texts such as John Climacus's chapter on obedience to support their views, and giving instructions such as: "A perfect disciple trusts his *abba*[124] totally; it is the *abba* who has wisdom, and everything he asks is necessarily a good thing. Thinking too much about what is asked is really rationalizing, and rationalizing is precisely what Eve did with the serpent, and hence it deceived her. It is for the *abba* to discern, but you, on the other hand, should not think too much about it; you have forgotten what it is to think about things. This is what it means to give up your intellect: to renounce all discernment, by means of a superabundance of discernment."

For the young, the all-encompassing nature of this kind of approach can be attractive. "You give yourself totally, you are giving up your responsibility and your understanding by submitting totally and unconditionally to someone who will embody the will of God for you. In this way you will be totally free, set entirely free from being enslaved to your own will."

A young person may throw himself into this for a time because it relieves him of the heavy burden of discernment. At the beginning the fruits are good, which is hardly surprising. The true meaning of obedience has become so damaged in our society that applying such an overwhelming remedy can prove effective. But at the same time, this remedy can cause another imbalance, worse than the one it was supposed to cure.

If we are to understand the words of John Climacus, they have to be read in their proper context. We would need a whole book for that, since the monumental work that is *The Ladder* contains a doctrine that is as precious as it is inimitable.[125] Trying to transpose this account of seventh-century Syrian monasticism to a twenty-first-century context could lead to grave dangers. John himself warns his reader, in his chapter on obedience:

---

[124] We will use this term here, so as to avoid having to choose between the various terms used in different circumstances and communities.

[125] *The Ladder of Divine Ascent*, by St. John Climacus, is the book that gave him his name. (Ladder in Greek is *klimax*.) An English edition is available: John Climacus, *The Ladder of Divine Ascent*, Classics of Western Spirituality (Mahwah: Paulist Press, 1982).

When it comes to bending our neck and committing ourselves to another person in the Lord, so as to acquire humility and, above all, salvation, before we even enter [the monastery], if we have any competency or prudence, we will have to examine our helmsman, scrutinize him, and, as it were, put him to the test, for fear that, by happening upon an ordinary sailor rather than a helmsman, upon a sick man rather than a doctor, upon a man subject to the passions rather than one who is free from them, and finding ourselves on the open sea rather than in a harbor, we should rush headlong into a ready-made shipwreck.[126]

Another temptation is to transpose the figure of the *staretz* into a Western setting. The words of Ignatius Brianchaninov on this subject will be no less severe! Fr. Labourdette, O.P., writes:

Obedience is a virtue of a free person. Any kind of subhuman obedience is counterfeit.... If we are really to be obedient, we must be capable of disobeying.[127]

These are strong words, but we can easily understand them. Can we say that a man being led to prison is *obeying* the police officers? On a physical level, perhaps, but this obedience is not free; it is endured, not willed. St. Thomas's distinction between an act of a human being and a human act, mentioned above, applies here. Religious obedience, following the example of Christ, is the free submission of a free will, enlightened by a free understanding. Any other kind is devoid of religious value.

We may swap the physical restraint of the police officers for another, more subtle kind of restraint: if you bind the understanding, you bind everything else, since the will is no longer free; it is like the will of someone under hypnosis, who has lost responsibility for his or her actions. Such a person seems to be obeying, but in reality he is not there as a person, having become more like a

---

[126]John Climacus, *Ladder*, (Paris, Éd. du Cerf, 2019), 57. [Translated from the French.]

[127]M.-M. Labourdette, *Cours de théologie morale*, vol. 2., Morale spéciale, (Paris: Parole et Silence, 2012), 739–740. Quoted in Fr. H. Donneaud's article, "Les enjeux théologiques de l'obéissance dans la vie consacrée," no. 2, 156.

robot. Isn't *giving away one's understanding* like a sort of spiritual hypnosis? In the final analysis, who are we giving it away to?

Can We Renounce Our Understanding?

As sublime as it may seem, this doctrine leads to the atrophy of a faculty that is essential for the spiritual life: discernment. How will someone who renounces the intellect be able to subject his own thoughts to discernment? We may answer: his *abba* will do it for him. But this response is just fine words, with little connection to reality. Struggling with one's thoughts is a constant feature of people's day-to-day lives; it involves all the movements of the soul. Even if he wanted to, the disciple would never be able to communicate even one percent of this to his *abba*. It is a strange spiritual paternity indeed that would seek to keep a monk in an immature state, without training him in that discernment, which was the true strength of the ancients.

Some will say: Look how beautiful it is, this monk has become a child, totally docile; he will do anything he is told to do! It is undeniable that there can be real beauty in a disabled person, as the potential of human beings is fathomless. But would that justify the deliberate creation of a handicap? "Human beings have been created in the Image of God, which means they are endowed with understanding, free will, and an autonomous power," writes St. Thomas.[128] If the understanding is one element of the Image of God within us, silencing it would amount to offending God. The Old Testament insists, sometimes powerfully, that people should not offer a blemished sacrifice to God.[129] Obedience without understanding is the obedience of a robot; it disfigures human beings in one of the ways in which they resemble God; it is unworthy of God because it is unworthy of human beings. Spiritual companionship should help a Christian to rediscover the fullness of his or her dignity as an image of God, just as God has desired it from the very beginning. In the second creation narrative, it is wonderful to watch God, as He brings to the man the various living things He has just created, "to see what he would call them: the name that the man gave to every living thing would be its name"

---

[128] Thomas Aquinas, *Summa theologiæ*, Prologue of IaIIae.
[129] See, among others, Lev. 22:21–25.

(Gen. 2:19).[130] God respects the work of Adam's understanding; He accepts the name that Adam gives to the creatures.

Even the loftiest spiritual life is no exception to this rule. Teresa of Avila draws our attention to this:

> In the mystical theology I have begun to speak about, the understanding stops acting, because God holds it in a suspended state.... To presume or decide to suspend it ourselves is precisely what I am asking people not to do; nor should we stop using it, on pain of becoming cold, stupid, and of gaining nothing; for when the Lord suspends and stops our understanding, He gives it something to fill it with wonder and keep it busy and, without the use of reason, in the space of a *Credo* He makes it understand more than all our earthly labors would attain to in many years. To occupy the powers of the soul and imagine that one can immobilize them [at the same time] is madness.[131]

A Formula of St. John Climacus

The formula of St. John Climacus, which states that "Obedience is a renunciation of discernment by means of a superabundance of discernment,"[132] cannot be applied indiscriminately. This paradoxical formula requires interpretation. But it should be clear that the essential thing is precisely the superabundance of discernment. To understand this formula as saying that *the absence of discernment is a superabundance of discernment* would be to commit a dangerous error. In reality, John Climacus is calling for a high level of spiritual discernment, which is capable of telling when the value of obedience matters more than the material result of the commanded action. In other words, even if the monk's idea was *per se* better than the superior's, the perfection of the monk's act of obedience, in

---

[130] This passage was directly translated from the French to maintain original emphasis. In the French edition, this comes from a translation by Osty, which is closer to the Hebrew than the scriptural version then in use in the French liturgy.

[131] Teresa of Avila, *Autobiography*, 12, 5 (Paris: DDB), 79. An English edition is available: Teresa of Avila, *Collected Works* (Washington: Institute of Carmelite Studies, 1976).

[132] *Ladder*, chapter 4: "On blessed and ever-praiseworthy obedience," no. 3.

setting aside his own thought (this is the "absence of discernment") will amply compensate for the lack of material compensation — so long as the result is not catastrophic, obviously. If the superior wants one of the brothers to paint a large room with a paintbrush rather than a roller, without the brother seeing any purpose in that, then there is no doubt that he is going to waste time. If, while he is painting, he spends the time telling the Lord he is happy that he has given up his own will out of love for Him, then the time becomes an opportunity for prayer. Everything that was apparently wasted has been regained, we might say; the practical matter was of slight importance. If the matter is serious, or if the good of others is at stake, an absence of discernment will no longer be a superabundance of discernment; it will be irresponsible (behavior). Discernment is in fact needed in every case, since the one who obeys must judge whether or not the matter is serious.

So we have to be careful with the formula of John Climacus. He speaks of a superabundance of discernment, which holds first place, and which in some cases results in what he calls an "absence of discernment," which we might translate more simply as a preferential option for the will of another over one's own will.

Obedience to the Church

So far, we have been considering obedience in the context of the relationship between superior and subject. But we must not forget that superiors have also taken a vow of obedience, which is not invalidated just because they have taken up a position of responsibility. In situations where the behavior of a community is becoming aberrant, we generally observe a curious dichotomy. On the one hand, we see an extremely demanding doctrine of obedience for the members of the community, which involves submission not only of the will, but of the intellect too, since every word of the superiors must be considered as a word of God. On the other hand, we find an extremely lax regime for the superiors themselves; there are no qualms about minimizing (or even completely and deliberately ignoring or setting aside) obedience to the Church and to canon law.[133]

---

[133] One religious woman noted humorously that in her congregation, canon law seemed like science fiction.

Abuses in the Religious Life and the Path to Healing

A particular reason is often invoked in support of such an approach: "The reason we don't obey is because the Church doesn't understand us." This explanation is very similar to the reactions of some novices who do not come from the same culture as their European novice master: *you don't understand us*. There can be no answer to that, since there is an element of truth in it, but it can be a very useful means of getting their own way.

The amusing little cartoon mentioned previously comes irresistibly back to mind, with the young sister on her knees before her prioress. We just need to change it a little: *We're very obedient toward the Church, provided the Congregation is sympathetic and we agree with what it proposes, after negotiation*. But even if the original cartoon makes us smile, there is nothing to laugh at in this adapted version, since it is too close to reality in some cases.

Fr. Henry Donneaud writes:

> I note this fact, as seen so often, particularly over the last decades, that those communities where there is the greatest number of abuses of power through manipulation, induced blindness, and infantilism can be the very same communities whose leaders do their utmost to escape regulation by the Church and, particularly when the noose is tightening, to avoid any real obedience to the Church.[134]

We mustn't let ourselves be deceived. So long as the sun shines, so long as the community is admired and applauded by the Church, demonstrations of submissiveness and deference in both word and deed may pull the wool over our eyes, but they don't count for much. What really counts is their attitude when the Church asks something of them that is not to their liking. Likewise, if the Church approves the rule, much insistence will be placed upon this approval to lend support to all the various small details, and to ward off all criticism, even if Rome has expressed reservations that we were able to pass over. The contrast between this insistence on submission to the Church (a divine voice, when it approves something) and the self-awarded freedom to refuse when it makes demands that are less congenial should be enough to show that there

---

[134] H. Donneaud, "Les enjeux théologiques de l'obéissance dans la vie consacrée," p. 42.

is considerable dysfunction here. We all know the version of the Lord's Prayer that reads: *Thy will be done, so long as it corresponds to mine.* Someone who has experience of this writes:

> When I pointed out this discrepancy to my superiors, I wasn't contradicted, only told that their behavior was legitimate, because "the Church does not understand us" (implying: "That is why we don't have to obey it"). I reacted rather provocatively, saying: "Okay then, so I can conclude that, if my prioress doesn't understand me (or if I simply think that she doesn't), I don't have to obey her!" It was clear that my superiors did not agree and were not very happy, but neither could they resolve this contradiction.

There are several overlapping dynamics in the situation described here, hence its relevance for detecting dysfunction. The culture of exception finds here one of its most conspicuous applications. Members of the community have a duty to obey, but this doesn't apply to the superior. If the superior is meant to be the voice of the Holy Spirit, he or she will believe this all the more — and others will believe it all the more about the superior — when he or she acts to defend the charism. This leads to assuming a position of superiority over the Church itself, which is now judged by the community: the Church is in crisis, decadent, and we are going to save it. The theme of Noah's Ark in the flood. People might even say: "We are disobeying precisely out of love for the Church, and for its good." One step further on, and the community will be presented as heroically suffering persecution by the Church, the highest proof of its fidelity to God.

There is something horrifying about this last stage, since, paradoxically, the affirmation is so enormous that it appears believable. They will trot out a list of all the saints who have had to bear opposition, distracting people's gaze from the real question. The logic of affirmation starts from an assertion that is unchallenged, because it is considered unchallengeable: the community is as pure as the driven snow. Consequently, our "enemies" are the enemies of God. Or to put it more simply: we are necessarily right, so they are necessarily wrong. We are back at the diagnostic test of Msgr. Carballo: when a community considers itself to be above all others and (to an even greater degree) above the Church, aberrant, sect-like behavior is already firmly in place. The witness quoted above goes on:

> For me, this question of obedience toward the Church, lived out concretely by superiors, and the obedience demanded at the same time in the heart of the community, is really the key question when it comes to detecting aberrant, sect-like behavior as soon as possible. I am absolutely convinced that, where there is no gap (or perhaps only a minimal one) between these two forms of obedience, there will be no great danger of sect-like aberrations.

Everything we have said concerning obedience also applies to superiors, which means they, too, are entitled to explain the difficulties of what is being asked of them, and to try to find an acceptable solution, in the context of open dialogue. But there also needs to be a real disposition to obey, since a charism needs to be discerned, both in terms of its object and in terms of the way it is pursued, and this discernment belongs to the Church. If the community rejects it, then it is closing itself in on its own vision of the Church and the world, to the exclusion of all else. It risks becoming increasingly cut off from the ecclesial body; alas, we have seen painful examples of this. It may be that the founder's vision is beautiful and prophetic, but it is nonetheless true that it will only bear fruit from within the Body of the Church.

The Royal Road of Obedience

Some might be afraid that this insistence on the limits of obedience may reduce it to something insignificant. They should take comfort; the space within the limits thus marked out is still vast. In our daily life, there are many opportunities to practice obedience even up to the third degree, so numerous are the situations where we may prefer someone else's opinion without fear. The choice of what we eat, which plants we should grow in the garden, which books we should buy, the liturgy as a whole (a place where there are constant opportunities for obedience and self-denial), the different forms of service we may have to render, the obsessions of this or that brother or sister that so set our teeth on edge, and so on. Here, too, we can say yes to the Lord. We know the famous example of St. Thérèse of the Child Jesus, with the sister who used to tap her teeth with a fingernail during times of prayer.[135] And then we must not forget the observance of the rule, which touches every aspect of the religious life. Every activity is filled with choices to be made that are neither critical nor questions of truth. In every one of these instances, it is possible to renounce our own will, freely and without the slightest hint of danger, by going even to the point of submitting our understanding, in a manner properly rooted in humility, which means considering that my brother is at least as intelligent as I am, and remembering the gift of charity, which allows me to go along with what he prefers, joyfully, in order to affirm him and please him. Connecting the different virtues together in this practical way will lead to a joyful and enlightened obedience, bringing a sense of fulfillment to our deepest self, because it is lived as a freedom and not as a constraint.

Dom Guillayume Jedrzejczak wrote that "learning to obey perhaps means learning to disobey." He explained that, without realizing it, we can be obeying a whole variety of processes that are either unconscious or out of control, generally egocentric in nature, all of which prevent us from being truly free. We offer our obedience blindly, without even realizing. To disobey these automatic compulsions, these reflex actions that have become deeply rooted, to disobey what we nowadays call addictions (and which used to be known previously — and more monastically — as vices): all of this is needed if we are to become free. For freedom is not simply a matter of choosing to do something; it also requires the ability to do it. It is not enough for someone choosing to become a pianist simply to say "I want this" for it to become a reality; a long period of training is needed. Obedience teaches us about the freedom of giving oneself, by teaching us to disobey the tyranny of "me." Christian obedience is a royal obedience; it is not the obedience of a slave or a passive instrument, since we are "a chosen race, a royal priesthood" (1 Pet. 2:9, but see also Rev. 1:6–9 and 5:10), and God calls us "into his own kingdom and glory" (1 Thess. 2:12). A religious obeys because he wants to obey, having sealed this choice by means of a vow, with the goal of learning how to love. But he is a king, or called to become one, and he knows it. Neither the Christian, called to follow the humility of Christ, nor the

---

[135] Thérèse de L'Enfant-Jesus, Manuscrit C (30v°), in *Œuvres complètes* (Paris: Éd. du Cerf, 1992), 275–276.

religious, who has chosen a more demanding path of obedience, must ever lose sight of their surpassing dignity as children of God, remembering at the same time the example of the one who allows them to share in His own filiation and kingship, and who reigns in a very unusual way, since He Himself washes His disciples' feet. "If therefore I, the Lord and Master, have washed your feet, you too must wash one another's feet" (John 13:14).[136]

To insist upon limits to obedience does not in any way make it less demanding; it simply allows us to see it in its proper place as a means, not an end, and teaches us to place the different things we owe obedience to in order of priority. If a martyr is to obey God, he or she must disobey a civil authority that is legitimate in the natural order but has overstepped the limits of its power. Apart from this extreme situation, the Christian remains under civil authority, as St. Peter reminds us (1 Pet. 2:13–18). In the same way, the limits we have discussed here leave a religious with enormous leeway to obey the rule and the superiors, when their commands are in accordance with the constitutions, and even the brethren, as St. Benedict recommends.[137] There is a lifetime's work in all of that.

So, there is nothing minimalist about this way of obedience. To be convinced of this, we need only read the texts we have cited. St. Benedict, St. Francis de Sales, and St. Ignatius all propose a way both high and difficult: the way of being conformed to the perfectly obedient Christ. As for the superiors, their response is also a way that can lead to holiness, if they discharge it as the Church recommends:

> Superiors are to exercise their power, received from God through the ministry of the Church, in a spirit of service. Therefore, docile to the will of God in fulfilling their function, they are to govern their subjects as sons or daughters of God and, promoting the voluntary obedience of their subjects with reverence for the human person, they are to listen to them willingly and foster their common endeavor for the good of the institute and the Church, but without prejudice to the authority of superiors to decide and prescribe what must be done.[138]

[136] This passage was directly translated from the French to maintain original emphasis.
[137] See *RB* 71:1–2.
[138] *Code of Canon Law*, can. 618.

7

Ascesis and Renunciation

Risks of a Spirituality That Is Taken to Extremes

To wander off the beaten track while walking through a forest in fine weather presents no risk for us; we may end up getting a little muddy, but that's all. If, on the other hand, we are on a mountain track that runs alongside a sheer drop, there is no longer any margin for error. Religious life, if it is fervent, is more like the mountain track. Many mistakes arise from excessive zeal combined with a lack of discernment. To try to get novices to progress more speedily, we can sometimes push traditional practices beyond what is reasonable, which would be rather like helping a plant to grow by pulling it upward. What should be docility to the Holy Spirit becomes a sort of forced voluntarism. The well-known story about the bow, in the collection of *apophthegmata* attributed to Abba Antony, illustrates this well:

> A hunter in the desert saw Abba Anthony relaxing with the breth-ren and he was shocked. Wanting to show him that it was necessary sometimes to meet the needs of the brethren, the old man said to him, "Put an arrow in your bow and shoot it." So he did. The old man then said, "Shoot another," and he did so. Then the old man said, "Shoot yet again," and the hunter replied, "If I bend my bow so much I will break it." Then the old man said to him, "It is the same with the work of God. If we stretch the brethren beyond measure, they will soon break. Sometimes it is necessary to come down to meet their needs." When he heard these words, the hunter was pierced by compunction and,

greatly edified by the old man, he went away. As for the brethren, they went home strengthened.[139]

Stretching the bow to breaking point is something that can happen in various ways in the religious life.

TAKE SEVEN TIMES AS MUCH

"This medicine cured me in a week. So take seven times as much, and you'll be better tomorrow." When presented like this, the idea makes us smile. And yet this logic is sometimes applied to the spiritual life. The religious who has spent forty years acquiring a virtue may seek to find a short cut for the person he is accompanying. Although there is nothing wrong with the intention, this approach does not really seem to have much regard for life, or the gradual way in which it develops. It might even end up being quite dangerous, since some of the ingredients that can be helpful in the ascetic life are rather like those medicines that are clearly labelled: *Do not exceed the prescribed dose.*

This virtue, which has become so dear to him, is not something the religious came by through forty years of effort. To be sure, he had his part to play, but almost all the labor was the work of the Holy Spirit, who can be neither commanded nor hurried. The religious had to go through a long process of coming to maturity, during which other virtues and aspects of the spiritual life had to be deepened; indeed, it would be truer to say he was being led along this path than to suggest that he found his own way along it. God is infinitely patient with us and, above all, shows infinite discretion. His action goes largely unperceived, and this can leave us with the illusion that we are doing all the work.

Jesus Himself experienced this slow process of development, something that may well surprise us. Out of His thirty-three years on earth, thirty were spent in a hidden life, during which nothing special happened: "[He] increased in wisdom and in stature, and in favor with God and man" (Luke 2:52). "With God": this slow process of coming to maturity has value in the eyes of God,

---

[139] Abba Anthony the Great, Saying 13, in *Sayings of the Desert Fathers: The Alphabetical Collection*, (trans. Benedicta Ward, S.L.G.), Cistercian Studies 59 (Kalamazoo: Cistercian Publications, 1975), 3.

otherwise the Father would not have chosen it for His Son. If we are to follow in His footsteps, we shouldn't desire to make quicker progress than Jesus.

Being "Traditional" Is Not Enough

Today, young people are often attracted by traditional practices, which in their eyes seem to promise security in a world that is constantly changing. They have to learn that this criterion is not enough. Any given practice, traditional or not, will only bear fruit if we engage in it at the right time and to the right extent. The important thing is not so much the practice itself (which might be more or less interchangeable with other, similar practices) but the wisdom behind it, a wisdom that manifests itself in a variety of ways, including: a balance of the different virtues and discernment; a breadth of vision that embraces the whole of Christian spirituality with its twenty centuries of history; the quality of listening and a respect for the human person, and many other ways.

This wisdom is also known by its fruits, not in terms of quantity, such as the number of vocations (a sign that can prove misleading), but in terms of the growth in the soul of the fruits of the Spirit: "Love, joy, peace, patience, kindness, goodness, faithfulness, gentleness, self-control" (Gal. 5:22–23), provided always that we understand these fruits at a sufficiently deep level, because the joy we are speaking of does not mean there will be no rough patches, and peace does not mean there will be no struggles. But within the difficulties and struggles, which Jesus told us about, there can exist a deeper sort of joy and peace, a joy and a peace that unite us to Him, while the incidents and accidents along the way remain, on the whole, part of something that is more external in nature. The novice or the monk who can tell his abbot "I am happy" gives him one of the best possible signs that he is at ease in his vocation. Whatever the difficulties, he did not enter religious life to find an easy option; deep in his heart, he perceives that this life is causing him to grow.

This life of growth offers us another sign that wisdom is present. God has "no pleasure in the death of the wicked, but that the wicked turn from his way and live" (Ezek. 33:11). "I came that [the sheep] may have life, and have it abundantly" (John 10:10). If, on the contrary, it seems that everything life-giving is disappearing, then that is a warning sign that must not be ignored. To desire, for example, to speed up the renunciation of self-will by eliminating everything that offers the religious a certain satisfaction can lead to a serious lack of balance, for "no one can live without some sensible and bodily pleasure."[140] To try to do so will push the religious to seek exotic compensations in inappropriate realms, such as an exaggerated aestheticization of the liturgy, or behavior that is more or less hypochondriac in nature; or it can lead to more classical forms of compensation, such as an obsession with work, or seeking out relationships outside normal bounds. On the other hand, it can also lead to a lack of self-worth, or to acedia.

> Our humanity was not even thought about. They spoke to us about the "fine point" of our soul and about our deep heart, which would be the only things that would pass into Heaven, while we left on earth all that belonged to the senses. So we immediately had to begin the business of adapting, of living life at the level of the deep heart, that is at the level of our deepest intellect and will; the rest had no importance. So the part of life that had to do with the senses was completely mortified, and, because of this mortification, there was no more life. We are alive when we can feel ourselves living, but when we no longer feel anything, well, in my own case, I came little by little to feel like a dead tree, like a tree that had had its branches cut off. After the branches have been cut off, there is only the trunk left, and when I spoke of things like this, they said to me: "That is really wonderful; this means that you are really being pruned for Heaven." So I said to myself: "It must be normal, then, but it seems strange that I feel less and less alive in terms of this world." But they said to me: "It is completely normal; it is the Cross. Look at the wood of the Cross; it is like a dead tree, and yet it is this that gives life." But in fact, without me realizing it, every sign of life within me was being snuffed out.

There was probably nothing superhuman about the renunciations that were being asked for, and no doubt they consisted of traditional practices, but the accumulation of negative actions, consisting of too many things being taken away one after the other, or at too early a stage, can overwhelm our human capacities.

---

[140] Thomas Aquinas, *Summa theologiae*, IaIIae, q. 34, a.1.

A lack of wisdom is revealed above all by the kind of interpretation that rejoices in death, imagining that it will somehow automatically lead to life. In this case, the person in danger did not receive any help; instead, there was a somewhat strange discussion, which seemed to ignore the cry for help, seizing instead upon the image that had been used — that of the tree — in order to say: it is a wonderful thing; you are dying, but Christ is alive. Can it really be the case that it is the nun who gives life to Christ by means of her death? This seems a very strange inversion indeed.

The problem with this sort of interpretation is that it is overly simplistic. The salvation that comes about through Christ does not consist in a simple paradoxical equation: death = life, particularly when this death is something that is endured, rather than desired. "I lay down my life, that I may take it again. No one takes it from me, but I lay it down of my own accord. I have power to lay it down, and I have power to take it again; this charge I have received from my Father" (John 10:17–18). At the heart of this dynamic of death and life, love is always present. Now, to love, we have to exist; we have to believe that we are someone, and that we are not only capable of loving, but also worthy of being loved. Those who do not believe themselves to be worthy of love cannot love in their own turn; on the contrary, it would seem totally incongruous to them, for it is impossible to love without desiring to be loved in return. And if one feels unworthy of this, what is to be done?

It may be that the person who caused this damage will say: "But I never said that!" Well, perhaps it is really true that he or she never said it, or even thought it, but all the same, that was what was communicated. If, as the fruit of long experience, such a person possesses the appropriate correctives, then he can sink into his own nothingness and think nothing of it; such people know perfectly well that this is only one way of looking at things, that this is only "nothingness" in comparison to the infinitude of God, and that the love of God for him is infinite. But if this is what they teach to a young soul that has not yet developed these interior correctives, a soul that does not yet know that he or she is loved by God, who has not yet had the experience of the gift of God, then the results can be catastrophic. It would be like a seasoned skier advising a beginner to take a black run by assuring him: "You'll see, it's easy!" For himself, perhaps, but not for the beginner.

Abuses in the Religious Life and the Path to Healing

Ascesis and Bodily Penances

Ascesis and bodily penances constitute perhaps the first area in which we may apply what we have just been saying. A vision that is too simplistic — such and such a saint has done such and such a thing, so it must be all right — inevitably leads to blunders that are of a more or less serious nature because of the great differences between us and the saint in terms of time and place, between the saint's way of life and culture and our own, and also between our own constitution and that of the saint. It is impossible to lay down rules that are valid for everyone, everywhere. Wisdom consists precisely in knowing how to apply general rules to specific situations, rules that cannot be valid for every particular case.

Here is the first mistake to avoid: the penances of a hermit cannot serve as a model for a community. The hermit takes them upon himself, and, since he experiences the consequences directly, it is relatively easy for him to modify them as necessary. If the same penances are imposed by a rule, or by a superior, the business of modifying them as necessary will be far less effective, especially if the superior is not a good listener, and especially if he thinks that he is himself dispensed from keeping them.

Amma Syncletica emphasizes another aspect of this: "As long as we are in the monastery, obedience is preferable to asceticism. The one teaches pride, the other humility."[141]

A common feature of situations where communities are manifesting some of the characteristics of sects is the extreme importance given to questions of food. It is true, the Desert Fathers gave an example of quite advanced asceticism in this regard, but to concentrate on this is to center on a concrete practice, whereas it is the result that counts. Does forcing the community to be hungry all the time really bear spiritual fruit? The old monks who lived through the war used to tell us they simply ended up thinking about how hungry they were all day long. Far from bringing forth spiritual profit, this simply uses up our strength and continuously forces the spirit back onto the body.

---

[141] Amma Syncletica, Saying 16, in *Sayings of the Desert Fathers: The Alphabetical Collection*, (trans. Benedicta Ward, S.L.G.), Cistercian Studies 59 (Kalamazoo: Cistercian Publications, 1975), 196.

St. Teresa of Calcutta asked herself what she should do regarding this question. Given that they lived among the poor, should they not share the way of life of the poor completely, including by being hungry? However, as her sisters were giving of themselves without counting the cost and, according to some accounts, were exhausted, she was advised to feed them properly, and she followed this advice. Hunger on top of fatigue would have been an excessive burden.

A text from the *Carthusian Statutes*, in the chapter on poverty, has something interesting to say, which is incidentally an allusion to chapter 55 of the *Rule of St. Benedict*:

> We exhort the priors to show themselves gracious and cooperative in providing for the needs of their community, in the measure that their resources permit. If they are moved by Christ's love, they will in no way leave themselves open to any reproach in this matter, nor will they, by being grudging, cause their monks to err by the vice of private ownership.[142]

By seeking to push to the limit a sort of poverty that is imposed, we simply cause the reflex action of hoarding, like the ant preparing for the winter, and the outcome ends up being the very opposite of the one desired. We could apply this to other situations. On the subject of food, a member of the community who is too hungry runs the risk of seeking out various means of getting around this, such as stealing what he can from the kitchen, and he will do this all the more readily if he perceives that the superiors scarcely submit themselves to the same ascetic regimes.

The text quoted continues along these lines, offering a deeper justification, which requires no further commentary:

> For the more willingly that poverty is embraced, the more acceptable it is to God. For it is the free surrender of the goods of this world that is praiseworthy — not the deprivation.[143]

---

[142] *Carthusian Statutes*, 28.10.
[143] Ibid.

Abuses in the Religious Life and the Path to Healing

BALANCE

All the Christian virtues are suspended between two extremes: the fact that we are creatures, drawn out of nothingness, and the infinitude of God, which draws us to Him. If one of these anchor points gives way, what was once virtue is transformed into folly. We do not have to make a choice between the human and the divine; Christ, who is our way, has united these two natures in His person, and spirituality ceases to be Christian (that is, in the image of Christ) if it does not accept both at once. The spiritual life is made up of a number of different balances, and this is the source both of its richness and its subtlety. Boldness and prudence, intimacy and transcendence in our relationship with God,[144] trust in God's mercy and consciousness of sin, fidelity to the rule and adaptation by means of dispensations, faith and works, grace and nature, the fact that everything comes from God and yet my cooperation is still necessary, prayer and work, abandonment to providence and the need to act with intelligence and foresight, and so on.

In chapter 55 of his *Rule*, St. Benedict writes:

> The beds are to be inspected frequently by the abbot, lest private possessions be found there. A monk discovered with anything not given him by the abbot must be subjected to very severe punishment. In order that this vice of private ownership may be completely uprooted, the abbot is to provide all things necessary: that is, cowl, tunic, sandals, shoes, belt, knife, stylus, needle, handkerchief and writing tablets. In this way every excuse of lacking some necessity will be taken away.
>
> The abbot, however, must always bear in mind what is said in the Acts of the Apostles: distribution was made to each one as he had need (Acts 4:35). In this way, the abbot will take into account the weaknesses of the needy, not the evil will of the envious; yet in all his judgments he must bear in mind God's retribution.[145]

---

[144] "You were more intimately present to me than my innermost being, and higher than the highest peak of my spirit." (*Tu eras interior intimo meo et superior summo meo.*) Augustine, *Confessions* (trans. Maria Boulding, O.S.B.), the New City Augustine (New York: New City Press, 1997), 83.

[145] *RB* 55:16–22.

This text illustrates the greatness of the tradition. This does not consist primarily in inspecting the beds, or providing strictly what is indicated on the list; this would be a literalist approach, forgetting that fourteen centuries separate us from the text, and that nowadays, people do not hide things under their beds. The greatness of the tradition is expressed in the balance of the text, which begins by indicating which objects are allowable within the bounds of poverty and which are considered superfluous, so as to give a clear lead. It then does not hesitate to point out transgressions, indicating an appropriate prudence and wisdom in order to avoid a situation where excessive frugality might push the monks into vices that are the opposite of poverty, and then concludes with an exhortation to kindness and mercy, especially toward the weak. This balance remains valid today, and it will still be valid in a thousand years' time. At the end, he adds one of the many exhortations the *Rule* makes to the abbot, urging him to remember that he, too, has a Judge. If it should happen, indeed, that he should leave his monks in a condition of meaningless deprivation, this Judge may well say to him: "I was hungry and you did not give me anything to eat, I was naked and you did not clothe me." And this sentence will resound all the more terrifyingly if he himself, during this time, had everything he needed. "Woe to you lawyers also! for you load men with burdens hard to bear, and you yourselves do not lift a finger to help" (Luke 11:46).[146]

The great tradition thus brings us back to this essential balance, which is both demanding but also full of mercy, which has both a firmness but also a kindness, and which is practiced under the watchful gaze of Christ, to whom we must render an account. And all of this in an apparently unimportant chapter which carries the title: *On the clothing and footwear of the brethren.*

Humility

This virtue has always had a particular place in Christian spirituality. St. Bernard writes: "Strive for humility. It is the foundation and guardian of the virtues; seek it out ardently, for it alone can save your souls."[147] In the text of which

---

[146] This passage was directly translated from the French to maintain original emphasis.

[147] Bernard, "First Christmas Sermon," *Sermons pour l'année* I.2, Sources Chrétiennes (Paris: Éd. du Cerf, 2004), 11. An English edition is available: Bernard

several passages have been quoted above,[148] Dorotheus of Gaza expresses this same thing by using the image of the mortar that must bind together the stones (the virtues), so that they do not come apart.[149] St. Bernard says again: "It is by humility that we acquire the other virtues; it is also by humility that we keep them. Indeed, it is humility that brings them to perfection."[150] Closer to our own time, the Curé of Ars writes: "Humility is to the virtues as the cord is to the rosary: take away the cord, and all the beads are lost; take away humility and all of the virtues disappear."[151]

And yet, it is far from certain that for a particular soul, at a particular moment, it would be right to expend all spiritual energy in the search for humility. If, behind this pressing search that is taking place in such a soul, we detect the image of a God who takes pleasure in humiliating His creatures, or maybe a psychological fragility such as a lack of self-esteem, then such a soul should, quite frankly, be redirected toward contemplating the love of Christ and of His Father for it, rather than toward the contemplation of its own nothingness, which will not lead it to God. A glance toward the grandeur of God is better for our humility than any consideration of our own nothingness.

To push a soul too zealously toward humility presents real risks, on both human and spiritual levels. True humility can only be established on the foundation of a healthy self-esteem and an understanding of the value we have in the eyes of God. The best solution to this problem of balance was expressed by St. Paul: "What have you that you did not receive? If then you received it, why do you boast as if it were not a gift?" (1 Cor. 4:7).[152] Now, what we have received is nothing less than divine sonship. Thus humility is not a question of saying, "I am nothing," but rather, "I have received everything, without any merit on

---

of Clairvaux, *Sermons for Advent and the Christmas Season*, Cistercian Fathers (Kalamazoo: Cistercian Publications, 2007).

[148] See pages 30–31.

[149] Dorotheus of Gaza, Instruction 14, "On Building up Virtues and their Harmony," in Œuvres *spirituelles*, Sources Chrétiennes (Paris: Éd. du Cerf, 1963), 425.

[150] Bernard, "Des mœurs et du devoir des évêques," chap. V:17, in Œuvres *complètes*, vol. 2 (Paris: Vivès, 1866), 202.

[151] F. Trochu, *Le Curé d'Ars* : St. Jean-Marie-Baptiste Vianney (1786–1859) (Lyon: Emmanuel Vitte, 1929), 537.

[152] This passage was directly translated from the French to maintain original emphasis.

my part." St. Paul remains the undisputed master of this path; he goes so far as to say that God "has given us his glory" (Rom. 8:30).[153] "Everything belongs to you, but you belong to Christ; and Christ belongs to God" (1 Cor. 3:22–23).[154]

Humility has its origins in the mystery of the human person created in the image of God. This phrase is repeated so often that we sometimes forget how profound a phrase it is: how can a created being be the image of the Uncreated One? How can one who has received everything he has, even his very existence, be called to enter into the life of the One who gives all things? The answer is to be found in the mystery of Christ, which is itself rooted in the mystery of the Word that is eternally begotten. A healthy humility will thus be filled with wonder at the incredible gift it has received. Far from destroying self-esteem, this sort of humility purifies it and elevates it to its highest level, by putting it on its proper footing, which is none other than God the Creator. "He who did not spare his own Son but gave him up for us all, will he not also give us all things with him?" (Rom. 8:32).

Humility is suspended between our dignity as children of God and the nothingness from which we have been drawn. We are not in a sort of vacuum here, since the unsurpassable humility of Christ has, once and for all, joined the infinitude of God to the limits of creation, and thus it is in Him that we find the balance that prevents us from becoming forgetful either of our origins (formed, as we are, out of dust) or of our proper end, which the Fathers of the Church love to call "divinization." Growth in humility can come about in a healthy way only in the context of this balance, with these two elements coexisting. "Humility is walking in the truth," says St. Teresa of Avila:

> Once I was pondering why our Lord was so fond of this virtue of humility, and this thought came to me — in my opinion not as a result of reflection but suddenly: It is because God is supreme Truth; and to be humble is to walk in truth, for it is a very deep truth that of ourselves we have nothing good but only misery and nothingness. Whoever does not understand this walks in falsehood. The more anyone understands it the more he pleases the supreme Truth because he is walking in the

[153] This passage was directly translated from the French to maintain original emphasis.
[154] This passage was directly translated from the French to maintain original emphasis.

truth. Please God, Sisters, we will be granted the favor never to leave this path of self-knowledge, amen.[155]

Yes, St. Teresa, of course; but if you want us to walk in the truth, don't forget the other half of the teaching that emerges from your writings: of ourselves, we are nothing, but by grace we are everything. At the beginning of the treatment of the Sixth Dwelling Place (from which this quotation is taken), you write: "Now the soul is fully determined to take no other spouse. But the Spouse takes no account of the soul's great desires that the betrothal should take place immediately."[156] Do not tell me that the soul seriously thinks it is made entirely of nothingness; if it did, it would not await its betrothal with such ardor but would rather flee far from the bridegroom, saying with St. Peter: "Depart from me, for I am a sinful man, O Lord" (Luke 5:8).

Spiritual authors often write of this nothingness of the creature. We have chosen to avoid this expression, which is admittedly quite legitimate when it is properly understood, but which is somewhat imprecise on its own. The creature has been drawn out of nothingness, but it now exists, and thus does not belong to that nothingness. Moreover, the human person is the image of God. But in the lived experience of the mystics, the chasm between the immensity of the divine and their own smallness is so great that it seems to them that they are nothing, hence the tendency to speak of their own nothingness. In the opposite direction, other (still perfectly authentic) mystics will speak of the union with God using language that seems almost to verge on pantheism, as though there were no longer any difference between God and themselves. Once more, it is a lived experience that is incapable of being placed within the all too narrow confines imposed by words. Union with God has taken these mystics over to such an extent that they no longer *feel* the difference between themselves and God; this is what they are trying to express. But this in no way eliminates the ontological difference between the Creator and the creature; and indeed such authors will quite often add an explanatory note to clarify this.

---

[155] Teresa of Avila, *The Interior Castle*, from *Collected Works of St. Teresa of Avila*, vol. 2, trans. K. Kavanaugh and O. Rodriguez (Washington: Institute of Carmelite Studies, 1980), VI.10.7, 420–421.

[156] *Interior Castle* (op. cit.), VI:1.1, 359.

An approach to humility that is too voluntarist in nature will often neglect this balance. Preserving only those texts that speak of our nothingness — and there are many of them! — such an approach imagines that the more we are convinced that we are nothing, the more capable we will be of accepting God's action upon us; this is in fact neither true nor false, in the sense that this condition is helpful and maybe even necessary but not sufficient by itself. To suggest that we are nothing of ourselves does not mean that we are nothing full stop. A one-sided insistence upon this latter formulation can inevitably lead to psychological as well as spiritual catastrophe. If I am nothing, then my life has no meaning, nor does my very existence, and I cannot be loved because no one, not even God, can love "nothing." To feel that one is "nothing" is to live the life of one who has been condemned. To push a person too far in this direction can even lead him to suicide.

One might almost say that humiliation is only part of the picture and, for this reason, is something that must almost never be sought out by the religious, and much less brought about by superiors. Humiliation can only lead to humility if it is lived in a fruitful way, which requires a spiritual maturity that is already quite well advanced. It can just as well lead to resentment, to bitterness, to an unhealthy contempt for oneself. Life offers us enough opportunities to be humbled; there is little point in wanting to bring such opportunities about ourselves — indeed, it would not be without risk. This method — the most dangerous of all — can only be properly brought to bear by divine providence. The royal road consists rather in learning to bear the various humiliations that life offers us as we seek to follow Christ. As long as it does not become an obsession, every religious should be keen to search for humility. But seeking humiliations is a far less reasonable prospect, and it runs the risk of cloaking an already hidden pride: am I sure that I will be able to bear humiliation in love and gratitude? Bringing about humiliations is such a high-risk operation that it must be asked whether it could ever be justified.

The opposite imbalance can also exist; St. Teresa of Avila warns us on this point:

> Since [the spiritual] edifice is built entirely on humility, the closer one
> comes to God the more progress there must be in this virtue; and if there

is no progress in humility, everything is going to be ruined. It seems a kind of pride to desire of ourselves to ascend higher since, in view of what we are, God does too much just in drawing us near to Himself.[157]

Fear of pride, though, must not lead a soul to be crushed beneath the feeling of its own poverty. When the prodigal son returns home, his father treats him like a prince. St. Basil, in his treatise *On the Origins of Humankind*, cries out, saying: "[Man], you were appointed ruler of creation!"[158] Yet at the same time, he does not neglect the proper balance:

God "took dust from the earth" and "molded the human being" (Gen. 2:7)... If you look toward our nature alone, it is nothing and worthy of nothing, but if you look toward the honor with which he was honored, then how great is the human person."[159]

Behind an apparently light-hearted and maybe even slightly self-important façade, the novices of today often conceal the great emptiness caused by our culture, which has stopped believing in the greatness of humankind. *Who am I?* This question occupies them more than they might think. To try too emphatically to explain to them that they are nothing simply cannot help them, so weak, in current Christian culture, is faith in the divine sonship that we all receive in Baptism.

Even in a religious setting, this faith tends to be rather weak, whereas it ought to form the foundation stone of a solid and balanced religious life. Really to believe that God loves us, with a faith that can survive trials and tribulations, is the fruit of a long journey. It is more appropriate, then, to begin by establishing or strengthening this foundation, not allowing the young enthusiast to develop a taste for humiliations that will simply not withstand the wear and tear that builds up over time. Such a game is not without risk, and in seeking to play it, we can get our fingers burned.

---

[157] Teresa of Avila, *Life*, in *Collected Works of St. Teresa of Avila*, vol. 1 (Washington: Institute of Carmelite Studies, 1976), 12:4, 120.

[158] Basil, *On the Human Condition*, trans. Nonna V. Harrison (New York: St. Vladimir's Seminary Press, 2005), I:8, 37.

[159] Ibid., II:2, 49.

The formator — who ought to have an understanding of these things — should begin with the fundamentals: creation in the image of God, the divine sonship that has been given to us in Christ and through Christ, the totally gratuitous love of God (a love that takes delight in us, not one that merely seeks to be benevolent to us), the mysterious relationship between the working of grace and our personal actions, the face of God (which has almost always been disfigured for us by things that have emerged from experiences in the family or elsewhere). There is ample material to be covered. True humility will come to birth naturally as a result of a journey like this, to a much greater extent and in a much better way than would occur if we were merely preoccupied constantly with our own poverty, that is to say with ourselves (in the final analysis), which would be the complete antithesis of humility. Let us listen to the great Teresa once more:

> In my opinion, we shall never completely know ourselves if we don't strive to know God. By gazing at His grandeur, we get in touch with our own lowliness; by looking at His purity, we shall see our own filth; by pondering His humility, we shall see how far we are from being humble.
>
> Two advantages come from such activity. First, it's clear that something white seems much whiter when next to something black, and vice versa with the black next to the white. The second is that our intellects and wills, dealing in turn now with self, now with God, become nobler and better prepared for every good. And it would be disadvantageous for us never to get out of the mire of our miseries. ... If we are always fixed on our earthly misery, the stream will never flow free from the mud of fears, faintheartedness and cowardice. ... So I say, daughters, that we should set our eyes on Christ, our Good, and on His saints. There we shall learn true humility, and the intellect will be enhanced, as I said.[160]

Sacrifice

The value of sacrifice in the Christian life, following the example of Christ, can hardly be overestimated. But the same reservations apply here as applied to the

---

[160] Teresa of Avila, *Interior Castle*, I:2.9–11, 292–293.

question of humility. The novice must be guided along this path with wisdom. Sacrifice must spring from love, which the novice is seeking to show. Even with the best will in the world, if this becomes tangled up with a desire for results, things become much more ambiguous. Our relationship with suffering is a very delicate matter, and it is always better to welcome any sufferings that providence might send our way, rather than to seek them out ourselves. St. Thérèse of the Child Jesus (who, incidentally, had a very great esteem for the value of suffering) wrote:

> The Good Lord gives me just as much as I can bear.[161] I would never want to ask the Good Lord for greater sufferings ... they would be my own sufferings, and I would have to bear them all on my own, and I have never been able to do anything all on my own.[162]

> I am very content not to have asked the Good Lord for sufferings; in this way, he will have to give me strength.[163]

The golden rule is to be found in the advice of St. Francis de Sales: *Never ask for anything, never refuse anything.*[164]

It is emphatically not, then, a question of devaluing sacrifice, but rather of keeping it in its proper place: it has to be at the service of love, which must always come first. And since God knows better than we do the measure that is appropriate for us, wise spiritual direction will teach the young religious that saying yes to all that life (that is, providence) asks of us is an incomparably safer path. The first sacrifice for the novice consists in faithfully following the rule of the institute. The effort involved in doing this is already more than enough; there is no need to go looking for things to add to it.

Again, we are not here making a case for lukewarmness but rather for sustainability. Expending a tremendous amount of energy in a way that spares no thought for what is still to come is not only pointless but can even ultimately be harmful; it can be a case of temptation under the appearance of good.

---

[161] Thérèse de l'Enfant Jésus, *Derniers entretiens,* Carnet jaune 25 August, 2, in Œuvres *complètes* (Paris: Éd. du Cerf, 1992), 1109.

[162] Ibid., Carnet jaune 11 August, 3, 1111.

[163] Ibid., Carnet jaune 26 August, 2, 1111.

[164] Francis de Sales, Conference 23, December 26, 1622.

Temptation Under the Appearance of Good

St. Ignatius of Loyola speaks of this temptation under the appearance of good in his "rules for the discernment of spirits," a fundamental text that every religious ought to be familiar with. These rules can be found in the *Spiritual Exercises:*

> It is characteristic of the evil angel, who takes on the appearance of an angel of light, to enter by going along with the devout soul and then to come out by his own way with success for himself. That is, he brings good and holy thoughts attractive to such an upright person and then strives little by little to get his own way, by enticing the soul over to his own hidden deceits and evil intentions.[165]

We can leave it to a Jesuit to comment on this text of his founder:

> We are, of course, in the hypothetical situation of a generous soul that is making progress along the right path. All the tactics of the evil spirit adapt themselves to this disposition: he presents himself, and acts under the cover of what is good, "he transforms himself into an angel of light." He keeps himself from revealing the goal he is pursuing, and from suggesting courses of action that would quite obviously be reprehensible. Rather, he strives, with a view to ends that are apparently praiseworthy, to cause the soul to turn from its original direction by an imperceptibly small amount. The soul believes it is still on the path on which it set out; perhaps it even believes itself to be more full of zeal, believes that it has made more progress, until at an unforeseen turn in the road, or some chance event, it no longer recognizes itself: it has wandered astray. The evil spirit had initially met the soul on its own path; now the soul is with him on his path. He has achieved his goal.
>
> There is, in the writings of St. Teresa of Avila, an echo of St. Ignatius's lucid description: "The demon arrives with all his tricks and, under the pretext of doing good, makes the soul separate itself from the divine will in small things, and draws it into other things, which he presents to

---

[165] Ignatius of Loyola, *Spiritual Exercises*, tr. George E. Ganss, S.J., Classics of Western Spirituality (Mahwah: Paulist Press, 1991), 206.

the soul as things that are not evil; little by little, he comes to darken its powers of understanding, and to cause its will to grow cold; he causes self-will to spring up within the soul, until eventually, by means of successive lapses, he draws it away from the will of God and snatches it away to do his will."[166]

An example of temptation under the appearance of good, which is an utterly classical feature of religious life, and which takes us back to the theme of this chapter, is treated by Fr. Jacques Fédry:

It is another sign of the presence of the evil spirit when people constantly feel pressured to take on more and more.... This is a restless obsession with doing more, which is really a distortion of the deeper call, not to do more things, but rather to do things with more fidelity; this concerns the quality of the way we live, the quality of our love. Satan presents things as good actions that should be carried out, and then turns people away from them, stops at nothing to hijack them.

One of the ways in which we can be tempted to avoid what God is asking of us is by multiplying the "things" that He is in fact not asking of us. For some, this will be things in the realm of pious practices, constant meetings of this or that Christian group; for others, it will be being scattered amidst a multitude of activities, bordering on overwork.[167]

The Adversary's strategy here is a tactic of diversion, designed to exhaust the soul's strength uselessly with practices of limited benefit, so that the soul no longer has any energy left for what is truly good, or simply so that it is exhausted and ends up collapsing. It is easy to fall into this temptation of "*always something more*" in a zealous community, as this saying (a favorite of a female superior) demonstrates: *Everything, immediately, intensely, until death.* This is a perfect example of temptation under the appearance of good, which pays no attention to human limitations.

---

[166] H. Coathalem, *Commentaire du livre des Exercices*, (Paris: Desclée de Brouwer, 1965), 310. The final quotation is taken from Teresa of Avila, *Interior Castle*, V:4.8, 357.

[167] J. Fédry, "La tentation sous couleur de bien," *Vie Chrétienne* no. 12, July 2011.

"The spirit indeed is willing, but the flesh is weak" (Matt. 26:41). If we are too quick to forget this, we will end up flat on our faces. If this serves as a lesson to us, all well and good; but if we lead others along this way, then we may start to ask whether the leader in this situation is not, quite frankly, dangerous.

Popular wisdom has summarized this in a formula: *slow and steady wins the race.*[168] There has to be some room for discernment here, since it is also true that if our pace is too slow, then we may never arrive. It is thus not only a matter of establishing a balance; it is even more important that we should prioritize, that we should set things in their proper order, and this is particularly important when it comes to the question of renunciation.

Renunciation Never Comes First

Nobody would deny that renunciation is an important part of the journey of the spiritual life, but all the same it remains necessary to know its proper place and set its proper limit. Renunciation never comes first. We only renounce one good for a greater good; attachment must always come before detachment. (Incidentally, this is the great difference between the Christian and Buddhist visions of detachment.)

When the sun comes up, the stars disappear. It is not this disappearance that makes the sun appear; the stars were not hiding it, and indeed they only seem to have disappeared — they are still there, sure enough, but they have become invisible to us because the sun has made the rest of the sky brighter than they are.

As we make progress on our journey of discovering God, the paltry "stars" of the world are blotted out, and progressively they lose their power of attraction over us, being bathed in the light of the divine Sun. Faced with the immensity of God's love, earthly goods suddenly seem very insignificant, and they lose their power of fascination. It is the sun that causes the stars to disappear. This simultaneity, when not properly understood, can sometimes lead us to imagine that turning off all the stars would be enough to make the sun appear — in other words, that it would be enough to separate oneself from all creaturely affections in order for God to fill us completely. Well, there is nothing automatic about

---

[168] "Qui veut voyager loin ménage sa monture." ["Those who want to travel a long distance should pace themselves." — Trans.]

that. Even if it were possible, turning the stars off before the arrival of the dawn would only lead to total darkness.

The profound misunderstanding inherent in such an approach stems from its lack of realism: self-forgetfulness can only be practiced when the person in question has a "self" that is robust and well established, at both the psychological and the spiritual level. Without this, emptiness will simply be emptiness. Through stripping oneself (or being stripped) of everything that gives value, a human person will see his or her spiritual energy dry up. Meanwhile, he or she also experiences the anguish of emptiness, the anguish of nothingness. One who is "nothing" — or who feels that he or she is nothing — has nothing to aspire to.

There are some ways of renunciation along which only God can lead a person, since He knows the soul in question and its limits, and because He can keep it safe when it finds itself on the brink of the abyss. No human being is capable of doing this. A spirituality that is based on being stripped of things, on being empty, a spirituality of annihilation, does not respect the workings of grace and even presumes to demand that God come and fill the void that has been created. This path runs the risk of leading to disillusionment and despair. If the one accompanying such a person spiritually does not understand how to read the warning signs (up to and including suicidal thoughts), but on the contrary interprets them in an apparently "spiritual" way, then the person being accompanied is being nudged even further in the direction of destruction. It is tantamount to soul-murder if a young monk, who is lost in a darkness that seems devoid of meaning, is simply told that everything is going well, on the grounds that the less he exists in himself, the more God will be present in him. In a specific context, this formula could make sense, but it can certainly not make any sense at all when the person in question is totally out of his depth and overwhelmed, perhaps even more on the psychological level than on the spiritual level.

The notion that we must begin by emptying the soul, so that God can come and be present within it, is a classic one in spirituality, but it must be properly interpreted. God cannot take the place of earthly things because He is not an earthly thing. Anyone who has experienced a conversion knows that God has burst into his or her inner chaos, and that it was precisely the presence of God and His light that transformed the chaos, that allowed a certain order to be established there, and gave the power needed so that any number of things that had lost their usefulness could be thrown away.

It is necessary, then, to bear clearly in mind precisely what it is that should occupy first place for us. It is much truer to say that sacrifice comes from love than that love comes from sacrifice. A spirituality of stripping things away quickly becomes unhealthy if we do not have a sufficiently clear understanding that being stripped of things demonstrates love but does not create it. The deepest source of sacrifice and renunciation is an all-encompassing love. In order to say to the Beloved that He is *everything* for us, we rid ourselves of all that is not absolutely necessary and (most of all) of all that is not Him. As we show our love in this real and concrete way, as we give it a certain breadth so that it does not simply remain at the level of being a nice idea, renunciation will help it grow and give it an indispensable perspective, but this renunciation will not actually give birth to love. Put simply, wanting to discover love by means of renunciation, by means of being stripped of things, by means of emptiness or sacrifice, is putting the cart before the horse.

We need to make a discernment. Attachment and detachment generally grow together. Sometimes one takes the lead, and sometimes the other does. Sometimes it is the love of God that breaks in first, showing us the futility of the things that hold us back, of which He is calling us to rid ourselves. Sometimes He will demand of us from the outset a painful renunciation and will only come afterward — sometimes a long time afterward — to fill the space that He has created. But if we pay careful attention, in every case attachment to God comes first; without this, it would be impossible to accept renunciation, or for it to bear fruit.

Renunciation is thus the consequence of a preference. This last word deserves to be underlined, as it points out the dynamic that occurs normally. A wise spiritual director needs to be sure that the work of detachment is being accompanied by a corresponding growth in the love of God. If this is not happening, then we will need to look again at the path being traveled.

The things of this world carry meaning: God speaks to us through them. We discover something of the love of God from any true love that we have experienced, whether this be the love of our parents, say, or a beautiful friendship. We will have to go beyond these mediations of God's love as we discover that His love is even greater than these other loves. God can ask us to have an experience of His love alone, by removing all supports from us. Because His love has already begun to fill our deepest heart, the process of being stripped of things, as painful as it might be, does not leave a void within us because the space created will be filled by the love of God. If, on the other hand, we create a void ourselves by systematically opposing our every desire, before God has become the soul's center, then the void will not be filled and the soul, no longer finding pleasure in anything, risks being swamped by acedia.

This royal road of renunciation, which prepares us for the stripping away that God may one day ask of us, has a name: abandonment. To want to strip ourselves of our own will by means of acts of that same will is somewhat contradictory and can end up making us more rigid instead of more flexible. Abandonment to the will of God — also called the abandonment to providence — leaves God as the potter to our clay, so that He can make of it whatever He wants (cf. Jer. 18). The goal is similar, but the route is very different: saying yes to things out of love, and not a sort of willful obliteration of ourselves. The route we are speaking of here carries no dangers, as the initiative belongs to God Himself. It leaves no place for pride or a desire for results. It respects the proper order of the spiritual life: saying yes to God comes before renouncing ourselves. Indeed, saying yes to God is really saying yes to my deepest self, which was made for God and which yearns for Him. This can often mean saying no to the more superficial self that has not yet been evangelized, but this is merely a consequence of the more fundamental yes.

Life offers constant opportunities to embrace renunciation; it is pointless inventing any for ourselves. An old brother from Montserrat once said to a young (and slightly overenthusiastic) novice: *Oh, brother: there is no point going in search of crosses; the Lord delivers them to the door!* So He does, and we don't even need to place an order! True formation is a matter of teaching the young to bear all of the small renunciations of day-to-day life with love: the neighbor in choir who sings badly, the work that I find boring, getting up in the morning, a none-too-friendly word that someone says to me, the gloomy weather that has been with us for a week now, the apples we have been eating for six months because someone gave us a truckload, and so on.

Saying yes to God in these small things that He sets before us each day in our ordinary life, turning them into acts of love for Him: this is what prepares us for great trials, should they come upon us one day, and perhaps in a particular way for the great trial that is certain to come: the radical detachment that happens at our death. All of this comes progressively to mold our will and our intellect, to fit them for the loving intention that God has for our lives. This sort of abandonment is a source of peace, joy, and deep love; it transforms the soul, and this radiates upon everyone around us; the whole community will receive the fruits of it.

The Spirituality of Substitution

The need for balance is no less necessary in our relationship with Christ. "It is no longer I who live, but Christ who lives in me" (Gal. 2:20). This saying, one of the most famous from St. Paul, has served as a guide for the whole of Christian spirituality, and it would be impossible to exaggerate its importance. All the same, we need to know how to understand it properly, so as not to make it say: "You are not worth anything; you need to do away with yourself completely, so that Christ can take your place."[169] Such an approach does not seem to have much to do with the love of Christ, and moreover it is psychologically destructive, since a healthy self-esteem is indispensable if we are to be able to live a normal life. This approach also represents a deeply wrong-minded teaching since, if we are going to hold out such an elevated ideal to people, we have at least to believe that they are capable of attaining it. This idea will have to be purified, through an awareness of all of the various workings of grace, but this should in no way reduce our appreciation of the immense esteem God has for His creatures. The Virgin Mary spoke to Bernadette as though she were a princess: "Will you do me the favor of coming here for a fortnight?"[170] Bernadette was astonished. Nobody had ever spoken to her like this. It was the first time that anyone had addressed her as *vous*.[171]

---

[169] That such an interpretation is possible is emphasized by the experience of Luther. For him, the human person is totally and utterly corrupted. Justification, then, can only come about from the outside, when, by faith, we are re-clothed in Christ's merits, which hide our corruption (which remains, however). Presented in a simplistic way, the idea of substitution conveys the same idea, the same refusal to believe that we can be purified, transformed.

[170] Voulez-vous me faire la grâce de venir ici pendant quinze jours?

[171] Translator's note: *Vous* in French, when used in the singular, is the polite form of address in the second person.

Abuses in the Religious Life and the Path to Healing

Through Baptism, the Trinity comes to dwell within us, making of our whole being a temple of His glory, making us children of God. There is no doubt that this temple needs to be cleansed of the cattle, chickens, and money-changers that can cause it to be so cluttered, but this is surely a matter not of emptying us of ourselves, but rather of emptying us of all that is *not* ourselves, so long as we understand correctly what we mean here by "ourselves": ourselves as images of God, sprung from the hands of the Creator; ourselves with all of the gifts, natural and supernatural, that He has bestowed upon us. He wants to dwell within us, not to replace us. He wants to make our temple worthy of His glory. "Do you not know that you are the temple of God, and that the Spirit of God dwells in you? If anyone should destroy the temple of God, God will destroy him. For the temple of God is holy, and you are that temple" (1 Cor. 3:16–17).[172]

If we meddle with self-esteem, the resulting damage can be serious, not only in psychological terms but also on the spiritual level: to destroy self-esteem is to destroy the possibility of entering into a relationship with God.

If I have to deny all my positive qualities out of fear that they may become a source of pride, if I am taught to consider everything that I do, all that comes from me, all that I am as "worldly" (in the negative sense) — with the impression that everything that is natural has to be replaced by something supernatural — how will I be able to keep alive the idea that God could actually love me? It would surely not be "me" that He loved, but rather the thing He so desires (apparently) to put in my place — in other words, Himself. And what am I in all of that? Nothing more than a sort of interloper, who must be turned out. Will I still be able to see Him as a Father?

It is worth underlining here how a mistake that could seem trivial can actually have serious consequences, once we begin to touch upon the fundamentals of the spiritual life. We know the mystical doctrine of the exchange of hearts; it is to be found, for example, in the life of St. Catherine of Siena. One day, while she was offering her heart to Christ, He appeared and took it from her. For quite a few days, it seemed to her that she had no heart. But then the Lord Jesus appeared to her again, holding in His hand a radiant, red human heart; He opened her chest, placed the heart inside it, and said: "My dearest daughter,

---

[172] This passage was directly translated from the French to maintain original emphasis.

just as one day I took that heart that you offered to me, so now I give you mine, and from now on, it will take the place of your own heart."[173]

But we cannot turn a mystical grace into a method. We cannot begin with this grace — a grace that was a totally free gift and the fruit of a long spiritual journey — and say to beginners: "When you no longer have a heart, when nothing of yourself remains, then Jesus (or Mary) will give you His (her) heart." It would be nonsensical to interpret St. Catherine's vision in a literal way; otherwise we would have to conclude that the heart of Jesus is now St. Catherine's heart, and the feast of the Sacred Heart would have to be changed! When He gives His heart, Jesus does not lose it, and this is why He can give it endlessly. In the same way, when we give Him our heart, He does not really take it away from us; He accepts it and transfigures it.

This is probably the key word that makes all the difference: not substitution but, rather, transfiguration. St. Catherine's visions show that her heart was so deeply buried in the heart of Christ that He gave it back to her, permeated with His own love, transfigured. But it was certainly the heart that belonged to her, to Catherine Benincasa, which was beating in her chest, and which now lives with the life and the love of her Beloved. "It is no longer I who live, but Christ lives in me."

[173] Raymond of Capua, *Life of St. Catherine of Siena*, chap. 6.

8

Spiritual Companionship

There is a painful and difficult question we still have to tackle. How is it possible that, in a fervent community, where everything seems to be oriented toward God, where firm insistence is placed upon the liberty of each person, where people are constantly talking of love, how is it possible that in such communities we can find religious men and women so sunk in depression that they are tempted to suicide? Yet this has happened to people who, when they subsequently left the community, have shown that they were, in themselves, perfectly balanced, and had no underlying illness. The discrepancy here is so profound that it is difficult not to look for a reassuring explanation, but the facts remain, in numbers too great to be ignored: a spirituality that was meant to bring life and perfect love could end up being both humanly and spiritually death-dealing, sometimes resulting in a complete breaking away from God. *If I don't die too quickly, maybe one day I will rediscover life with the Good Lord ...* that is how it was expressed by one former sister, an ex-member of a fervent congregation, even though more than twenty years had passed since she left. Today she has rediscovered that life. Working to uncover the truth about her experiences in the community allowed her to free herself from an image of God in whom she — quite rightly — could not believe.

Obviously no two cases are exactly alike, but we can identify some danger areas. One woman who prefers to remain anonymous presents a startling account:

At the time, I was regularly accompanying consecrated religious who had been forced to leave their congregations, most often for health reasons.

I accompanied them as they looked for work. I was closely involved with one contemplative community who sent me about fifteen such people. What struck me particularly was that these religious women had often had suicidal thoughts. And yet none of them was depressive or unbalanced. Something else was going on. Here is my analysis: they felt they were in an impossible situation. They were being asked to strip themselves of all the things that made them individuals: their interests, their talents. So they learned to overcompensate so as to become the perfect, smiling, bland sisters they were expected to be if they were to enter the way of holiness and self-transcendence to which they aspired. The directives coming from the community pointed one way, while their own consciences inclined in a different direction. And the more they sought to conform, the more their doubts, struggles, and poor self-image became magnified. They were each progressively erasing their identity as a child of God, their identity as a unique person. As their sense of guilt grew, the impression that they were possessed by the devil increased their sufferings enormously.... Only death could set them free from these torments. What was the good of living? They held a negative view of the world, a world that had, in their estimation, progressively become so toxic, such a source of defilement, so oppressive. But the life they lived, a life of withdrawal from that world, had become so complicated. Their natural energies might well have often encouraged them to act in a particular way, but they were told not to listen to this inner dialogue. It was not of God ... They were in a double bind. Only death could set them free. They all seemed to be imprisoned in the same scenario, even though their personalities were all quite different.

And yet this was presented quite sincerely as the most perfect way of the love of God. It is no longer merely a question of asceticism; here the interior life, the images of self and of God are all affected. What explanation can we find for this?

The search for the Face of Christ, who is after all the one who said "he who has seen me has seen the Father" (John 14:9), is a feature of any Christian life, and it marks those who have given their whole life to this search in a special way. Everything in the tradition speaks of the necessity of having a guide on this path. It will be sufficient for us to quote Cassian, who spent years listening to the elders he encountered in the desert.

> All professions, all the arts invented by human genius, certainly require a master, if they are to be practiced competently. What about this hidden and invisible discipline, then, accessible only to a heart that is perfectly pure, where a mistake doesn't simply lead to some temporal damage, easily repaired, but to loss of the soul and eternal death? Is this to be the one discipline where we can manage without a guide?
>
> Remember: we are contending here, not with visible adversaries, but with invisible enemies, who are merciless. It is combat by night and by day, a spiritual combat, not against one or two enemies, but against innumerable legions; a combat whose outcome is awe-inspiring, if we consider how persistent the adversary is, and how secret his attacks.
>
> We cannot be too diligent in following in the footsteps of the elders, nor in revealing to them the thoughts that arise in our hearts, despising the false sense of shame that would lead us to conceal them.[174]

Nevertheless, this advice does raise the enormous question of the trustworthiness of the guide.

Spiritual Fatherhood

We can only rejoice that there has been a certain rediscovery of spiritual fatherhood. It never really disappeared from the West, but renewed contact with the traditions of the Christian East has breathed new life into it. The tradition of the Desert Fathers was well acquainted with the idea, and Barsanuphius and John of Gaza have left us a very substantial witness to it.[175] Anyone who has found a spiritual father, in whom he can have full confidence and with whom he feels free to say anything, has found a real treasure. Opening the very depths of the

---

[174]John Cassian, *Conferences* 2:11. For an English edition, see: John Cassian, *The Conferences*, Ancient Christian Writers 57 (Mahwah: Paulist Press, 1997).

[175]Barsanuphe and Jean de Gaza, *Correspondance*, vols. 1 and 2, Sources Chrétiennes (Paris: Éd. du Cerf, 1997 and 1998). For an English edition, see: Barsanuphius and John, *Letters* (two volumes), Fathers of the Church 113/114 (Washington: Catholic University of America Press, 2006 and 2007).

heart is an experience of real beauty, but it is one that is relatively rare, since it demands a spiritual mother or father who is blessed with a wholehearted openness, a finely tuned discretion, and a total respect for the freedom of anyone who entrusts himself to him. The mission of such a guide will be simply to assist the action of the Holy Spirit in a soul, leaving total freedom not only to the soul being guided but above all to the Holy Spirit, whom the guide must never seek to replace. This is a delicate task, which can only be undertaken by people of great humility who accept in advance that it may turn out that other guides are more perceptive than they are. Such a guide will help a monk to become more and more docile to the inner voice, by means of which God reveals Himself. And progressively, the guide will help the monk to stand on his own two feet.

But we have to keep our eyes open, since this area carries risks, especially the risk of incompetence. People are not spiritual fathers and mothers just because they say they are. In general, anyone who insists on offering his or her services should be approached with at least a modicum of caution. St. Jane Frances de Chantal had a bitter experience of this.

The Caged Bird

Here is an account of how she was literally caged by her first spiritual director.

At that time, "a good religious man" [history, happily, does not record his name] enjoyed great success as a director of consecrated souls. Jane met him by chance, we are told, one day when he had gone to pray at Notre-Dame-d'Étang, a shrine two leagues from Dijon; he at once advised her to place herself under his direction. Jane realized that he was not the guide she had seen in a vision; but in the disarray in which she found herself, she agreed: "Like a humble sheep, believing that it was the will of God, she allowed herself to be bound by this shepherd, who bound her to his direction through four vows: firstly, that she would obey him; secondly, that she would never leave him for another director; thirdly, that she promise faithfully to keep what he would say to her secret; fourthly, not to discuss her interior life with anyone other than him." This went on for two years. Jane, being generous, strove to keep up with all the prayers, fasts, methods, practices, and so on that the imprudent shepherd enjoined on her. It sounds fanciful ...[176]

The intention behind these demands is perfectly clear: this "religious man" wanted to enjoy exclusive and perpetual rights over the soul of this woman, providing us with a perfect example of one of the causes of aberrant spiritual direction: power. It is worth explaining just how powerful was the dictatorial grip that this religious had over St. Jane de Chantal.

We know that in 1602, Jane, in a state of great spiritual distress, had begged God to give her a director, and God had answered her prayers with a vision. Although she did not know who she was seeing at the time, she saw St. Francis de Sales exactly as she would recognize him two years later in Dijon. For his part, he, too, had seen the young widow, whom he did not know either, as yet. When she saw him in the pulpit in Dijon on the Friday after Ash Wednesday of the year 1604, she recognized him immediately, and he recognized her. On several occasions, he came to dinner at her father's house, and she was "dying" to reveal her interior sufferings to him, but she couldn't do it, since she was bound by the fourfold vow she had made to her director. On Wednesday of Holy Week, "Our Lord visited upon her such a furious attack of temptation," writes Mother de Chaugy, "that, since her own director was absent, she was absolutely compelled to seek some respite from our blessed father." Yet she did not dare to speak freely because of her vow. Later, she underwent such a terrible attack of scruples that she had to solicit the aid of Fr. de Villars, who was her confessor. He reassured her completely. "It seemed to me," Jane said, "that the mountainous burden that had been weighing upon my heart was lifted." The "good, religious man," with whom she was completely open about it all, was furious, and he behaved in such a way that she was immediately plunged back into her scruples. He even went so far as to ask her to renew her vow of obedience to him. For her eventually to feel that she had at last been set free from this obligation required the repeated interventions of Fr. de Villars — who declared to her quite frankly that, if she didn't seek to disentangle herself from this man's direction, she would be resisting the Holy Spirit — as well as the clear declaration by St. Francis de Sales

---

[176] A. Ravier, *Petite vie de Jeanne de Chantal* (Paris: DDB, 1992), 39. The rest of the story is a summary of the same book.

that the four vows imposed on her by the first director were "good for nothing, except maybe for wrecking the peace of someone's conscience." "O God," she would later say, "how happy was that day for me! It seemed to me that my soul was changed completely, and escaped from that inner captivity in which the counsels of my first director had held me until that point."

Inner captivity is a strong expression, but it is accurate. Spiritual fatherhood, which ought to be a school of inner freedom, can become a kind of slavery when it seeks to impose itself in an exclusive way. This is an extraordinarily strong, and wrong, turn, since it is tantamount to taking the place of God, who is the only real master of souls.

In the case of Jane's director, the signs of this wrong turn were clear enough: he sought to bind her to himself for ever, exclusively, with no intervention from anyone. To that end, he exploited her uprightness of soul, hijacking it and turning it into an instrument of servitude; she is bound by her own uprightness, by means of a sense of guilt. If she approached anyone else, she would feel she was being unfaithful to God because — as she thought — it was to God that her vow bound her. The purer and more upright the soul, the more insidious the trap. The will to have an exclusive influence over someone is clearly related to the desire to possess.

Liberation from this captivity was not simply achieved by recourse to yet another exclusive influence, since divine providence did not make use of St. Francis de Sales alone. The word that set her free belonged to Fr. Villars. Jane was not simply moving from one set of chains to another, and St. Francis de Sales made sure she didn't go back into another cage, even a gilded one. Their relationship was marked by very long periods of separation, sometimes lasting several years, due to their various journeys. St. Francis de Sales never lost sight of the ultimate goal, which was to lead her to God alone, and at the time of the Pentecost retreat in 1616, which marked a turning point in Jane's life, he wrote to her: "Think no more about the friendship or the unity that God has created between us." She replied to him: "My God, my true Father, how the sword has pierced!"[177]

---

[177] A. Ravier, *Jeanne-Françoise Frémyot de Chantal, sa race et sa grâce* (Paris: Ateliers Henry Labat, 1983), 114.

Ida Friederike Görres puts well what happened that day:

All of the great spiritual directors have always known that the priest has
the task of helping the soul to become free and independent, even independent of the priest himself: his role is to be the one who introduces;
gently, but firmly, he must detach himself from this need [the one being
directed has] to give up his or her own freedom, clinging to him and
never wanting to leave him. In this struggle too, it is his responsibility
to lend the woman assistance against her feminine nature, and often
against himself.[178]

In the case of St. Jane Frances de Chantal, the evil did not reach catastrophic
proportions, since the original director had no interest in her inner life; it was
enough for her that she should be obedient to him. The bird was caged, but it had
not been killed. These days, it is no longer common to find such an externally
focused approach, but the desire to attach oneself to a soul has not disappeared
at all. The sickness has simply changed form.

FREEDOM AND CONSTRAINT IN COMPANIONSHIP

An image may help us to understand the process. A glider can't fly on its own;
it needs a plane to help it take off. So the glider can be grateful to the plane for
allowing it to take off. But if, once it has reached the necessary altitude, the
plane says to itself that, really, it has provided a great service to the glider, and
it is absolutely necessary to continue providing it with this service, refusing to
let go of it, the situation becomes absurd. The service the plane was supposed
to render the glider was to let it experience the freedom of flying, yet here the
glider finds itself literally captured.

In the realm of spiritual direction, in a first phase, which is often very beautiful, the person receiving direction discovers the spiritual life. Opening the heart
bears fruit and gives access to new perspectives. The one receiving direction
discovers how beautiful it can be to allow oneself to be led to God, to listen

[178] I.-F Görres, *Sur le célibat des prêtres* (Paris: Éd. du Cerf, 1963), 96. The quotation
is found in the second part, "Considerations on the meeting between the priest
and women."

to God as mediated through the word of another. This may last for months, often years. The progress made in the spiritual life is real, and there are tangible fruits — until something begins to grate. In those early years, precisely because of his inexperience, the young religious slips quite easily into the director's way of thinking and spirituality. But when his own spiritual personality begins to emerge, when the Lord begins to speak to him directly, and the director becomes less of a guide and more someone providing support, someone who invites the other person to keep moving forward, someone who takes a step back, all will be well so long as the director recognizes this change and somehow knows how to hand things over to the Holy Spirit, who is the only real Master of the interior life. In short, all will be well if the plane accepts the need to let go of the glider when the moment comes.

But if the plane is anxious to hold onto its role, if the director does not wish to let the soul in his care reach maturity, for fear that he might lose it, then all the elements needed to keep it in his power are to hand. It will be easy for him to suggest to such souls, seeking to follow the interior Master wherever He is leading them, that they are really following self-will, and that if they are seeking to abandon the openness brought about by the total obedience that had been promised up until this point, then it must be the Enemy who is drawing them away from that gentle path of total surrender that Jesus Himself followed.

And thus, in the subtlest way, is set the trap into which Jane de Chantal fell. In just the same way, the soul is caught in the director's nets and can no longer escape. If they obey the director, they will have to abandon their own convictions and the promptings of the interior Master, who has begun to lead them, and will inevitably have to endure the disquieting feeling that something is not right. If such a person decides to follow the interior Master, he experiences feelings of guilt and perhaps scruples, since he has abandoned obedience and openness. Such a person is therefore caught in a continual struggle between, on the one hand, what he finds at the deepest level within himself (misrepresented to him as the work of the Evil One), and on the other hand a submissiveness he has been taught to regard as the will of God, but which — in a confused way, without being able to articulate it clearly — feels more like a kind of slavery. The only way to escape a trap like this would be to approach someone from outside the community, who might be able to give an objective view. But what can be done if this option is denied by the community itself, since people from the outside can't understand its charism?

So there is no recourse. A deep sense of loneliness, psychological tensions, feeling that one is caught in a trap that one senses is there without being able to put one's finger on it: all of this risks plunging a person into depression. Where is this God, who seems to be contradicting Himself by calling to one in the depths of the heart but blocking the way to Him by means of the practice of obedience? Who is this God who is asking the person to renounce all those deepest aspirations that used to lead to Him? When the feeling that something is not right gives rise to feelings of guilt, and guilt (it is understood in some obscure way that this is unwarranted) reinforces the feeling that something is wrong, then the vicious circle closes, stripping the soul of all the light and joy it knew at the beginning.

If the director interprets this as a trial from God, as some kind of purification, inviting the person to submit, citing the example of Jesus in Gethsemane, this will only serve to increase the torment, since the soul senses that it is not God who is tormenting it but rather the bonds that the director is keeping so tightly secured around him, rather than letting him take flight. But a terrible scruple prevents him from letting this idea arise in his mind in any clear way because then he imagines he would be fighting against God, who (he is told) is the source of this inner darkness. In circumstances like these, people can begin to imagine that death is the only way out.

The Risks of Importing Models of Spiritual Direction from Elsewhere

What has just been described may seem unreal to some people, and it is true that it only occurs, thankfully, in quite exceptional cases, but nevertheless such cases are still too common for us to neglect them. For the vast majority of those who accompany others in the spiritual life, the need for a spirit of service and a respect for people's freedom is obvious. But we need to exercise some caution concerning the fascination some feel for the figure of the *staretz*, as found in the Russian tradition, since often what fascinates them is precisely the submission to the *staretz* in a way that is total, unconditional, and, apparently, without discernment. An imprudent interpretation of this will bring us back to the unacceptable kind of blind obedience. In *The Brothers Karamazov*, Dostoevsky writes:

Abuses in the Religious Life and the Path to Healing

What is a *staretz*? The *staretz* is someone who absorbs your soul and your will into his own. Once you have chosen a *staretz*, you give up your will and you entrust it to him in all obedience, with complete resignation.[179]

Dostoevsky is not a specialist in matters of the spiritual life; what he writes here has more to do with a popular interpretation of the role of the *staretz*, which fixes upon some of the visible aspects in a way that is not necessarily very balanced. Literature has thus disseminated the image of the *staretz* figure, a kind of archetype of the charismatic spiritual master, to whom blind obedience is promised, since he speaks in the name of the Holy Spirit.

Such a trustworthy master as Ignatius Brianchaninov is careful to lay down some conditions by first quoting Cassian: "It is good to be directed by people who are really wise," and then explaining: "A fallen will cannot successfully be set straight by the fallen will of some master who is himself still enslaved to the passions." He emphasizes this once again, this time quoting Simeon the New Theologian:

> If you want to renounce the world, do not entrust yourself to a master who is inexperienced or under the sway of the passions, for fear of learning from him not the way of the gospel, but the way of the devil. For the teaching of good masters is good, but the teaching of bad masters is bad.[180]

Nothing here, then, resembles blind submissiveness on the part of the disciple.

To present a sound explanation of these matters, Fr. Pavel Syssoev — a Dominican of Russian origin — has offered a short text on the subject, for the benefit of our work.

THE *STARETZ*

The word *staretz* comes from the Russian Orthodox tradition. A *staretz* is an old man (that is the literal meaning of the word) who is recognized as a spiritual master and who is often a charismatic figure.

---

[179] F. Dostoevsky, *The Brothers Karamazov*, part I, ch. 5 (*The Startzi*).

[180] I. Brianchaninov, *Introduction à la tradition ascétique de l'Église d'Orient*, (Paris: Éditions Présence, 1978), 63.

The *staretz* is a man of immense experience, often tried and tested in holiness, after decades of seclusion and life as a hermit. He is known to have received from the Holy Spirit gifts such as those of healing or prophecy and, in particular, the ability to give spiritual advice concerning the ways of the interior life.

The *startzi*[181] are not appointed by anyone, and they would never describe themselves in these terms. They are simply recognized by the faithful as authorities on the spiritual life. It is thus the *vox populi* that recognizes them. Outside of their periods of recollection or voluntary solitude, they receive visitors (some traveling great distances), who come to receive their blessing but particularly to open their hearts to them. Many of them have the reputation for knowing the interior life of visitors they have never met before.

True *startzi* will never say: "I am a *staretz*, a vessel of the Holy Spirit, and I will give you a word of life." That would be totally ridiculous. They are recognized by the holiness of their life, their humble obedience, their heroic gentleness, the way they eschew all power, their extreme discretion; by all these things we recognize them as extremely rare gifts to us from the Lord.

Submission to a *staretz* is totally free but often very deep in Russian culture. In this sense, the term *staretz* doesn't cover the same ground as the term *spiritual father*; it goes quite a bit further. This is why true *startzi* are rare. They are not to be found necessarily in every monastery, since God's grace does not answer to our demands. The way in which people hand themselves over to the *staretz* demands that the *staretz* himself be utterly transparent to grace.

TRUE AND FALSE *STARTZI*

Just as the Old Testament recognized that there were true and false prophets, there are also true and false *startzi*. The Russian tradition has even given them a name, *mladostartchestvo*, "the young old men": those who play at being a *staretz* without having the experience, the vocation, or the charism of a *staretz*. It is worth paying attention to the strict warning of Ignatius Brianchaninov, who enjoys immense authority in the Russian tradition. In his book *Introduction to the Ascetic Tradition of the Eastern Church*,[182] in the famous chapter 12, "On the

[181] The plural of *staretz* in Russian.
[182] The Russian title literally means: "What the spiritual life is, and how to live in accordance with it."

life of obedience to an elder," he warns us against false elders and insists that "in our time,"[183] it is often wiser to follow the tried and tested advice found in books than that of false masters, who proclaim themselves to be vessels of the Holy Spirit. A monk will make more progress through obedience to the rule, to the superior, and to ordinary teaching than by seeking out self-proclaimed *startzi*.

> Those elders who take it upon themselves to assume the role — we are quite deliberately borrowing this unpleasant term from the language of the secular world, in order to paint a clearer picture of this business, which is in reality nothing more than a kind of grotesque spiritual play-acting and the most deplorable pantomime — these elders, then, who assume the role of the holy *startzi* of former times on their own initiative, though lacking the spiritual gifts that these latter possessed, need to understand that their intentions, their thoughts, and their conception of obedience (that cornerstone of the monastic life) are all false. Let them understand: their way of thinking, their wisdom, and their knowledge are nothing but blindness and demonic illusions, which cannot fail to produce the same kind of fruits in those to whom they give direction. Their exaggerated pretense can only go unnoticed for a certain time even by inexperienced beginners who find themselves under their direction, so long as these have a modicum of intelligence and give themselves to holy reading with a sincere desire to be saved....
>
> It is a terrible thing to take to oneself, through presumption and on one's own initiative, obligations that can only be accomplished through a commission from the Holy Spirit and with His support; it is a terrible thing to present oneself as a vessel of the Holy Spirit, when the bonds to Satan have not yet been broken and the vessel is contaminated by him. Such a pantomime, such hypocrisy, is truly appalling. It is disastrous both for [the fake *staretz*] himself and for his neighbor. It is a crime, a blasphemy before God.[184]

---

[183] And yet he was writing at a time (1861) when the monastery of Optina had some *startzi* whose reputation endures even today.

[184] I. Brianchaninov, *Introduction à la tradition ascétique de l'Église d'Orient*, 64–65.

It would be difficult to find more vigorous language than this. The commission from the Holy Spirit, which is mentioned here, clearly marks out the *staretz's* discernment as a charism. This charism is rare, so much so that Ignatius Brianchaninov continues:

> We must recognize that we cannot take on all the many practices of the Fathers in their entirety. Indeed, it is already a great blessing of God and a source of great happiness that we are able to feed on the crumbs that fall from the table of the Fathers. These crumbs may not be the most satisfying sort of food, but they can keep us from spiritual death, even if we are still left with feelings of frustration and hunger.[185]

In the following chapters, he covers those teachings of the Fathers of old, which should ordinarily serve as our guide in times when God does not raise up *startzi* for us.

The Holy Spirit is the sole Master of all charisms. He springs up to confirm us in our faith, or to clear up our doubts, but He is not under our control at all. The Holy Spirit never leaves us destitute, for He works even through ordinary means, institutional means that have been given us directly by God (Scripture, the priesthood, and so on), or through the tradition of the Church (the great richness of different spiritual traditions, the teachings of the saints, the rules of different religious orders, and so on). These various means possess a certain diversity, a richness, a balance. They support one another, shed light on one another. Superiors are given their responsibility by means of election or nomination; they receive what is called the *grace of state*, that is to say the grace God gives them for accomplishing the mission entrusted to them. This is a particular grace, but we can describe it as an ordinary grace, as opposed to an extraordinary grace, which is what a charism is. This grace enables them to serve the community despite their limitations and weaknesses, to present a teaching that they first put into practice themselves, without overestimating their wisdom or spiritual gifts.

Occasionally, the Lord raises up in a community a Padre Pio, a Catherine of Siena, an Ignatius Brianchaninov, a Seraphim of Sarov. Sometimes He will give a confessor some enlightened piece of advice in a specific situation, while leaving him to his own judgment in ordinary situations. Simply being named

[185] Ibid., 67.

superior of a Capuchin community does not turn a brother into a Padre Pio. Conversely — and this is fundamental — someone like Catherine of Siena could doubtless never have been the prioress of a Dominican convent; she was too big a personality, too exceptional, too intense, lacking the particular discretion that is necessary in a superior. Closer to our own time, the same was true of Fr. de Foucauld; the Abbé Huvelin had to tell him several times that he was not cut out to be a founder. On the other hand, there can also be an Agnès de Langeac, a Catherine de' Ricci: mystics and gifted superiors under God. But finding these two characteristics in the same person is even more of a miracle than a charism!

A believer does not relate to an institution in the same way he relates to someone with a special charism. I am bound to obey my superior, but no one is bound to go and consult a Padre Pio figure. Conversely, I can tell someone like Padre Pio deep secrets that my superior has no right to know. My superior will guide me in the business of sanctifying ordinary, everyday life, but it is only for extremely rare decisions that I will go to see a *staretz*. From the *staretz* I receive advice, not orders; from my superior, I have to be ready to take orders, with all the objectivity of the rule, of Tradition, and of the teaching of the Church.

There are excellent and holy superiors, but these do not claim to be a Curé of Ars or an Antoninus of Florence. They are appointed or elected, but this does not confer upon them the advanced spiritual experience of a *staretz*. If they do have this, it will be a blessing for the community, but they themselves would certainly be the last to assert such a thing. As for the young superior who aspires to play at being a *staretz*, he runs a real risk of being nothing more than a *mladostartchestvo*, a "young old man."

Fr. Pavel Syssoev, whose contribution comes to a close there, thus brings us back to the ideas of balance and the interdependence that exists between charism and institution, without separation or confusion of these two things.

The Role of the Abbot or the Prior

This does not mean that an abbot or prior lacks a pastoral role toward his monks. As father of all,[186] he must be attentive to the material good, of course, but far

---

[186] This expression is appropriate in the context of a monastic community and may need to be nuanced or modified in other forms of community.

more to the spiritual good of his monks. It is absolutely part of his job to speak
with each of the brothers about every aspect of his life, and especially, therefore, about his relationship to God and his brothers. He must be able to sense
whether or not his soul is at peace, whether he is walking joyfully along the ways
of God or if, on the contrary, he is making his way with a millstone around his
neck. But he doesn't become his guide simply by virtue of this, and he can in
no way impose his services upon them.[187] The superior may not necessarily be
the most advanced in the ways of the spiritual life nor the most capable when
it comes to companionship.

St. Benedict deals with superiors that are elected "for life" or "for an indeter-
minate period," and his example is illuminating. The spiritual fatherhood of an
abbot in this sort of situation will necessarily be deeper than that of a superior
elected or appointed for three or six years. The brethren cannot be completely
open with someone who may only be there on a relatively short mandate. Such
a superior does exercise real spiritual paternity in the community and in relation
to individuals but in a way that is generally less radical than a "life abbot." For
this reason, St. Benedict reminds us, on two occasions in his *Rule*,[188] that he is
not necessarily everyone's spiritual father; there are other spiritual fathers in
the community too. The paternity exercised by the abbot is of a different order.

Through the decisions he makes for the whole community, he will either
make the brothers' spiritual lives easier or more difficult; his choices will have
an effect on their souls, either helping or hindering their relationship with God,
helping them grow or not. This is equally true, of course, for decisions he takes
concerning each individual brother: these will either foster their life with God,
their spiritual growth, or not. Therein lies a real paternal mission.

However, for all that, it is not required of him that he provide spiritual
companionship to each and every brother, which is good, since this would
be practically impossible in large communities. Furthermore, there can exist
between souls various affinities (or, indeed, differences), which it would be
foolish to ignore. If the superior is not possessed of this humble realism, he
risks exposing the community to grave dangers.

[187] Perhaps he shouldn't even propose it; would a monk be free to say no?
[188] Chapters 21 and 46.

This is not to say that it wouldn't be extremely profitable, perhaps even necessary, for the brother to have a basic level of openness toward his superior, to prevent the relationship from being based purely on work. If we want to establish a family atmosphere in a community, we need to allow the superior to have sufficient knowledge of us so that he can adapt the way he treats us accordingly; otherwise he will just be like the boss of a company.

The superior, then, has to be sensitive in the attentiveness he shows his monks. He should like speaking with them of God, of His love, of the ways that lead toward Him and those that lead away. If he has been chosen as the abbot, it is because his brethren have recognized in him a wisdom that he not only may, but ought to share with his monks. But he cannot require his monks to expose the depths of their hearts to him. If any of the monks asks him to be his spiritual father, in the full sense of the term, then that, of course, will be a source of joy for him, but a responsibility too.

As for the rest, his whole desire should be that each of them should advance on the way to God, without his having to know all the details of this way. Attentive but without intrusive curiosity, available to the brethren but with no strings attached, he will realize that he is by no means the holiest in the community, since it was probably not for that reason that he was chosen as abbot, and he will know how to remain in the background whenever a monk chooses a guide other than him.

Discernment and Companionship

Welcome

With regard to the youngest candidates [for religious life], those who have responsibility for them need to have the same sensitivity. Pushing someone to enter the institute, or trying to hang on to someone who is suffering too much under the weight of the burden of the life and is thus asking legitimate questions, would be to respect neither his personal liberty nor God's call. Marie-Laure Janssens reports how the novice mistress, who hardly knew her, said to her right from the start: "Your case is crystal clear; your place is among the sisters. When do you want to enter?"[189] With one sentence, she had robbed her of the basis

---

[189] M.-L. Janssens, *Le silence de la Vierge,* (Paris: Bayard, 2017), 40.

of her vocation. For even supposing the Lord had really called Marie-Laure to join the sisters, when He calls, He is looking for a *Yes* from the one He is calling, not from anyone else. Someone already formed might understand the abuse of power in that kind of comment and might be minded to escape, but a candidate who is not forewarned might fall into the trap without seeing it.

> Her words were so clear and spontaneous that I welcomed them, not as the fruit of some human reflection, but as a dazzling response from Heaven to the attraction, a very ambivalent attraction, that I was feeling. So I jumped in, full of confidence.[190]

Someone with responsibility for formation can never say to a candidate: *you are called to enter our community,* for by expressing it like this, though maybe not in so many words, the message is: *You must.* When the formator issues calls with such certainty, it is no longer possible to discern the call of Christ. The formator may say: *If you ask to enter our community, we can't see any objection to that.* But that's as far as he can go. The starting point for a vocation, on which everything else depends, is an intimate relationship between Christ and the candidate, a relationship in which nobody may intervene, since the freedom must be total. It is the direction of a whole life that is at stake!

Difficulties En Route

To encourage someone to stay too long, when she clearly wants to leave, is another example of the same lack of respect for the human person. When a difficulty arises, it is quite normal to take some time to see if it can be overcome. But if months go by and the doubt remains, continuing to insist only ties her down, and the community may become a prison.

An abrupt interpretation, along the lines of, "It is a temptation," or "it is the devil," shows an absence of discernment, not only in relation to what is going on with the young religious but also regarding the motivation behind these words. If these words are accompanied by exorcism — it may seem surreal, but it has been known to happen — the violence exerted becomes unbearable. The one accompanying this person is here treating her like a child who is incapable of

[190] Ibid.

discerning for herself, and, most importantly, is imposing a pre-formed opinion on the candidate. The difficulties of the way are a part of life and growth. Novices can never know whether their vocations are solid if they do not go through the first storm. It is not a question of abandoning them just when they most need help but of allowing them to walk the path themselves, and if they are looking for a mommy or a daddy who will tell them what they should do, then the guidance needed at that moment consists in showing them they have their own resources, their intelligence, a certain measure of experience, and must begin by using these before looking for someone else to do all the work for them. At that point, the role of the one accompanying them is often to provide reassurance, since he knows there is nothing unusual about storms, and to encourage, because he knows the novice is not made of sugar and won't melt in the rain. The message to pass on at that moment could be something like this: *There is a storm. You endure it, and then we will look at what it means; this is how you will learn to discern.* Doesn't the seasoned sailor say to the young cabin boy who is facing his first storm: *Now you will see what the sea is all about!*

IDEALISM, AND IGNORANCE OF WHAT IT IS TO BE HUMAN

The cabin boy will also learn what a boat is, and why a sailboat has to have a keel. To the sailor who is used to freshwater, a keel can seem a real bore. It is heavy, deep, and risks touching the bottom in the shallows. Wouldn't it be better to get rid of all that in order to sail along more merrily? On a peaceful lake, perhaps; but our cabin boy in the storm will understand just how indispensable this heavy keel is, if the boat is not to capsize and sink.

In terms of the spiritual life, it would be tempting to say that we have to get rid of everything human, so that the divine can appear, but this dichotomy would not respect God's plan. *Gaudium et spes* opens with the affirmation that "there is nothing that is truly human that does not find an echo in the heart of the disciples of Christ,"[191] because it has found an echo in the heart of Christ, who was gripped with compassion for the widow of Nain, for the leper, for the blind, for the sick, for the crowds who were like sheep without a shepherd; Christ who is the Good Samaritan, moved with compassion for the man he met on

[191] *Gaudium et spes*, 1.

the road; Christ who shows how His Father is full of compassion for His son, returning after a life of dissipation.[192] Jesus loved John, wept for Lazarus, and how delightful it is to see Him get cross because the disciples are pushing away the children people are bringing to Him for Him to touch them.[193] He wept over Jerusalem, He was deeply distressed by the hardness of heart of those who observed Him.[194] Contempt for human nature is contempt for Christ. *The Word became flesh* — not an angel. To us in our short-sightedness, becoming an angel might have seemed much more fitting for a God who is pure spirit, "but the foolishness of God is wiser than human beings" (1 Cor. 1:25).[195] The temptation of angelism distances us from the Incarnation, just as Docetism failed to understand how the divine could really unite itself with what is human. Religious life — which is often termed *sequela Christi* (following of Christ), and not "following of the Word" — is entirely based on the Incarnation, as expressed by the Council of Chalcedon, when it spoke of Christ who was "consubstantial with the Father in His divinity, and similarly consubstantial with us in His humanity, in all things similar to us — except in sin."[196] He says to Mary Magdalene: "Go and find my brothers, and tell them that I am ascending to my Father and your Father, to my God and your God." In our loving response to Him who has thus loved us, what place would there be for an *angelic life*,[197] as though the angels were higher than Him? The source of the religious life is Christ, both God and Man, who comes by His grace to join our humanity to His divinity,

---

[192] See Luke 7:13, Mark 1:41, Matt. 20:34, Matt. 14:14, Matt. 9:36, Luke 10:33, and Luke 15:20.

[193] John 13:23, John 11:35.

[194] Mark 3:5.

[195] This passage was directly translated from the French to maintain original emphasis.

[196] Denzinger, *Symboles et définitions de la foi catholique* (Paris: Éd. du Cerf, 1996), no. 301.

[197] Anyone who has lived in a community knows that there is nothing angelic about it. No criticism is meant by this remark; the intention is simply to stress that there is something incongruous about this expression when it is applied to the religious life, especially as we know nothing of the angelic life. And if only what is excellent, sublime, utterly pure, celestial, divinized, is to be considered as really human, we may well fear that the image thus constructed is not that of an angel, but that of a superhuman figure, with no relationship to the human being that is willed by the Creator. Could this be a sort of spiritual transhumanism?

and to lead us into God, us men and women, for by His Incarnation, human nature — not angelic nature — has even been introduced into the heart of the Trinity. It is only as a consequence of this that the whole of creation, including the angelic creation, is thus found in God, but the mysterious choice of God was that the Word should become a human being, setting up a woman of our race, His Mother, as Queen of the Angels.

In this way, it was revealed that everything that makes up the human person is compatible with God, a natural consequence of the human person's creation in the image of God, but our day-to-day experience of life tends to call this into question, so much does our life seem anything but divine. Yet the only exception to this is sin. The humanity of Christ is not a mutilated humanity; it comprises flesh, our sensible nature, the world of the emotions, imagination, the passions,[198] pleasure, a complete psychology (the unconscious is no exception to this) — and all of this not only during His earthly pilgrimage but in His glorified humanity too, to this very day. Any assertion to the contrary would have a whiff of Docetism about it. In rising from the dead, Christ restores life to His body, He does not become an angel, and all that is human comes back to life; did He not even eat in front of His disciples, according to St. Luke? In going up to Heaven with her body, the Mother of God does not leave half of her humanity on earth. Truly a man, truly a woman in glory, Christ and His Mother are today, at this very moment, the firstfruits of that glorified humanity that is so difficult for us to imagine, the utter splendor of a humanity that is entirely in harmony with God, like Adam and Eve on the first day and indeed more than they were. The Glorified Christ and His Mother are not less than man and woman; on the contrary, they are man and woman to an even greater extent, with the whole mysterious union of flesh and spirit, of mind and grace, of sensible nature and divine light that make up the human being in its fullness. All the powers of our humanity make up the life of Christ just as they make up our life, it is all united forever through His person to the divine nature, something theology calls the "communication of idioms" (*communicatio*

---

[198] The passions are neutral in themselves. Thomas Aquinas quotes Augustine: "Saint Augustine writes on the subject of the passions: 'They are bad if the love involved is bad, good if it is good.'" *Summa Theologiæ* IaIIae, q. 24, a. 1, *sed contra*.

idiomatum).[199] Now all this, in our case, needs to be purified of the stain of sin and its likeness to the divine nature restored — but purified, not scorned or done away with, which is impossible. *Consubstantial with us in His humanity:* this bold formula of Chalcedon must not be toned down, as the astonishing episode of the temptations in the desert shows us. If the words mean anything, then they mean that Christ felt — but did not follow — the attraction of evil. Christ wanted to enter completely into our experience, since temptation is not sin; rather, it gives us the opportunity to fight for what is good.

Using the term "angelic life" to describe the religious life thus seems at best inappropriate, even if we think of it as simply an unrealistic ideal. Canon law says of religious that they "foretell the heavenly glory."[200] Pope Francis's Apostolic Constitution *Vultum Dei quærere* speaks repeatedly of the prophetic life.

> Consecrated persons, by virtue of their consecration, "follow the Lord in a special way, in a prophetic way." They are called to recognize the signs of God's presence in daily life.[201]

Prophetic does not mean idealized or angelic. It means religious life tends toward that Life of the Kingdom, without which the religious life would be meaningless, and in doing so proclaims that Kingdom. A prophet proclaims what has not yet come about. Isaiah never saw with his own eyes the country where "the lion lies down with the lamb" (Isa. 11:6),[202] since he died a martyr,

---

[199] This expression means that what is proper to each of the two natures of Christ can be attributed to the person who subsists in both of these natures. "By virtue of this unity of person, which we must recognize in the two natures, we say at the same time that the son of man came down from heaven, when the Son of God assumed flesh (taken from the Virgin of whom he was born), and conversely the Son of God is said to have been crucified and laid in the tomb, although he suffered these things not in that divinity through which the only Son is coeternal and consubstantial with the Father, but in the weakness of human nature." Leo the Great, *Tome à Flavien §5; trad. Festugière,* 35. The "Tome to Flavian" is Letter 28 by Pope St. Leo the Great. An English edition of the letters can be found at: Leo the Great, *Letters,* Fathers of the Church 34 (Washington: Catholic University of America Press, 1963).

[200] *Code of Canon Law,* can. 573 §1.

[201] Pope Francis, *Vultum Dei quærere* no. 2.

[202] This passage was directly translated from the French to maintain original emphasis.

cut in two by the impious Manasseh, at least according to tradition. To reduce the history of Israel to a realization of prophecies would be an obvious mistake; the same goes for the religious life.

Furthermore, the Life of the Kingdom cannot properly be called "angelic"; it will be a life that is human, fully human. Our bodies are called to rise again, and even Christians too often forget this. This is the source of the respect that the Church has always had for the body. The religious life must be marked by a similar respect for all the various dimensions of the human condition, including the bodily dimension.

This is why St. John Paul II opens *Vita consecrata* with a meditation on the Transfiguration:

> Those who are called to the consecrated life have a special experience of the light which shines forth from the Incarnate Word. ... How good it is for us to be with you, to devote ourselves to you, to make you the one focus of our lives![203]

The ideal of the religious life is not de-incarnation but transfiguration.

Thus, any spirituality that involves contempt for human nature is not truly Christian; its connection with Christ has been distorted. Only sin can turn us away from God, and since sin can infiltrate the entirety of our life, our whole being is marked by it, and we need a Savior to free us from it — free us, that is, from sin, not from human nature — to purify our human faculties from sin, not to replace them with faculties that are supposedly angelic.

> Gregory gave great prominence to Christ's full humanity: to redeem man in the totality of his body, soul, and spirit, Christ assumed all the elements of human nature, otherwise man would not have been saved.
>
> Disputing the heresy of Apollinaris, who held that Jesus Christ had not assumed a rational mind, Gregory tackled the problem in the light of the mystery of salvation: "What has not been assumed has not been healed,"[204] and if Christ had not been "endowed with a rational mind,

---

[203] John Paul II, Post-synodal Apostolic Exhortation *Vita Consecrata*, March 25, 1996, no. 15.

[204] Gregory Nazianzen, Ep. 101, 32: SC 208, 50.

how could He have been a man?"[205] It was precisely our mind and our reason that needed and still needs the relationship, the encounter with God in Christ.

Having become a man, Christ gave us the possibility of becoming, in turn, like Him. Nazianzus exhorted people: "Let us seek to be like Christ, because Christ also became like us: to become gods through Him since He Himself, through us, became a man. He took the worst upon Himself to make us a gift of the best." [206]

Too much asceticism, too much renunciation, not enough regard for the gradual way in which things progress or for the time that is needed, a lack of attentiveness to things that are necessary for the psychological life (such as a healthy self-esteem, or the feeling of being useful), a mistrust of healthy initiative and of legitimate autonomy, a lack of awareness of the essential need to be loved and recognized, or even a systematic discrediting of human qualities: long indeed is the list of those areas where a refusal to take the human conditions of life into account can have serious consequences, in the long term, for a person's human and spiritual balance.

The idealism that lies behind this arises in part from an ignorance of the laws of growth. If someone has really discovered deep down the infinite love of God for him, even if he is stripped of every support, he is standing on immovable rock, which can weather any storm. What can be lacking to anyone who is filled by God? "They are too greedy by far, for whom God is not enough," Tauler used to say, and this expression was enough to bring about the conversion of Mme. Acarie.[207] And yet this is about aiming for completion, not just a beginning; we are talking about a path along which God leads anyone He chooses and not a mere method; about renunciation for the sake of a greater love and not out of contempt; we are talking about something more, not about something less.

[205] Ibid., Ep. 101, 34: SC 208, 50.
[206] Benedict XVI, General Audience of August 22, 2007. The quotation is from Gregory Nazianzen *Orationes* 1, 5: SC 247, 78.
[207] J. Tauler, *Institutions spirituelles,* chap. 20. See A. du Val, *La Vie admirable de la bienheureuse sœur Marie de l'Incarnation* (Paris: A. Tauminart, 1647), 27.

Abuses in the Religious Life and the Path to Healing

GRACE DOES NOT DESTROY NATURE

"Grace does not destroy nature; it brings it to perfection."[208] The most wonderful realization of this adage of St. Thomas Aquinas comes in the Incarnation of the Word, who did not destroy the human nature that He assumed. Indeed, it remained so true to itself that the people of Nazareth, for 30 years, noticed nothing out of the ordinary and were astonished when Jesus returned there. St. Mark writes that "they were deeply shocked by him" (Mark 6:3).[209] In Jesus, every human faculty — without exception — found its fulfillment in God. By means of Grace, the sacraments, and the way of conversion, we are all called to enter into this transformation, which is accomplished in Him and which the apostles glimpsed on the mountain of the Transfiguration. In Jesus, and in ourselves, no divine faculty comes along to replace a human faculty; rather, the human faculty will, in His case, find its total fulfillment in God; and, in our case, it will progressively become worthy of God once again. "Once again," because by nature it *is* worthy of God, having sprung forth from His hands, and it is part of His image, even if it has been disfigured by sin. Playing on the expression from the book of Genesis — "Let us make man in our image, after our likeness" (Gen. 1:26) — the Fathers of the Church stressed that divinization causes us to recover the likeness we had lost, but the image has remained intact, even when we have become submerged in unlikeness.

Grace, then, does not destroy nature and does not replace it; rather, it leads it back to the perfection proper to it and raises it infinitely higher because of the Incarnation. "O God, who wonderfully created the dignity of human nature, and yet more wonderfully restored it," says the liturgy.[210] To restore, to lift up, to accomplish, to purify, to straighten out: there are so many terms that have something to tell us about the path of the spiritual life, a path which a spiritual father accompanies, all the while knowing that he is only at the service of grace; a deeply positive path, along the course of which we discover who we are. St. Leo the Great says:

---

[208] Thomas Aquinas, *Summa theologiæ* Ia, q. 1, a. 8, ad 2.

[209] This passage was directly translated from the French to maintain original emphasis.

[210] Christmas, Collect of the Day Mass. Before the reforms of Vatican II, this collect was said at each Mass.

Christian, recognize your dignity and, now that you share in God's
own nature, do not return to your former base condition by sinning.
Remember who is your head and of whose body you are a member.
Never forget that you have been rescued from the power of darkness
and brought into the light of the Kingdom of God.[211]

I hope the reader will forgive this rather heavy-handed insistence on one
element essential to the spiritual life. The higher the spiritual edifice is to be
built up, the more solidly it will need to be rooted in the Incarnation and in the
extraordinary dignity that has been bestowed upon human nature. It is this path
to fullness that will allow us to bear the difficulties and dryness of the journey.

THE FOUNTAIN IN THE DESERT

"The journey is long, and the way dry and barren, that must be traveled to attain
the fount of water in the promised land."[212] Desert, *acedia*, night … spiritual
tradition recognizes these different states, and they must not be confused with
one another. The passage through the desert is a part of the spiritual life. Acedia,
on the other hand, is a spiritual sickness, which the *Catechism of the Catholic
Church* speaks of as a "form of depression."[213] Gabriel Bunge defines it in this way:

Acedia, then, is above all a certain lifelessness, a kind of catastrophic
drop in the soul's natural resilience, which makes a person unable to
defend him or herself from the "thoughts" that are attacking at this
particular moment.[214]

As for the authentic kind of night, it can only come from God; it can never
be the fruit of human effort, which can only produce a dangerous, counterfeit

---

[211] Leo the Great, Sermon 21, 2–3 (PL 54, 192A), quoted by the *CCC*, no. 1691.

[212] *Carthusian Statutes*, 4.1. See Deut. 32:20, Wis. 11:2, Ps. 62:3, Rev. 7:17, Gen. 12:1.

[213] *CCC* no. 2733, summarized in no. 2755.

[214] G. Bunge, *Akèdia, La doctrine spirituelle d'Évagre le Pontique sur l'acédie,* (Bégrolles: Bellefontaine, 1983). An English edition is available: G. Bunge, *Despondency: The Spiritual Teaching of Evagrius Ponticus on Accedia,* (New York: St. Vladimir's Seminary Press, 2011).

version. In reality, however, discerning between these different states is not easy, particularly if there are elements of depression in the mix.

A mistake at the stage of diagnosis can have serious consequences, at least if the mistake becomes entrenched. This subtle question, full of nuances, cannot be covered here, but let us at least flag one essential thing: the one accompanying must bear in mind that there are different possible causes. If he has a ready-made interpretation, seeing the spiritual "night" in every situation, a young religious who is not at home in the community (and shows this in a tendency to depression) can expect to suffer a lot. If, on the other hand, he sees depression in everything, someone under his direction who is undergoing one of the spiritual nights will also suffer. And if he interprets a "night" or depression as acedia, and treats it by means of encouragement or reproach, he will certainly not be helping anyone he is accompanying. Wisdom recommends that a spiritual companion suspend judgment for a while, observing how the situation develops, that he take advice from experienced people, and that he allow the young religious to take advice from other people too. This will avoid many an error and much needless suffering.

A few elements can help us understand whether the path is still sound, even when the going is hard.

First of all, exceptional cases apart,[215] there has to be a balance. The portion of the *Statutes* that was quoted at the beginning of this section is immediately followed by a quotation of William of St. Thierry, which speaks of intimacy with God in solitude:

> There the faithful soul is frequently united with the Word of God; there the bride is made one with her spouse; there earth is joined to Heaven, the divine to the human.[216]

---

[215] When God Himself leads a soul into the night, nobody will be able to bring it light. But even so, a balance still remains: the soul that is being led in this way will itself radiate light on everything around it.

[216] William of St. Thierry, *Lettre aux frères du Mont-Dieu* 35, Sources Chrétiennes (Paris: Éd. du Cerf, 1975), 173. The full text of this paragraph of the *Carthusian Statutes* 4.1, reads: "Our principal endeavor and goal is to devote ourselves to the silence and solitude of the cell. This is holy ground, a place where, as a man with his friend, the Lord and his servant often speak together; there is the faithful soul

These two things must never be separated.

Joy is probably the clearest sign of spiritual health — not necessarily a perceptible, exuberant joy, but the joy of love, even in the midst of pain. Love loves to give, and giving what does not cost anything seems deficient. But when it's nothing but cost, when pain is only pain, when renunciation is only renunciation, questions have to be asked.

A deep sense of peace, despite the trouble that is experienced on the surface, takes joint first place with joy.

Meaning, which lies at the root of these two things, is less a sign than a condition. When we love, any suffering we must endure has a meaning, and because it has a meaning it can be part of the expression of our love — this is precisely what sacrifice is. Missing a football match because we have run out of fuel through lack of preparation is difficult to accept because there's no meaning to it.[217] Missing a football match because your wife is tired and you don't want to leave her alone in the house, when she would clearly prefer you to stay, doesn't reduce the cost of the renunciation, but the price we are paying here has meaning: the joy of being able to show your wife that your love is real and concrete. As we have said, renunciation finds its meaning in the love behind it.

The signs we have just discussed are nothing more than the first fruits of the Spirit, according to St. Paul: "But the fruit of the Spirit is love, joy, peace, patience, kindness, goodness, fidelity, gentleness, self-control" (Gal. 5:22).

We find these same signs in the famous description of *acedia* in the *Praktikos* of Evagrius: "The demon of *acedia*, which is also known as the 'noon-day devil,' is the hardest to bear of them all ... " After the colorful description we know so well, Evagrius concludes by saying: "After this struggle, the soul finds itself at peace, experiencing a joy words cannot describe, for no other demon can

---

frequently united with the Word of God; there is the bride made one with her spouse; there is earth joined to heaven, the divine to the human. The journey, however, is long, and the way dry and barren, that must be traveled to attain the fount of water, the land of promise." An English text of the original letter can be found: William of St. Thierry, *The Golden Epistle: A Letter to the Brethren of Mont Dieu*, Cistercian Fathers 12 (Kalamazoo: Cistercian Publications, 1971).

[217] Unless we can see the thing in the light of providence: *Lord, what are you saying to me?*

resume the attack straightaway."[218] We are not being asked, here, to find joy and peace in the heat of the battle, but to see them as a kind of stable foundation, whose existence can be sensed in the heart of the silence.

An important sign that a path of renunciation is the right one can be found in a paradox, expressed in various terms: light-darkness, joy-suffering, peace-trials. St. Thérèse of the Child Jesus writes:

> My soul felt a PEACE so sweet and so profound that it would be impossible for me to put it into words and for seven and a half years, this inner peace has been my lot; it has not abandoned me even in the midst of the greatest trials.[219]

St. John of the Cross puts it even more strongly in his poem "Without and With Mainstay":

> Without and with mainstay,
> no lantern, light of day,
> burning, I burn away.
>
> My spirit in free flight
> breaks from the pull of earth,
> tie of its human birth,
> to breathe a keen delight
> suspended on God's worth.
> Let the world hear: I hold
> my heart's one wish today,
> knowing my very soul
> without and with mainstay.[220]

---

[218] Evagrius Ponticus, *Traité pratique ou Le moine*, no. 12, Sources Chrétiennes (Paris: Éd. du Cerf, 1971). An English edition is available: Evagrius Ponticus, *The Praktikos & On Prayer*, Cistercian Studies 4 (Kalamazoo: Cistercian Publications, 1970).

[219] Thérèse de Lisieux, "Manuscrits autobiographiques," Manuscript A69, recto and verso in *Œuvres complètes*, (Paris: Éd. du Cerf, 1992), 186. The capitals are in the original.

[220] Written in 1585–1586. Translation from *The Poems of St. John of the Cross: New English Versions*, trans. John Frederick Nims, (New York: Grove Press, 1959).

The poem will go on to speak of darkness, but darkness that comes from the blinding light of love; it speaks of being consumed but also of the *most blessed life*, of *the life of Heaven*, of *pleasure*, and of a *delightful flame*. The paradoxical formula expresses something of the intimate experience of the soul that does not feel God but knows He is there, of a knowledge that is more experiential than intellectual, a mysterious and elusive experience that leaves us with the feeling of being supported by "nothing" but a "nothing" that can support everything.

Night or depression? At an external level, the symptoms can seem very similar, but St. Paul will come to our aid yet again. "Patience, kindness, goodness, fidelity, gentleness [or: humility] ... " When we see a soul experiencing the night but nevertheless spreading light around itself, when we see it accomplishing with great fidelity — sometimes heroically — what love requires of it, without deriving any joy from it, but being in a state of deep peace, then we can be sure that the Spirit is leading it and supporting it. It is going through the desert, but an invisible fountain is following it and allowing its presence to be sensed, if not by the soul itself, at least by others round about. If, on the other hand, we can only find lassitude and disgust in such a soul but no fruit, we are in the domain of *acedia*.

Opening the Heart

How Necessary It Is

How can we allow ourselves to be guided if we do not open our heart? The *Carthusian Statutes* put it in a discreet but firm way at the end of the chapter on conversion of life. It is worth quoting this paragraph in full:

> For the continuing quality of our life will depend more on the fidelity of each individual than on the multiplication of laws, or the updating of customs, or even the zeal of priors. It is not, indeed, enough to obey the commands of our superiors and observe faithfully the letter of the *Statutes*, unless, led by the Spirit, we savor the things of the Spirit. Each monk is placed in solitude from the very beginning of his new form of life and left to his own counsel. Now no longer a child, but a man, let him not be tossed to and fro and carried about with every new wind, but rather let him try to find out what would please God and do it of his

own free will, enjoying with sober wisdom that liberty of God's children, concerning which he will have to render an account before God. Let no one, however, be wise in his own eyes; for it is to be feared that he who neglects to open his heart to an enlightened guide, will lose the quality of discretion and go less quickly than he ought, or too fast and grow weary, or stop on the way and fall quite asleep.[221]

Balance is important. It is recommended that we open our hearts, but the goal of this is clearly indicated by what comes earlier: learning how to savor the things of the Spirit,[222] how to make the right choices, to discern for oneself what is pleasing to God, to put into practice the freedom of the children of God. This is as good as saying: learning to be a spiritually mature man or woman, who will perhaps one day be capable in his turn of guiding his brothers or sisters. This balance is the same as the balance that is found in education: offering guidance and support for as long as necessary but no longer than that. If a monk is still a child after ten or fifteen years of religious life, then his education (human and spiritual) has failed.

In addition, there are different degrees of opening the heart. Perhaps a minimum of openness is all that is needed. The Jesuits, for example, must render on *account of conscience* each year to their provincial. Were it not for this, they might risk being totally independent, and obedience, so important in the Society, would become something theoretical. But it is only once a year and in a very particular context. Nobody has the right to demand total openness; this can only be offered once a relationship has gone on long enough for someone to discern whether complete trust is possible. This is why it can never be institutionalized or demanded.

CAN OPENING THE HEART BE ENCOURAGED?

This is a very delicate question, and everything depends on what we mean by "encourage." In a certain sense, the text of the *Statutes* quoted above encourages

---

[221] *Carthusian Statutes*, 33.2.

[222] Translator's note: in the French text, the Latin phrase "nisi, Spiritu ducti, quæ sunt Spiritus saperemus" is rendered as "si nous ne savions aussi nous laisser conduire par l'Esprit, pour sentir et vivre selon l'Esprit," or "unless we also know how to let ourselves be led by the Spirit, to feel and live according to the spirit." This is rendered more literally in the English translation of the *Statutes* as: "unless, led by the Spirit, we savor the things of the Spirit."

opening the heart but in a very general way. With anyone looking for a greater depth in companionship, we must, of course, explain what opening the heart is and help the person, if it seems appropriate, to move in this direction, since this kind of openness is not easy for everyone. We can teach such people that, as St. Bernard says, "anyone who is his own master is the disciple of a fool."[223] We can speak to them of the Desert Fathers, who show how necessary it is to have a guide.[224] Someone with no idea of what opening the heart is must be introduced to the idea. But the guide must be freely chosen, and the whole of the companionship must be characterized by great freedom. There are also people who find it difficult to speak of their inner life, something more commonly found among men than women. This must be respected.

But if someone should encourage a person directly: *You ought to open your heart to me*, or even demand: *Open your heart to me*, then dysfunctionality is already present, and the motive is not pure. Even if the initial fruits are good (since opening of the heart helps people to know themselves), in the long term the person will feel that his privacy has not been respected. In serious cases, the person may feel violated (violation of the conscience) because he will have the feeling that someone has invaded his innermost self without his consent.

But, people may say, *the person must have given consent, since it was he who opened his heart.* This would show a lack of awareness of how possible it is for consent to be obtained by seduction, manipulation, abuse of power, or other means. We are speaking here not about things of the flesh but those of the spirit, which are more subtle. It is possible to force someone without his being aware, or without his daring to say no, since he is in the presence of an authority he respects, even if, in his internal forum, he senses something is not right. The breach of trust would be even more serious if it came from the superior, since the authority and trust involved would make refusing far more difficult, and his freedom would not have been respected.

The suggestion may not necessarily be direct, or at any rate, it may be accompanied by an acceptable justification. For example, the director will say:

---

[223] Bernard of Clairvaux, *Lettre 87*, 7 in *Lettres* vol. 2, Sources Chrétiennes (Paris: Éd. du Cerf, 2001), 465.
[224] For example, Cassian, *Conference* II, 11.

Abuses in the Religious Life and the Path to Healing

"If I am going to guide you, I need to know you, so you have to open yourself totally." Or again: "You are free, but if you do not open yourself, you will not be the disciple whom the master has led to sanctity, and you will remain trapped in mediocrity." Despite the affirmation — *You are free* — such an expression constitutes a demand when it is addressed to someone who, by his vocation, obviously wants to aim for sanctity. Deep down, the formula is a paradoxical demand: *You are free, but you do not have any choice.*

True opening of the heart — the sort that seeks to leave no shadow because there is total trust — requires an exceptional encounter. If we force it even a little, the injury will be terrible. One sister who had experienced this describes it this way: "That feeling, which is impossible to describe, of being violated inside, ravaged, pillaged, of no longer having any right to an interior life lived before God and for God alone."

TRANSPARENCY OR CONTROL?

Speaking of transparency in the realm of the spiritual life is not without risk. Derived from civil life, where it is used today to cover almost any eventuality, the term describes a simple reality: not hiding things. We demand transparency of banks; we demand that politicians and business leaders exercise transparency in relation to their income, and so on. Yet most of the time, the transparency in question is an obligation. Is the prison warden, who demands that the inmates hide nothing they are doing, not demanding transparency? In all these cases, the transparency has two characteristics: it is required (it is a law) and it is a means of control. Is it any different in the spiritual life?

Asking for transparency about things people do can be normal to a certain point and in a certain context. The superior has a right to know what the bursar is doing within the limits of his remit. Asking for transparency in the realm of his thoughts or his conscience, on the other hand, is an abuse of power. All the various forms of totalitarianism have sought to control people's thoughts.

> Psychology teaches that the urge to control and dominate is a neutral urge, that is to say, it can be used positively — to organize one's own life, attain a goal, discover a method that will obtain results — or negatively, in a defensive way, to cover up an insecurity or affirm one's own omnipotence.

Forcing the transparency of the brothers or sisters can be interpreted as a way of affirming oneself and protecting oneself from the risk of failure, of rebellion or of anything that might dent the esteem in which superiors are held. The hidden thought, probably present at an unconscious level in the mind of the community's guide, could be expressed like this: "If I know everything that is going on in everybody's head, I will be in control of everything, nothing will escape my gaze, nothing can happen that I have not foreseen. This will give me a sense of security and allow me to keep on exercising power." This attitude recalls the parable of the rich man who amasses his goods in his barn, only transposed from the context of riches to the context of knowledge.[225]

Breaking Confidentiality

When a spiritual father tells another person what he has heard in direction, even outside the sacrament, the one being accompanied feels betrayed. The person who hears the indiscretion may also be shocked, and if it is someone being accompanied by the same priest, he may be afraid that he could be the next to be betrayed. This is sometimes enough for someone to abandon spiritual direction with a particular priest. In the context of an openness that has been forced, indiscretion generally becomes the rule, springing from a feeling of having rights over the other person's inner life: *I have the right to know everything and the right to do what I want with what I know.* In a pyramid structure, the violation of confidentiality is, moreover, part of the structure itself, given the requirement to relate everything to the head of the community. Intermediaries have to pass everything on, so nothing can be kept confidential. Experience shows that if someone lives long enough in this kind of atmosphere, the very meaning of confidentiality is lost, and many people are unable to keep themselves from saying what, deep down, they know they should be keeping to themselves. Even the seal of the confessional may be broken.

What is at work in these situations is an abolition of boundaries. If the boundary of another person's personal life is no longer respected, why should we imagine the boundary of discretion would be respected? If the one providing

[225] Sr. A. Bissi, unpublished text.

spiritual companionship imagines he has the right to look into the inner world of the other person, but given that, in his own eyes, this information belongs to him now, how will he understand that he may not pass on what he hears to other people? These questions are more serious than we might think; does the other person still have a separate existence as "other" here?

In a healthy situation, two boundaries should be respected. On the one hand, the one being accompanied has the freedom to decide what he passes on (or not) to the spiritual companion. The companion, however, does not have any rights; he is a servant here. On the other hand, the one being accompanied alone has the right to grant the companion permission (or not) to mention anything he has heard to a third party, whether this relates to individual things that were said, or areas that were covered. The companion does not have the right to demand disclosures from the other, nor to pass these on. What he receives does not belong to him.

In practice, trust reigns supreme in this situation. The more there is a real trust [between the companion and the one accompanied], consisting in mutual respect and esteem, the more the first boundary will open naturally. And the more natural it will be for the companion to understand that the second boundary — the one that is between them and other people outside the companionship relationship — is an integral part of respect for the other person's privacy and therefore must not be violated.

Aspects Particular to Female Communities

The dynamics of relationships are not always experienced in the same way in male and female communities. Without wishing to establish hard and fast distinctions, it is nonetheless helpful to recognize some nuances. To describe the difference in approach, we needed a female pen, so a mother abbess will now explain to us how she sees things:

> Women are certainly more sensitive to a sense of guilt than men, in that they have a more visceral sense of responsibility in relation to the life (maternity) that is entrusted to them. It is thus easy to make a woman feel guilty at an emotional level, as though her femininity (and thus her deepest being) were directly affected.

For this reason, pressure to open the heart can be purely affective in nature. The need to be valued, to be the favored one, can in fact be a feminine weak point. In general, more than might be the case with a man, a woman needs to be welcomed, seen, chosen, the favorite. She may picture to herself what she needs to do to be seen, noticed, preferred. Now clearly the superior can use this feminine need for her personal gain, without even realizing it, under cover of genuine motherliness: *You are my favorite daughter, or the one who is closest to me; the sister I love more than anything else,* and so on. It is very difficult to resist this kind of pressure, since doing so can feel like ingratitude. Shouldn't I open my heart to this person who is showing me such care? And if we do put up resistance, despite everything, then blame steps into the picture, possibly accompanied with words such as *After everything I have done for you …*

One of the greatest sources of security for a woman is the possibility of opening up to someone, of speaking, of being listened to. She understands that she cannot become herself unless she has someone to relate to. Time given to her sisters, spiritual conversations with them can be seized on and turned into a real instrument of pressure and manipulation. A sister who does not know when her superior is going to ask her to come to her office may end up thinking of nothing else. This can easily be used by the superior to destabilize her daughters completely and make them even more dependent. Manipulative personalities frequently use things like blowing hot and cold, violent and unexpected tempers, to weaken resistance and recruit followers.

A sense for detail, which is particularly developed in women, can make a woman think that she hasn't said everything, or even that she has not told the truth if she didn't share all the details. In the same way, a female superior could even demand, in the name of the truth, this same kind of detailed self-disclosure. The more we open up in detail, and the stronger the bonds between us, the greater the extent to which dependency may be established.

Women also have a very developed sense of "totality": when a woman gives, she gives everything. If she maintains a certain distance (which is very healthy), she can have the feeling of not being honest in her self-giving. This can also be manifest in her relationship with the superior. The superior can, for her part, demand exclusivity for the sake of authenticity, for the sake of the quality of the relationship.

On the other hand, a woman, made to be a bearer of life, feels the need to establish relationships of real quality with those to whom she is close. In a monastic community, of course, this is expressed by the superior toward her daughters but also by the sisters, who will find it difficult to live in a mediocre relationship with their superior. A sister may do everything to ensure her superior's attention, which plays to the maternal instinct of the one in charge. A superior may demand great openness from her sisters, which plays to their need for a special relationship.

Another aspect of emotional blackmail engaged in by the superior may take the form of prolonged or regular periods of sulking. If the superior starts sulking for long periods, all the sisters become ill at ease and find it hard to endure such a breakdown in their relationship with their "mother." When she deigns to come out of her self-isolation and asks a sister to do something, that sister will do anything to meet expectation, simply so as to recover a living bond with her. If this situation repeats itself two or three times, most of the sisters will not dare cross the superior for fear of causing a new "shutdown."

The reflections of this mother abbess may be illustrated by these words from one witness: "I had come to be in the presence of God. I ended up in the presence of the prioress and was defined by her. It was very difficult, and utterly absurd."

9

Spiritual Abuse

Given its multifaceted nature, and the ways in which it can deftly mask itself behind the noblest of pretexts, spiritual abuse deserves to be treated separately.[226] "I left X twenty years ago, but I am marked for life. A few exceptional occasions aside, I don't think those in charge deliberately intended to destroy or break us." But even if they didn't mean to, that was exactly what they did, at least in the case of the author of this testimony, who can only broach the subject of her past with great difficulty: even talking about it causes great pain. The reality of the harm done in the realm of the spiritual life is usually the thing that is most difficult for leaders to accept. Moreover, this harm almost always comes back to a single principle: the distinction of the internal forum from the external forum, which in cases of abuse is, unfortunately, insufficiently clear. This is a most valuable principle in its proper place, and here too much is being allowed to slip through the net.

In origin, this separation of the different forums was a response to a particular problem, in a particular context: "The forum is the context in which judgment is pronounced on a person's vocation to the priestly ministry."[227]

[226] This chapter takes up in part a study that was published in the collection *Vie Religieuse et liberté, approche canonique, pastorale, spirituelle et psychologique,* published by CORREF (the Conferences of Religious of France), Paris 2018. The aspect of the internal forum is treated in greater length there. Dom Dysmas de Lassus, *La paternité de l'Abbé et l'accompagnement des frères,* 51–149.

[227] B. Pitaud "L'école française de spiritualité et la protection du sujet: for interne et externe dans les séminaires," *Revue d'éthique et de théologie morale "Le Supplément,"* no. 222, September 2002, 117–130. The quotation comes from page 118.

The goal of separating the forums is to allow a judgment to be reached that is informed while still respecting the privacy of the person concerned. It provides protection against abuses of power from any authority figure who might seek to exercise control over people's consciences. Yet it cannot offer any protection against spiritual abuse when this occurs in the internal forum. We need, then, to take a broader look at this.

Reading the Landscape

One thing that emerges when we look at conversations between victims of spiritual abuse is their use of the expression "internal forum," together with associated terms.[228] What crops up most clearly is the notion of an intrusion into the internal forum, the conscience or the innermost thought [of victims], these three expressions generally being synonymous: *Putting pressure on me in the internal forum.* This *pressure* is experienced not only as something violent but as a real lack of respect: *My internal forum was trampled underfoot.* More descriptively: *Wanting to intrude directly into my conscious or subconscious mind.* And the witness adds a phrase explaining how that was experienced: *The aim was to destroy me as a person.* The word *rape* or *violation* is often used: *Raped in my inner self,* or again, *the "chastity of the heart" was violated.* This forceful intrusion occurs when there is an *obligation to reveal the internal forum.*[229]

The consequences of this kind of violation are described as a disappearance of the "I."

> I don't know who I am anymore. We had to be reduced to nothing to the extent that the "I" that was giving itself seemed as it were to disappear. I didn't exist anymore. So little of oneself is left.

Online. See *idem.,* "Les rapports du for interne et du for externe dans la tradition de l'École française de spiritualité," Bulletin de Saint-Sulpice, 2004, no. 30. This text has been reproduced as an annex in the collection already quoted at pages 112–123.

[228] More than 150 pages of this exist in total. The authors have allowed these conversations to be quoted, provided that this is done anonymously.

[229] Translator's note: Here the author is referring not principally to the internal forum in the seal of sacramental confession but to the innermost thoughts of the person being directed in general, which may of course include this.

Breaches of confidentiality are mentioned and condemned as a scandal, but they are not placed on the same level as more serious abuse. The central point here is the forceful intrusion into the sanctuary of a person's inner life in the name of authority. The expression "spiritual abuse" can seem a bit strong on account of its resonance with the term "sexual abuse," but it is the victims themselves who use these terms when they speak, for instance, about violation of the conscience. It is an abuse of trust, which takes advantage of the person's openness so as to force a way into his or her deepest, most intimate thoughts and, eventually, to hold sway over his or her conscience, using the pretext of the spiritual life. In the worst cases, people may end up in a real stranglehold.

Three main themes emerge from this analysis.

First Theme: Claiming Authority over Conscience

In the context of the religious life, abuse occurs when a relationship of companionship is based on a relationship of authority. The case of St. Jane Frances de Chantal, discussed previously, may seem to be something of a caricature, and yet several recent cases have been quite similar to that caricature.

Four vows demanded by Jane's director	A community with aberrant, sect-like behavior
The first: that she should obey him	A spiritual guide is imposed. Obedience is invoked in the internal forum. Pressure to open the heart.
The second: that she would not substitute him with another director	Pressure to prevent people from leaving the community.
The third: to keep confidential what he said to her	What is taught within the community is kept secret from the outside world.
The fourth: not to confer about her interior life with anyone other than him	It is forbidden to speak with external confessors.

Here, the community or institute has taken the place of the director, but otherwise nothing has changed. This could also be true of someone in the community — a founder, a superior, or some pseudo-spiritual master who sets up a relationship like the one imposed on Jane. The story goes that Jane's first director was a "good religious man." We may well believe that he acted out of foolishness rather than malice; nevertheless, the result remains the same, and Jane de Chantal experienced such a relationship as crushing; she spoke of a "mountain on her heart."

Nobody Has Authority over Conscience

By its very nature, the vow of obedience does not cover the spiritual life because it is concerned with actions rather than with someone's inner life. From this, we may establish a fundamental principle that allows no exceptions: no one has authority over another's conscience, since if anyone did claim to have such authority, he or she would be competing with God. A text of the Second Vatican Council, taken up by the *Catechism of the Catholic Church*, gives us the reason for this:

> In the depths of his conscience, man detects a law which he does not impose upon himself, but which holds him to obedience. Always summoning him to love good and avoid evil, the voice of conscience, when necessary, speaks to his heart.... For man has in his heart a law written by God; to obey it is the very dignity of man; according to it he will be judged. Conscience is the most secret core and sanctuary of a man. There he is alone with God, whose voice echoes in his depths.[230]

The fact that this law is written within us comes from our being created in the image of God. No human being is capable of desiring evil for the sake of evil, for if anyone aims at something evil, he does so to the extent that it appears to him as something good. The fact that we are incapable of committing a conscious act without using our reason also shows that conscience is fundamentally oriented toward what is true. This represents the conscious emergence of that mysterious law, the "spark of the soul," at the heart of the conscience, where the image

[230] *Gaudium et Spes*, no. 16, taken up by CCC, no. 1776.

that we are finds itself in the presence of its Model. From this it emerges that God has authority over the conscience, not as an external authority, dictating its laws, but as the source of being, and particularly of the free being that is the human person. The conscience is thus shown to be the locus of a fundamental relationship with God, which explains why it is inviolable.

> No human authority has the right to interfere with anyone's conscience. Conscience bears witness to the transcendence of the person, also in regard to society at large, and, as such, it is inviolable.... To deny an individual complete freedom of conscience — and particularly the freedom to seek the truth — or to attempt to impose on it a particular way of seeing the truth, constitutes a violation of that individual's most personal rights.[231]

It does not follow from this that the conscience is an infallible oracle. The depraved also have a conscience, which doesn't reproach them for anything because they have disfigured it or stifled it. We have to follow our conscience, therefore, but we also need to ask: what sort of conscience is it? The conscience of a saint, or of a convicted sinner?

> It is insufficient, therefore, to say: "Always obey your conscience," without immediately adding: "but ask yourself whether your conscience is telling you the truth or a lie, and never tire of seeking to know the truth."[232]

In a short article, Fr. Servais Pinckaers explains the distinction (which deserves to be better known) between the conscience and that light of the conscience known as *synderesis*, the "spark" of the conscience or the "spark" of the soul.

> *Synderesis* is a direct participation in the light of God, which shines in each one of us since we are created in His image. Every conscience enlightened by it therefore reflects God's light in how we judge our deeds.... *Synderesis* is the light of our first principles about good and evil;

[231] John Paul II, *Message for the World Day of Peace*, January 20, 1991.
[232] John Paul II, *General Audience* of August 17, 1983.

Abuses in the Religious Life and the Path to Healing

conscience puts these principles into practice with the help of reason, reflection, questioning and deliberation about our acts according to their content, their end, and their context; it leads to a judgment as to the nature of the actions we are about to make, or have already made, expressed in terms of obligation or prohibition or remorse ... As a result of ignorance, for which we can be responsible at least through negligence, it may happen that in our conscience, we judge that something is good, when in reality it is not, or judge something to be bad, when in reality it is good or neutral, such as for a Christian to eat meat offered to idols.[233]

The light that illumines our conscience is imperishable and "[St. Thomas] judges that *synderesis*, which he understands as the original light of good and evil in the human heart, cannot be wrong, cannot sin, and cannot be extinguished."[234] The judgment of our conscience is not infallible, since our limitations, our ignorance, our torpor, and our sins form a more or less opaque veil over the light it gives. In the beautiful expression of Fr. Pinckaers, the conscience is "a seeker of truth," specifically, "*of truth in regard to what is good*," a tireless seeker after what is truly good. A seeker though, not an oracle.

But then why must we always obey our conscience, even if it can be in error? Illumined by this law/light, binding it to the God who is all good, the conscience cannot be deliberately mistaken; it judges what it believes to be good. To depart from it, therefore, would be to choose deliberately what we believe to be bad.[235] Hence the importance of forming and refining our conscience, like mined gold that must be purified.

These considerations are necessary if we are to reach a better understanding of why nobody can have authority over someone else's conscience. If any human authority wished, even with good motive, to impose itself on someone else's conscience, then that authority would be placing its own light above that

---

[233] S. Pinckaers, *La conscience de l'erreur, Communio*, no. 109-5 — Sep./Oct. 1993, 31–32. See also CCC no 1778: "Conscience is a judgment of reason whereby the human person recognizes the moral quality of a concrete act that he is about to perform."

[234] Ibid., p. 31,

[235] St. Thomas Aquinas, *Summa theologiæ*, IaIIæ, q. 19, a. 5,

of the other person's *synderesis*, which is impossible. Anyone submitting to such pressure would find himself in a battle between two "divine" voices. Which one should he follow? If he follows the exterior voice, which claims to speak to him in the name of God, then he must stifle that *spark of the soul*, which is the place of a mysterious but most intimate relationship with God. He would cease, in fact, to act in a human way because he would no longer be free or in control of his own actions. And yet it is precisely by being free and in control of one's own actions that human beings act as creatures in the image of God. So, whatever one's good intentions, anyone seeking to impose himself on someone else's conscience is not treating his fellows like human beings.

Nobody, then, should impose himself on another person as a spiritual director, and a spiritual companion who has been freely chosen has no authority to issue commands.

And yet we must distinguish between two situations that are fairly similar. In the first case, a superior may be imposed as spiritual companion, either by the rule or by his own authority. This authority, which is legitimate at the level of community life, is used to deprive the person of freedom of choice in the realm of spiritual companionship. In such a case, the proper limits to the obedience due to a superior have been transgressed. We must not imagine that such an act of authority is always direct, since the pressure can also be indirect — by invitation, encouragement, reproaches for a lack of trust, and so on, thereby conveying the message we are already familiar with: *you are free, but if you don't comply, you are not a good monk.* This case typically arises from a confusion between the internal and external forum, the separation of which (when properly respected) ought to prevent it.

Another kind of situation may exist, however, in which the spiritual father acts within the relationship of spiritual companionship as though he had authority over the other person's conscience. Here, it is a matter of spiritual abuse properly so-called, regardless of whether or not he has authority in the external forum.

What must be respected, then, is not the difference between persons but the difference between relationships. The relationship appropriate to spiritual companionship is entirely different from that involved in leading a community, and the danger arises from transposing into the relationship of spiritual companionship a way of working that is proper to an authority relationship. People used to speak of *directors of conscience*, which was not without ambiguity and led to many an abuse.

Collaboration on the Part of the One Receiving Direction
It may also happen that the one receiving direction collaborates with this phenomenon. Fr. Adrien Candiard points this out with great clarity:

> I think particularly of young people, who are perhaps asking questions about their vocation, or at least about how to take their Christian life seriously, because (with the exception of the most mature among them) they may often almost court this kind of abuse of their conscience. When caught up in dizzying and often worrying bouts of questioning, they may appear very happy when a word of authority descends on them from Heaven, not so as to lend them support with the business of illuminating their own conscience, but in order to replace that conscience. But we help them not by complying with their demand, but rather by helping them to establish clear limits to it.[236]

This important observation explains how an abusive companionship relationship can come about. At the outset, it may be well received and even bear fruit. The negative consequences only begin to appear later on.

Second Theme: Demanding Total Self-Abandonment

When an authority relationship is established in the context of companionship, it can be used to bring about the complete self-surrender of the one being accompanied.

> Fr. X asked me to "submit" myself entirely to him. I noted down the following quotation only a few minutes after I heard it from him: "I expect total loyalty from a novice. Otherwise, I will not be able to work with that novice. You have to accept what I say to you, with no contradiction

---

[236] Conference of Fr. Adrien Candiard at the General Assembly of CORREF at Lourdes, November 13, 2018, on the theme "power and spiritual companionship must not be confused."

from within yourself. You need to realize that I am here for you as your novice master, the representative of Christ." "I sense that you are loyal in your head, but not in your heart. There is still a resistance there that you must conquer totally." "I am asking you to totally change your heart and your spirit." "Open yourself to me unreservedly. I don't know you at all. Show me yourself just as you are."

The abusiveness comes from the demand for totality. It is normal to expect a novice to open the heart, to the extent that this is possible for him; indeed, without this it is difficult to help the novice, but it is unacceptable to demand that this openness be total. The *unreserved* openness demanded by Fr. X already constitutes an abuse. What is more, this unreserved openness is at the service of an unreserved submissiveness, as though the novice master were Christ in person. We are now in the same category as blind, unconditional obedience, without reflection, only this time at the level of the interior life. In the name of a supposed spiritual renunciation, nothing remains of what constitutes the dignity of the human being, as recounted by the victims of such an approach in the quotations given above: *I hardly exist anymore.* All that makes me "me" before God is in another's hands. Taken far enough, it may end up in the sort of control that destroys liberty.

But this is not immediately apparent since, at first, it may bear real fruit:

At first, revealing my thoughts was a great help to me. But what I didn't like was the "obligation" to reveal, the fact that we weren't free, that we were made to feel guilty (and made ourselves feel guilty) if we didn't reveal everything. There was too much pressure on a sister to "change," to be "transformed," and openness of heart was sometimes used to arrive at this goal "efficiently," "quickly" ... By applying this sort of pressure, the opposite result is achieved. It was at times like these that I felt violated in my inner self — when people were using their knowledge of my inner life to "shape" me, change me, transform me ...

This text underlines just how the opening of the heart can be exploited for another end. The beautiful experience at the beginning — the experience of a kind of discovery of the interior world that had been so poorly understood until then — progressively turns into a way of controlling someone's life. The tipping point is revealed when the center of gravity is seen to shift. A healthy opening of the heart is simply the opportunity for someone to discover the ups and downs of his interior world. Everything is for the benefit of this person, not for the benefit of the one who is listening to him. But when the listener begins to use what he has heard as leverage on someone else, everything changes, because the center of gravity has shifted: openness of heart is now being placed at the service of someone else's agenda. Even with the best intentions in the world, he is *using* someone else's inner world, which can be compared (in this situation) to an act of violation. And if the intention here is to force the person opening himself up in this way into the mold of some "official" spirituality or way of thinking, then the feeling that his conscience is being violated will be even greater, since the center of gravity has been totally reversed. The one listening is no longer at the service of the person who is opening up; rather, this person is now at the service of the listener, or at least at the service of what the listener stands for. It is a complete reversal of roles.

Third Theme: Spiritual Doctrine

Fr. Adrien Candiard observed above that "they may be almost courting this kind of abuse of conscience." But it can also be the case that the spirituality of the house or the institute requires it.

If the prevailing spirituality places too strong an emphasis upon the will of God regarding everything, it is almost certain that confusion will arise between the will of the superior and the will of God. If I ask God whether He wants me to wear a sweater, He is certainly not going to give me an answer. By the same token, if the prevailing mode of thinking is that we must seek the *will of God* in all things, it inevitably follows that this *will* must be expressed by one's superiors; how else? The italics signify that this supposed *will of God* is not the will of God at all, since God is not some overprotective mother, telling me what I have to do every step of the way, and, since He has absolutely no *will* concerning whether or not I should wear a sweater, He gives me an intellect so that I can work out the answer to this sort of question myself. This punctilious approach to the *will of God* is thoroughly infantilizing, since it leaves no room for the exercise of freedom and responsibility. We recognize here the very heart of abusive behavior: the will of God concerning you seen as something external to you, requiring you to submit like a child to everything asked of you.

From here on, all manner of things may be demanded, and the seriousness of the abuse will depend on the nature of what is being asked. The common feature in all these situations is that the person being accompanied is stripped of responsibility for his own life, at the level not just of his spirituality but of his humanity more generally.

If the danger comes from a particular person — an imprudent or dangerous spiritual father, say — then we may be talking about spiritual abuse, but not of aberrant, sect-like behavior. The superior ought to be aware of the danger, and anyone around should be able to enlighten the victim on the question, so long as the victim is still able to speak, despite any confidentiality a director may attempt to impose on him, for whatever reason.

On the other hand, if this dangerous approach is no longer the work of a single person only but has become a culture running through the whole community (or its superiors, at any rate), then all attempts to raise questions will be nipped in the bud, since it is very difficult for him to insist on being right over against everyone else. The internal immune system will have ceased to work properly, and only outside intervention will have any effect.

Naming the Evil as Precisely as Possible

Spiritual abuse is a dangerous evil, and it is completely opposed to the idea of religious life. If we are to succeed in avoiding this danger, we must be aware of it. To this end, we need a more precise vocabulary to describe what is going on. The expression "spiritual abuse" describes the evil itself and helps us reach a better understanding of what is going on than an expression such as "confusion of the internal and external forums," which only describes a possible cause.[237] Jacques Poujol gives several definitions, which, taken together, form a useful overview:

---

[237] Far be it from us, here, to minimize the importance of maintaining a separation between the internal and external forums. This precaution is indispensable for avoiding abuses, but in itself, this is a means of doing something, and we need an expression which describes the evil itself.

Abuses in the Religious Life and the Path to Healing

Behind the words "spiritual abuse" lurks the reality of suffering, incomprehension, and deep wounds for those who have experienced it.... Spiritual abuse can be defined as the spiritual and psychological maltreatment of someone, with the effect of weakening (or even destroying) the person, making him psychologically and/or spiritually dependent.... Spiritual abuse occurs when someone (pastor, priest, shepherd, or any other Christian in a leadership role in a prayer group, community, or parish) uses the authority of his position to control or dominate one person or several people.... Again, spiritual abuse occurs when a Christian leader exploits someone else to satisfy his own psychological or emotional needs, or the needs of the institution he runs. Spiritual abuse is an abuse of authority, rendered the more serious by the way it makes use of divine authority to dominate one person, or several people.[238]

The Image of God Disfigured

This abusive use of divine authority has dramatic results. All consecrated religious have thrown themselves into the religious life with a great love deep down in their hearts, and happily, in normal situations, this love will find space to blossom. But for those people who have fallen into an institute where they have ended up being oppressed, things are very different. In the correspondence of those who have managed to escape, we regularly find this kind of painful statement: *I don't know how to pray any more, I can't pray any more.* Their relationship with God has been broken, often completely, such as in the case of those who have gone so far as to lose their faith; but more common are cases where, in a particularly painful way, though the desire for God remains, the victims' image of God is so disfigured that a relationship with Him is no longer possible.

Jacques Poujol described this *erroneous and warped image of God:*

The victim has a view of God as someone demanding, unpredictable, never satisfied, strict, ready to punish or humiliate, a tyrant-God, who

---

[238] J. Poujol, *Abus spirituel, S'affranchir de l'emprise* (Paris: Empreinte temps présent, 2015), 9–12.

sets unattainable goals, and seems to have a *quid pro quo* approach. Victims imagine that His Spirit recoils at the slightest sin, like a spiritual alarm bell going off as soon as a bad thought occurs. They don't believe God is their advocate; they see Him rather as the accuser.[239]

A painful observation from one witness confirms the last sentiment: "For me, God had become 'the eye in the tomb, watching Cain.'"[240]

The drama arises from the way in which the words (and even the deeds) of authority figures have been invested with a sacred character, and presented as representing God in the strict sense. If the superior's every word is supposed to be a word of God, if every expression of the superior's will is supposed to be the will of God, then in the overall context of abuse, God can be perceived as the abuser. The image may vary — from the overprotective mother (reluctant to let her children grow up, keeping them instead in a state of dependence because she wants them for herself), to the perverse God who takes pleasure in humiliating and crushing His creatures, or there again, the irresponsible despot who plays with human beings according to his fantasies. A culture of lying is often experienced as the ultimate scandal. "If these people who speak in the name of God lie like this, how can we have confidence in the God they represent?"

This disfiguring of the image of God is strengthened by the fact that, in all these situations, from the most trivial to the most serious, the arguments offered rest on Scripture, on the Gospel, St. Paul, the great mysteries of the faith, the image of God. Even sexual abuse is justified in terms of the greatest mysteries of the faith. The evil done to people is no longer simply psychological: it is also spiritual. Some people will retain a real aversion to certain realities of the faith, or even to God — at least to the God they have been shown.

And they will be right to do so, since to believe in a perverse God is an offence to God.

Believing in Jesus Christ is good in itself, and necessary for salvation; but the will only inclines toward what the reason proposes. So, if this faith

[239] Ibid., 72.

[240] The terrible poem "La conscience" by Victor Hugo needs to be read if we are to understand the dramatic force of this observation.

is presented by the reason as something evil, then in this case adhering to that sort of faith would be adhering to something evil.[241]

This is true when the image of God has been so disfigured that it no longer has anything to do with Him.

Victims, then, will need reassurance. What they are rejecting is really just an idol, and rejecting idols is part of the honor we owe to God. Nevertheless, their scars are so deep that it is not clear whether they will ever be able to overcome their aversion, over which the reason has no control. But God knows and understands, and He knows that He is the one they desire in the end, when they aspire to what is good and true, to what is awe-inspiring.

Precautions That Need to Be Taken

The witness who was quoted above on the subject of being forced to reveal things goes on:

> After I left, I also had an experience of transparency in a relationship of spiritual companionship, only this experience was very good, for three reasons:
>
> 1. I had total freedom at all times. I could simply say nothing, if that was what I wanted. I said just what I wanted to say, without doing any violence to myself. And, even if it were something important, I never forced myself to say anything I did not want to say.
> 2. The person I was confiding in had no other authority over me.
> 3. The person I confided in had very considerable powers of discretion and discernment, wisdom and prudence, and was detached from any desire to seize authority or control.

[241] The quotation is from Thomas Aquinas. The text, which is somewhat difficult for the modern reader, has been paraphrased. Here is the literal translation: "Believing in Jesus Christ is good in itself, and necessary for salvation; but the will only inclines toward what the reason proposes. So, if this faith is presented by the reason as bad, then the will will incline as though towards something evil, not that it really is evil in itself, but only accidentally, by means of the idea the reason has conceived of it."

These few lines, which are the fruit of experience and more particularly of an encounter with a companion who bore a real witness to the goodness of God, give us almost all of the most important themes. Concerning the last sentence, isn't it true that one of the most surprising aspects of the spiritual life consists in discovering more and more how our God, even though He is our creator, is *detached from any desire to seize power or control over us?*

Guaranteeing Freedom: Canon 630 of the 1983 *Code of Canon Law*

The wisdom of the Church has already been brought to bear on the question of spiritual abuse. In the nineteenth century, the unfortunate imitation of the Jesuits' "manifestation of conscience" by newer congregations had led to abuses. Rome reacted strongly, with the decree *Quemadmodum* of December 17, 1890. The 1917 *Code of Canon Law* took up the question again in its canon 530. The *Code of Canon Law* of 1983 refined its approach to the question still further in its canon 630.

This canon provides a strong guarantee of the freedom to which anyone being accompanied has a right: freedom to choose one's confessor and spiritual father, freedom to reveal things to superiors, or not. This canon has found a point of balance in what is a difficult question.

> Can. 630 §1. Superiors are to recognize the due freedom of their members regarding the sacrament of penance and direction of conscience, without prejudice, however, to the discipline of the institute.
>
> §2. According to the norm of proper law, superiors are to be concerned that suitable confessors are available to the members, to whom the members can confess frequently.
>
> §3. In monasteries of nuns, in houses of formation, and in more numerous lay communities, there are to be ordinary confessors approved by the local ordinary after consultation with the community; nevertheless, there is no obligation to approach them.
>
> §4. Superiors are not to hear the confessions of subjects unless the members request it on their own initiative.
>
> §5. Members are to approach superiors with trust, to whom they can freely and on their own initiative open their minds. Superiors, however,

are forbidden to induce the members in any way to make a manifestation of conscience to them.[242]

This canon stands in opposition to two forms of excess: that of forcing the members of the community to have a superior as their spiritual director and that of reducing a superior to a purely external role. Freedom is affirmed by section 1. Section 5 forbids a superior from "induc[ing] the members in any way to make a manifestation of conscience to them." This is a strong expression, and it includes all forms of pressure, however subtle they may be. Trust is recommended; it is always possible to be open with the superior, provided this is really free and spontaneous. If a religious feels forced, no matter how slightly, to manifest his conscience to a superior, the freedom demanded by the Church is no longer being respected. It should be emphasized that the canon excludes the possibility that any rule could impose the superior as spiritual director for the whole community. A very careful article by Fr. Gonçalves explains where this canon comes from, beginning with the decree of 1890.[243] It also explains the exception that is the "Jesuit manifestation of conscience."

Being free to choose also means being free to leave; this applies to spiritual direction just as it applies to the sacrament of penance. Nobody can be forced to stay with a spiritual director that doesn't suit him. As for the freedom to be open, this concerns both who we choose to be open with, and what we might choose to say or not say.

The Proper Kind of Companionship

Freedom of choice and the proper separation of the forums give us a first level of protection against abuses. Obviously, these are not sufficient to ensure that the quality of any companionship received is good. Some will have more talent than others; there is nothing unusual in that. Nevertheless, we must pay

---

[242] *CCC*, can. 630.

[243] B. Gonçalves, *For interne et autorité.* This lecture, given at the Institut catholique de Toulouse on April 27, 2015, has been published in L.-M. Le Bot (ed.), *Autorité et gouvernement dans la vie consacrée: Des ordres religieux aux nouvelles formes de vie consacrée,* (Langres: Les Presses Universitaires/Institut catholique de Toulouse, 2017), 95–121. An abbreviated version can be found in *Vie religieuse et liberté,* Appendix 2, 124 ff.

some attention to our model of the companionship relationship, which may be conceived of in two ways. In the first model, the director communicates with God and receives His word, which he passes on to the one receiving direction. This model is linear:

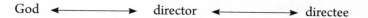

God ⟷ director ⟷ directee

The director here acts as a sort of intermediary in the relationship and in the decisions to be taken. By virtue of his position, he acts as a screen. Everything occurs as though the one receiving direction, not knowing how to hear the will of God, is going to turn to the director, who will undertake to pass on the questions and answers. In reality, since directors are not totally transparent, they may end up passing on a lot of themselves. This is not bad in itself, but what is bad is that everything is declared to be "divine," though a great deal of what is human is mixed in with it. This model doesn't favor a relationship between the one receiving direction and God; as a result, it presents fertile ground for serious abuses. In the gravest cases, the director acts as a total screen, all the while uttering spiritual formulae, and ends up bringing everything back to himself; this can even result in sexual abuse.

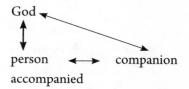

God

person accompanied ⟷ companion

In the second model, there is a triangular relationship, and the triangle is not symmetrical. The privileged relationship is the one between God and the one receiving companionship. The companion (who is no longer described as a director), stands to one side, like the bridegroom's friend, according to the saying of St. John the Baptist: "He who has the bride is the bridegroom; the friend of the bridegroom, who stands and hears him, rejoices greatly at the bridegroom's voice; therefore this joy of mine is now full. He must increase, but I must decrease" (John 3:29–30). The companion is in a relationship with God by means of his own spiritual life, which gives him experience he can use to help the one being accompanied, who is still proceeding somewhat hesitantly along this path. He will also have a relationship with the one he is accompanying, but this relationship will not act as a screen. His mission is not to give orders but rather to provide encouragement when the road seems dark or dry, to confirm the intuitions of the one being accompanied while they are still afraid to trust themselves, and to give reassurance when they feel a bit lost.

The difference is summed up in this brief comment:

> Even if we are good persons with the best intentions in the world, it is possible to do a great deal of harm. This is always the case when priorities become confused. The priority, the only one, is that the person who is confiding in me in some way or other should grow in freedom, that he should love God more freely, that he should listen to the voice of the Holy Spirit who is speaking to him (and not to me).[244]

And not to me. This is the key to the second model, where the companion truly believes that the Holy Spirit, the Spirit of Jesus, has first place when it comes to speaking to the person being accompanied, and thus to the companion too, whom he will enlighten with his gifts, but without turning himself into a kind of intermediary, acting as a screen.

TEMPTATIONS OF SPIRITUAL DIRECTORS

It goes without saying that the distinction between these two approaches is not clear cut and that every kind of intermediate position exists. But being aware of them can help each of us to understand whether our way of working is helping souls to grow in freedom in their relationships with God and whether it helps the action of the Holy Spirit, leaving Him all the space and all the initiative. Various temptations, more or less serious, threaten to beset anyone who considers himself to be a spiritual director.

Efficiency

> One problem is that, when I accept someone who wants to confide in me, I may want to be efficient. I want to solve his problems, because I am a problem solver! There is no hanging around with me. And yet, we

---

[244] Conference of Fr. A. Candiard to CORREF.

know that the Holy Spirit often takes His time, and that the pace of an authentic spiritual path can be slow — or at least, it never seems to follow the growth patterns we may have planned out in advance. I don't always have the necessary patience. I am afraid that people might judge me to be useless, because I don't solve the problem. So there is a great temptation to jump with both feet into the conscience that is being presented to me, so that I can solve his problem, especially when I can see exactly what needs to be done. It would be so easy to put pressure on him, for his own good! I think the shortcut is the devil's signature way of working: if you manipulate things a bit, you can attain your goal more quickly.[245]

The Prophet-Director

The Prophet-Director behaves like an oracle who is a transmitter of the divine word, and so nothing he says can be objected to. A Dominican priest was right when he wrote:

> I cannot help but remember the sorts of things that were being said at the beginning of the [Charismatic] Renewal: "The Holy Spirit is saying to me," or "is saying to you" ... One day, one of my Dominican brethren said to me: "Say 'I am' instead of 'the Holy Spirit is,'" and I immediately realized just how a desire for power can conceal itself behind such expressions, which could be fairly terrifying for people not yet formed to any great degree ... To be clear, I do not believe at all in a "great plan of God" for anyone, and I think that evoking such a thing is often a kind of trick, which allows people to pass off their own desires as God's desires, as a way of giving them more weight.[246]

Nobody is denying that the Holy Spirit is able to provide assistance to a spiritual counsellor. But this assistance doesn't come directly; the counsellor doesn't receive messages for which he is merely a loudspeaker. This assistance comes about within the counsellor's own processes of reflection, without him having an immediate perception of it.

[245] Ibid.
[246] The quotation has been slightly altered, for reasons of discretion.

Abuses in the Religious Life and the Path to Healing

Though it is more subtle than "the Lord is telling you to," the formula "it came to me in prayer that the Lord is saying to you/asking you," is hardly less dictatorial. There was a person who, from time to time, used to take part in the public prayer meetings of one of the new communities. One day, one of the members of the community came up to her during the evening and said to her: "It has come to us in prayer that the Lord is calling you to join the community." She fled, but others might well have been dazzled by the thought of being specially chosen like that.

We are wrong if we think that an approach that respects the privacy of the other's inner life leads to a mediocre spirituality. In the following letter, written by a lay person who was one of the great spiritual directors, even directing Carmelites, we can see that a thoroughgoing respect for personal freedom in no way prevents us from presenting a very high spiritual path:

> My style has always been, and still is, not to propose to souls anything that may daunt them, but to wait instead for grace to incline them to it first. Until that moment, I leave them in freedom, and do not seek to force them to do anything. If you go on not wanting to open your heart to N., don't beat yourself up about it. It is true that I had thought that he might have been helpful in bringing you to perfection, and I think he possessed the talents, the grace and the disposition for this. For I can assure you that, if you want to be a stranger to creatures, or to live in death, separated from all things, nobody could have suited you better, his method being to lead souls without letting them know what they are, or what they do, so as to remove from them any strength they could attribute to themselves. He has written to me to say that, not having found this total openness of heart with you, he has not committed to helping you, waiting instead for God to give you both the dispositions needed for that.[247]

Monsieur de Bernières Louvigny could sense that the person confiding in him was a soul called to a very high path, hidden and highly ascetic. He

---

[247] *Les œuvres spirituelles de Monsieur de Bernières Louvigny, ou conduits assurés pour ceux qui tendent à la perfection: Seconde partie contenant les lettres qui font voir la pratique des maximes.* Third edition (Paris: Charles Robustel, rue Saint-Jacques au Palmier, 1690), Letter 45 of September 4, 1653, concerning the conduct of directors, 122–123.

proposes a demanding kind of accompaniment, but neither he nor Fr. N. want to force the person; instead, they both wait for the grace of God to show the way. A voluntarist asceticism would be the complete opposite to their approach because it would encourage the soul to find strength in its own will — and thus in itself — and in the director's method. Even the initial impulse comes not from him but from the person seeking direction: *If you want...* Is there, in this desire, a message from God? He thinks it is possible, but he waits until the person is able to hear it and, having heard, suggest a way forward himself.

The Particular Case of the Novice Master

The particular case of the novice master might be a cause of embarrassment; isn't it an exception to canon 630? The novice doesn't choose his novice master, even though he is going to have a significant influence on his religious life and will expect a certain measure of openness from the novice. Of course, the novice can freely choose his confessor, at least when there *is* a choice, since in women's communities, for example, this choice is often restricted. The novice master cannot be reduced to the role of a kind of master of ceremonies; he is not charged with responsibility only for external things. The need for formation in depth is obvious, given the growing fragility of vocations. Becoming a religious is not simply a matter of strictly following the rule; people need also (and perhaps need above all) to learn to know themselves, and how to recognize the fragilities and wounds will come to light in the common life, just as they do in personal life; people need to learn how to enter into relationships with other people, with God, and with themselves; they need to learn how to practice asceticism (which is not first and foremost about external things); they need to learn how to discern the twists and turns of their thoughts, and so on. No serious formation can occur without all this. Where does the internal forum end and the external forum begin? It can be difficult to identify a boundary, especially in the realm of learning how to pray, i.e., how to enter into a relationship with God.

The novice master is at once a formator, with the authority implied by that term, but also someone who provides companionship. It is particularly important for him to understand the different kinds of relationship implied by these two aspects of his role, aspects which are, moreover, asymmetrical. The first cannot be avoided. He exercises this authority over all those in the novitiate; there can be no exceptions to this. But there may be exceptions to the second aspect. A novice master could, and sometimes should, suggest that a novice who has real difficulties with him might find someone else for spiritual companionship. The formation may suffer a little because of this, but all the same it would be hindered to an even greater degree if the novice were to remain trapped when it came to spiritual conversations.

There are several reasons that justify this exception to the rule. A novice arriving in the monastery will have a hard time choosing a spiritual father. He doesn't know the monks yet and often hardly knows himself. He can only have confidence in the fact that the novice master has been chosen for his qualities. He knows he won't be perfect, but that's life. A novice master is appointed; he does not impose himself on people, and he remains subject to the superior's authority. Lastly, the novitiate has a limited duration, and this aspect is of essential importance, since an exception to the rule can't go on forever.

The abbot needs to remain watchful. Abuses have occurred in the past and are certainly still occurring. One abuse concerns the discernment of vocations, by seeking to attract and retain some people and reject others on spurious grounds, just because "I like person A and not person B."[248] Prudence requires that this discernment should be overseen, since it is neither reasonable nor honest to entrust the future orientation of candidates' lives to a single person. A second possible form of abuse comes from the great influence the novice master has. If he does not use this influence for its proper purpose, this may end in cases of spiritual or even sexual abuse. The best protection here will be to raise awareness in the community of the different mechanisms of abuse, which will allow possible misdemeanors to be identified more easily.

That being said, the role of the novice master is of enormous importance in the life of the young monk, and his responsibility is great. The frequent warnings addressed to the abbot in the *Rule [of St. Benedict]* might also be applied to the novice master. He, too, will have to render an account to God for the way in which he has guided the novices in his care.

He should be a deeply religious man, a lover of quiet and silence, gifted with prudence and good judgment, aflame with genuine charity,

---

[248] This latter case is of course rarer these days, but it remains a serious matter, since even here it concerns the life of a human person who is perhaps being called by God.

radiating love of our vocation, having an understanding of the diversity of spirits, and in open-minded sympathy with the needs of youth.[249]

In other words, such a person is difficult to find.

God, the Source of Our Freedom

God created us free. When we look at what we do with this freedom, we might think He took a foolish risk, but since He does all things with wisdom, we have to conclude that He has a tremendous esteem for this liberty, since "the foolishness of God is wiser than human beings" (1 Cor. 1:25).[250] This is shown in a striking way by how His providence operates, so rarely choosing to intervene directly in our lives; appearances on the road to Damascus will always be the exception. And yet, a strange account of the way God acts in our lives is widely presented, well beyond the confines of the religious life. In this account, God has produced a roadmap for our life, which we have to follow. To be sure, this roadmap has been produced by a Father who loves us and who does all things for our good, but produced all the same, and our principal job can be summarized as twofold: discovering the map, and not straying from it too seriously. Everything has been written in advance, but the key to understanding it has not been given us, which makes a human life seem a bit like a treasure hunt. When Boy Scouts play this sort of game, the leaders have previously left along a route a certain number of slightly mysterious clues that have to be found and then decrypted in order to discover the location of the next message. This is thus a work of the intellect, but the players have no choice regarding the route.

In such an approach, the *will of God* takes an interventionist turn, which is justified in terms of divine goodness and wisdom. *He knows better than us.* There's no disputing that, but it doesn't alter the fact that this vision only focuses on the doing and not on the relationship; the essential thing is following the plan. This conception of things may be found in the context of vocational discernment, though not only here. But is this really the way God deals with us?

This conception of human destiny conveys the image of a God who is a bit like the conductor of an orchestra. The score is already written and the

---

[249] *Carthusian Statutes*, 20.1.

[250] This passage was directly translated from the French to maintain original emphasis.

musicians — men and women — have to follow it. Any deviation will lead to wrong notes and thus to dissonance. Others might prefer the image of a play for the theatre, but the result is the same. The scope for interpretation is a bit broader, but the play has already been written. But in no sense does the history of the People of God provide us with such an image. In that history, we see God accompanying His people tirelessly and maintaining His own fidelity, despite the countless infidelities of the people. For example, God did not directly will the exile; He sent Jeremiah to warn the people and show them how to avoid it. But the book of Jeremiah is shot through with a lament: "I have spoken, but you have not listened." The people will thus go into exile, and God will accompany them, in order to turn this exile into a new opportunity for a complete renewal of the relationship of Israel with its God; after the exile, we hear no more about idols. The history of Israel is our history, and God accompanies us — yes, us — along the path of our life, shot through as it is with choices that, we might say, are often not His choices. He tells us His preference, in Scripture, through the Magisterium, through our conscience, but the choices are ours — nothing is written in advance.

We have to get rid of this "treasure hunt" idea if we want to understand the way God acts in our lives, a way that is worthy of Him — and of us. Our respect and esteem for our freedom need to be in proportion to the respect and esteem God Himself has for it. "Man is rational and therefore like God; he is created with free will and is master over his actions," writes St. Irenaeus.[251] We would not be like God if He decided [all the details of] our lives for us.

God's call invites us to a path of light, but the response is ours because a free response is too precious in God's eyes for Him to use coercion in any way. Throughout our lives, He accompanies us, He gives us advice, and if we take a poor route, He will be with us there too, right to the end. Far from the image of the treasure hunt, the image that gives us light here is that of Jesus walking alongside the pilgrims of Emmaus, without their knowing it, opening their minds and warming their hearts (See Luke 24:32–45).

---

[251] Irenaeus, *Contre les hérésies*, IV, IV, 3. Quoted in the *Catechism of the Catholic Church*, no. 1730.

10

Sexual Abuse

Thinking about spiritual abuse has opened us up to the phenomenon of those hidden forms of abuse that relate to a personal relationship. It is in this context that the most serious types of abuse can occur, abuse that can remain undiscovered for a long time, since it often has no direct impact on community life. The painful question of sexual abuse — whether of children, or of adult men and women — has shown us just how real is the possibility of living a double life as a consecrated religious. But indeed, this is a worse sort of double life than, for example, that of a priest living with a mistress, since in this case people are left scarred for life. The work of rebuilding may take many years and may never be able to erase what happened in the past.

The revelations of recent decades have concentrated almost exclusively on pedophilia. And yet, for a long time, various people have been emphasizing that the question of adult abuse also needs to be examined. And indeed, this area is now beginning to receive attention in both the civil and religious spheres. The motu proprio *Vos estis lux mundi* gives the same degree of protection both to minors and to *vulnerable people*, who are defined as follows:

> [A vulnerable person is] any person in a state of infirmity, physical or mental deficiency, or deprivation of personal liberty which, in fact, even occasionally, limits their ability to understand or to want or otherwise resist the offence.[252]

---

[252] Francis, *Vos estis lux mundi*, of May 7, 2019. Art.1, §2, b.

Abuses in the Religious Life and the Path to Healing

What we have just said on the subject of spiritual abuse allows us to understand how a relationship of spiritual companionship can end up limiting a person's ability to understand or to want or otherwise resist the abuse. This means that a religious, even as an adult, can effectively be a vulnerable person. The same is true of novices with regard to the novice director, even in the context of an entirely normal relationship.

Many studies of this phenomenon have been published, and here we will only present the most important elements, asking what insights the particular context of the religious life might bring to this process of reflection.

The Dynamics at Work

Abuse of Power or Abuse of Trust?

Abuse of power is a notion that is of crucial importance in any attempt to reach an understanding of abuse, but the expression can lead to confusion, since, in legal terms, abuse of power occurs when someone goes beyond the legal powers conferred on him by law or by his particular role. In religious life, the equivalent would be that of a cellarer giving monks orders in an area that properly comes under the authority of the superior. This is all still at an external level. If a spiritual father were to issue orders to couples regarding their married life,[253] we could speak of abuse of power, but the expression is already verging on the inappropriate, since we would be talking here about something rather different from power; really, it would be more of an illegitimate intrusion into the couple's private life. Spiritual and sexual abuses are really just more extreme versions of the same phenomenon. The idea of "intrusion" is important, but it is not really adequate, since it is dealing with what is occurring at the level of acts, without really touching on the dynamics that underlie this behavior. In their excellent document *Sexual Abuse in a Church Context*,[254] the Swiss bishops begin by defining several fundamental ideas:

---

[253] Of course this does not mean that the priest cannot speak to them of Christian morality.

[254] *Abus sexuels dans le contexte ecclésial: Directives de la Conférence des évêques suisses et de l'Union des supérieurs majeurs religieux de Suisse*, 4th ed. (Fribourg, March 2019), 1.1.2 "Mise à profit d'un ascendant moral."

In the case of abuse of a sexual nature, it is generally a question of a perpetrator exploiting an imbalance of power.[255] He finds himself in a position above that of his victim in various ways, for example on account of his hierarchical position, his role, his age, his emotional independence, his skills, the esteem in which he is held as a pastor. In this sense, we can also speak of abuses of power with regard to "dependent" people.

In this context, then, "abuse of power" means that a person exploits the imbalance of power he has over someone else, in order to exert control over this other person (having him in one's grasp), and to insinuate his way into an intimate relationship with him, either on the spiritual or physical level, in a way that is illegitimate or even criminal, by drawing the person to take part in acts that, in the normal course of events, he would have refused to be involved in. Although it is not entirely unambiguous, the term "abuse of trust" perhaps seems to come closer to the reality of what is happening here, rather than abuse of power, but the most precise term is still that of the Swiss bishops: "exploitation of an imbalance of power."

Trust Can Weaken the Critical Sense

An abuse is not an ordinary crime, given that when it is committed by a priest, a teacher, or a parent, it necessarily occurs in the context of a relationship of trust, relating as it does to what is most intimate and personal to [the victim].[256]

Trust can weaken or totally stall the critical senses. One community had come to hold a high opinion of a young, foreign candidate, who had visited several times to make a retreat and had even thought of entering. The community spontaneously placed its trust in him when he asked, later on, for financial help for a foundation he claimed he had begun in his own country. The total disconnect between the destitution of his community and the enormous, brand

---

[255] Translator's note: This translates the French *ascendant moral,* and is the technical term generally used in the English-speaking safeguarding milieu.

[256] K. Mertes, *Verlorenes Vertrauen. Katholisch sein in der Krise* (Frankfurt: Herder Verlag, 2013), I, II, 2.2.

new building that had apparently been constructed for the novitiate should have been blindingly obvious. It did cross some people's minds, but they had built up such trust in him that this suspicion could not develop into a real question. In the end, it required a doubt expressed by someone outside the community to initiate a process of checking, which revealed that it was all false. In an overall atmosphere of trust, any doubt that might arise is always met with the same instinctive response: *it's just not possible.*

Obviously, we are not advocating mistrust here; indeed, a world without trust would be inhuman. But this example shows that a spirit of healthy criticism can almost be anesthetized by trust, since it can be a very painful thing to express doubts about someone we trust, especially if he has been good to us, which leaves us feeling obliged to him. To entertain doubts seems ungrateful, so our doubts are pushed into the background by a natural defense mechanism. An abuser will exploit this mechanism to the full.

This changes the whole concept of consent. If the father of a family suggests having a sexual relationship with his son, even if the son offers no resistance, we clearly cannot say that it is consensual. Quite simply, he lacks the psychological means necessary to resist, or even really to understand what is going on, and the father may take advantage of this. A priest might induce a woman to have a sexual relationship with him and later say, in his defense, that she consented, since she was an adult. But in reality, she was blinded, as it were, by the inner conviction that this holy man couldn't possibly have bad intentions, so she must simply go along with it.

> The priest made certain gestures just before *Absolution.* And you should know that when a priest is hearing confessions, and we come to the moment of absolution, the priest is acting "in persona *Christi*" — on God's [sic] behalf. I always told myself that when he made these gestures, he was acting in the name of God, so I couldn't have any doubts; this was what God wanted for me. Also, the whole thing took place in a chapel, so there was no challenge to be made.[257]

---

[257] *Religieuses abusées, l'autre scandale de l'Église,* a documentary produced by É. Quentin and M.-P. Raimbault, ARTE productions, March 5, 2019, 45'10".

The priestly aura leads a child or a member of the congregation to think that whatever a priest suggests must be good. It only needs to be wrapped in a few good words, or some spiritual justifications, and the real intention will remain hidden.

> There is something particular about crimes of sexual violence, in that they are committed in the context of a relationship of trust. In this relationship, the perpetrator manages to pass off the act of violence as an act of love, a means of imparting teachings, a punishment that has been merited, or he manages to find some other justification. To be sure, the victim "is aware" of all the details of the abuse, but he is often not yet in a position to be able to call it what it is.[258]

SPIRITUAL JUSTIFICATION

The notion that people use the holiest things to justify the unjustifiable may leave us speechless, but it is a common feature of abuse that occurs in a religious context. Jacques Poujol gives several examples of this: "See it as a blessing from God"; "God has told me that it is a good thing; our love is special"; "It is a privilege for you that I have chosen you"; "By loving me, you are loving Jesus."[259] Acts that are ambiguous or even frankly sinful are presented as an expression of God's love, which needs to be incarnate if it is to reach people. *You need this if you are to discover God's love.* The witness quoted in the appendix heard this as: "My holiness — how shall I put it? — my very raison d'être depends on my allowing myself to be my spiritual father's prostitute." This is really moving in the direction of blasphemy. Pope Benedict XVI wrote:

> A young woman who was a [former] altar server told me that the chaplain, her superior as an altar server, always introduced the sexual abuse he was committing against her with the words: "This is my body which will be given up for you." It is obvious that this woman can no longer hear the very words of consecration without experiencing again all the horrific distress of her abuse.[260]

---

[258] K. Mertes, *La confiance perdue*, II, 5 "Complicité et responsabilité."
[259] J. Poujol, *Abus spirituel, S'affranchir de l'emprise*, 38.
[260] *The Church and Sexual Abuse*, Letter of Benedict XVI, published April 11, 2019.

Abuses in the Religious Life and the Path to Healing

Presenting the abuse as something mystical also provides the easiest way to justify keeping it secret: *What happens between you and me is a special grace, which others would not understand.* This is a simple way of presenting immoral violence as the summit of union with God.

Moments of doubt may spring up, but at such times, the victim may be reassured by the notion that this is an exception to normal rules: "It's allowed for us. The grace that we are living is so high that it sets us above ordinary laws. The degree of love that we have reached allows us to do anything." To be able to persuade the victim with such assertions, the abuser himself has to be convinced [that they are true]. If it was all only a game, the impact would be less. This loss of any consciousness of the harm being done to another makes conversion almost impossible.

The Progressive Approach

In cases of child abuse, the blinding effect of all this is sufficiently powerful for things to happen quickly. With an adult, steps leading toward abusive behavior will be much more cautious; the victim may be prepared according to a process that has been demonstrated in an experiment with frogs. A research team threw a frog into a pan of boiling water. In a reflex action, the frog immediately jumped out of the pan. It was a bit groggy but still alive. The team then took the same frog and put it in a pan of cold water, which was then warmed very gently. The frog ended up cooking, since there was no sudden crossing of a threshold, which might have made it react. It was disarmed little by little, to the point that it lost all awareness of danger. In the witness testimony given in the appendix (included because it is a good illustration of all the elements of sexual abuse),[261] this gradual approach can clearly be seen.

Inappropriate Canonization of Obedience

The abuser's intention is to bring it about that the future victim is totally subject to him and thus really to have the victim in his power. Something that regularly crops up in testimonies is the idea that the vow of obedience requires this total and unconditional submission, particularly to priests: "For a religious sister who had

---

[261] Although there was no sexual relationship, properly so-called.

been abused, the horror of having broken her vow of chastity is mixed with a fear of committing perjury. To denounce a priest is to cause damage to the Church, to violate the vow of obedience she made."[262] This is a tragic error. There is no need to go back over this, as we have discussed it enough already, but it underlines how the notion that the vow of obedience requires unconditional submission can so easily place an all-powerful weapon in the hands of the abuser.[263]

Fear is also invoked to support this so-called obedience. Pascal Ivy, a psychotherapist, quotes this testimony: "The fear that I would be cast down into Hell if I disobeyed him was just too powerful; in the end, I gave into him."[264]

WHAT IS IMPOSSIBLE DOES NOT EXIST

Here we should underline how powerful is the paralyzing effect of abuse. What happens is so crazy, monstrous, and unimaginable that the victim is no longer able to think, or even to leave, to shout, or to defend himself.

Jacques Poujol says the same thing: "Being unable to understand [what is happening], the victim finds him- or herself stupefied, denying the true nature of what he or she is in no position to understand."[265]

The ARTE[266] documentary speaks of a bird that is hypnotized by a snake and is thus unable to fly off, although physically, of course, it had the necessary means.

The author of the testimony given in the appendix writes: "Nothing works any more. It is as though, all of a sudden, I lost my senses. The system crashes. What is impossible cannot exist. It just can't. Nothing happened."

This reaction is highly significant, since it comes into play in all controlling relationships: *It's just not possible,* leading to the corollary: *What is not possible does not exist.* Considered from this distance, it seems nonsensical, but in fact it is a kind of defense mechanism, invoked when a person's world is threatening to collapse. Since this awareness is too much for the psyche to cope with, it erases the facts. *The system crashes.* This was how parents refused to believe

---

[262] *Religieuses abusées, l'autre scandale de l'Église,* 19'00".

[263] See chapter 5.

[264] J. Poujol, *Abus spirituel, S'affranchir de l'emprise,* 38.

[265] Ibid., 30.

[266] Translator's note: ARTE is a French/German TV channel, with a focus on themes related to art/culture.

their children when they were trying to explain what a priest was doing: *You don't speak about priests like that*. It's just not possible, so the child must be talking nonsense. This sort of reaction in response to pedophilia doesn't exist in France anymore, precisely because everyone knows that abuse is possible, but it remains very much present in other areas, within religious life, and to an even greater extent outside of it. One of the goals of this book is to fight against this very reaction, which prevents victims from defending themselves. Knowing that what they are seeing or experiencing is possible and being able to put words to these experiences may help them find the strength and the clarity of mind to say *no*. Likewise, people from outside, whose advice they might seek, will be better able to listen to them.

Feelings of Guilt

This blinding mechanism may also become a source of guilty feelings for the victims, who often reproach themselves for not seeing what was going on, since abusers often induce the victim to cooperate. Or worse still, the abuser may seek to shift all responsibility onto the victim. In the second part of his book *A Listening Heart*, in a section entitled "Victims and Their Tormentors," Msgr. Ravel writes:

> We never forget acts for which we feel responsible. In a way that is quite different from other forms of violence, sexual abuse "shifts" the responsibility for the violence that takes place; it tends to switch the guilt of the tormentor and the innocence of the victim. We often find the victim has feelings of guilt, while the torturer considers himself innocent, boasting a conscience that is entirely at peace. The sorrow of guilt is not where it ought to be. This state of affairs, for which there is plenty of evidence, makes it very difficult for victims to report the crime, since they often feel that reporting the facts of what took place is like confessing to a crime they themselves committed. It is as though, by violating their body, [the abuser] has made their soul unclean. The feelings of guilt generated in the victim last just as long as the feelings of denial in the perpetrator.[267]

[267] L. Ravel, *Comme un cœur qui écoute, la parole vraie d'un évêque sur les abus sexuels* (Paris: Artège, 2019), chap. 3, 68. In chap. 4, entitled "Le mineur victime"

That final observation is crucially important because it shows that, even when the victim is no longer in contact with her tormentor, he still has a certain power over her and an influence over her life, through her memory of the trauma.

This reversal of guilt is not limited to sexual abuse. Jacques Poujol makes the same observation: "Indeed, victims tend to take upon themselves the guilt of those who manipulate them."[268]

> The theologian Lytta Basset has given a good description of the victim's feelings of guilt. When someone is the victim of inexplicable suffering that he doesn't understand, or when his distress is neither understood nor recognized [by others], he blames himself for the suffering. There are often very strong feelings of guilt in victims of spiritual abuse. It is paradoxical: an evil that someone suffers in a state of powerlessness can easily make them feel guilty, particularly if the abuser shifts his own responsibility onto the victim. Feelings of guilt here are deceptive or parasitic; they take the place of another feeling, which would be more appropriate to the situation: anger.[269]

We should note the following words, from the middle of the quotation, "when his distress is neither understood nor recognized," because they describe what we might call a guilt-inducing way of listening to someone. Even if no explicit assertion is made, refusing to consider the genuine possibility that the abuser might be guilty ends up making the blame fall back on the victim.

People close to the victim, who might know some of the details of what took place, may end up leaning in the same direction by asking, "Why didn't she put up any resistance?"

("Minors as victims"), of his book *L'église catholique face aux abus sexuels sur mineurs* (Paris: Bayard, 2019), 191, M.-J. Thiel provides a detailed analysis of victims' experiences and underlines that the influence that "child victims" are under is stupefying, which explains — at least in part — how the aggressor can continue to perpetrate the abuse, by making the child think that he/she is the seducer.

[268] J. Poujol, *Abus spirituel, s'affranchir de l'emprise*, 27.

[269] Ibid., 71. We should remember that Jacques Poujol is speaking about spiritual abuse, not sexual abuse. The similarity in vocabulary used is very striking.

Abuses in the Religious Life and the Path to Healing

Regarding the ARTE documentary,[270] I must say it shook me up enormously. Perhaps all the more when I came to understand that people (and in particular those around me, including my oldest friend, who has since supported me since I left the community) simply didn't understand the phenomenon of control at all. "How did they let this happen to them? I would never have let it happen to me. I'd have given them a good slap, and walked out."

This is how people who have never themselves been caught in the trap of a controlling relationship think.

Controlling Behavior

The business of one person being controlling toward another is complex; today, it has been analyzed by people with appropriate skills, but it remains poorly understood by people at large. And yet we must address it in a rigorous and clear manner, since things are made much easier for predators if potential victims are unaware of how these things work. It has not been a major topic of this book, since the authors consider that this subject lies beyond their competence. It needs to be handled by specialists in another volume, which would complement the present book. Nevertheless, we can share some thoughts, beginning with some witness testimonies.

In a Personal Relationship

The painful testimony that is quoted in the appendix shows how this hold develops. All the dynamics that we have just explained can be found there. It all begins with a great sense of trust. *The painful shipwreck, on the [rocky] shore of my childhood; your light has given meaning to my existence again.* The appeal for *a great docility to the Holy Spirit* contains a clear invitation for her to let herself be guided blindly, to abandon herself totally in trust, which is of course a prelude to the abuse of that trust. *The love that occurs between two people who give their all in the religious life is a divine love.* This allows the submission to the abuser's hidden intentions to be invested with a sacred character, justifying all

---

[270] *Religieuses abusées.*

232

the deviances. *We are joined to one another by a secret. It wouldn't be good to share it, since others won't be able to understand it.* This avoids any prying eyes. *Jesus loves Mary Magdalene in particular, the prostitute, precisely because she can receive His forgiveness fully.* Thus, the exceptional nature of the situation is justified.

He has my mind, my heart, my soul, my spirit, and my body in his hands. This sentence sums up the phenomenon of control in a single line. We should note that the body comes last. The revelations that are coming out at the moment may well concentrate in a particular way on the sexual aspect of abuse, but the sentence would be no less terrible even if we were to omit the last item: *He has in his hands my mind, my heart, my soul, my spirit.* This is slavery without visible chains. The abuser now has total power over the other person, which is evidenced by the short comment: *And I come back to see him. Regularly.*

Someone who has not encountered the phenomenon of control will find this difficult to understand and may interpret this submissiveness as consent; this is a tremendous misunderstanding, making us incapable of really listening to this tragic story.

> It took me fifteen years to resolve this crashing of the system. Fifteen years to accept the pain of recognizing that this person — once a hero in my life — was actually a very sick man. To understand, also, that it hadn't been a case of stupidity on my part but of manipulation, of control, of brainwashing. Even today, more than a quarter of a century later, I am sometimes plunged back into the nightmare, and I feel even more keenly the depth of the betrayal. Other young girls from my time are still held under his sway.

In a Community

The film *Emprise et abus spirituel*[271] gives an excellent summary of the phenomenon of control in a way that is accessible to everybody. In it, Dr. Isabelle Siben explains:

> If spiritual abuse is to take place, there must already be a hold over someone, a manipulative hold, because people are not stupid, and if it were merely a case of ordinary mistreatment, they would realize this

[271] The details of this film are given in an earlier footnote.

and leave. When someone has a hold over you, it is as though someone else's thinking has been injected into you.[272]

Marie-Laure Jannsens calls it "breaking into a person's life by means of a spiritual lever."[273]

Xavier Léger refers to a model that has been developed by the psychologist Steven Hassan "to explain how a person can end up being manipulated, and her identity changed. In his opinion, it is sufficient to control four factors: the member's behavior; her ability to reflect; her emotions; the information she receives."[274] We have already dealt with control over someone's ability to reflect and over the information one receives. We have not spoken quite so much about control of the emotions. Xavier Léger speaks of the practice of "love-bombing"

the new arrival, so he has the feeling of being the center of attention. Love-bombing is a weapon that is particularly effective when people are isolated in emotional suffering. Then, once the bait has been taken, this euphoria gives way progressively to feelings of guilt and terror. Steven Hassan explains that "instilling feelings of guilt is probably the most important emotional lever, when it comes to getting someone to conform and submit."[275]

In a religious community, the practice of the Chapter of Faults[276] can be diverted from its proper purpose and become the forum for public accusations. The same goes for the practice of fraternal correction sessions, which have been abandoned almost everywhere because of their ambiguous nature.

A Strange Likeness

Although the preceding paragraphs (with the exception of the last) considered only the dynamics of sexual abuse, experienced in the intimacy of a two-person

---

[272] I. Siben in *Emprise et abus spirituel.*

[273] M.-L. Janssens, ibid.

[274] X. Léger, *Le statut épistémologique des concepts d'emprise, de manipulation mentale et de secte,* II, II, 1, 38.

[275] Ibid., 42.

[276] A monastic practice, which consists of recognizing one's own faults during a meeting of the whole community.

relationship, we cannot fail to notice that these same dynamics have already been encountered in the context of aberrant, sect-like behaviors in communities and in the context of spiritual abuse. Pope Francis has underlined this connection, particularly in his *Letter to the People of God*,[277] where he constantly places together sexual abuse, abuse of power, and abuse of conscience. Msgr. Ravel shows that, in a certain sense, all these forms of abuse resemble one another:

> By being diverted from its goal, [spiritual] power is hijacked for personal profit, whether it be a case of power (over souls), glory (over communities), or sex (over persons).[278]

The similarity between the various post-traumatic symptoms should cause us to take the consequences of non-sexual control more seriously, since in both cases, these can extend as far as suicidal ideation. It is perhaps a matter of regret that there is currently a tendency to regard abuse within the Church and clerical sexual abuse as the same thing, a tendency that points too exclusively toward clericalism as the major cause. Gathering everything together under a single term (whose connotation is purely masculine, and that covers a range far broader than the problem of abuse) is allowing one part of the problem to elude us. Msgr. Ravel defines clericalism as a sliding away from power *for* the sheep toward power *over* the sheep. Fortunately, not every cleric affected by this sickness is an abuser! We might say that clericalism — understood in a broad sense to include everyone with religious authority: men and women, priests and laypeople — provides the context necessary for abuse to occur. In other words, doing away with clericalism would also eradicate abuse. But a more exact analogy is needed if we are to understand the precise causes of abuse.

Msgr. Ravel puts us on a better footing:

> Spiritual discernment can identify two elements for us, and highlight them as twin conditions associated with the beginning of abusive activity. These are an egocentric mentality and the misuse of spiritual authority.[279]

---

[277] August 20, 2018.
[278] L. Ravel, *Comme un Cœur qui écoute, la parole vraie d'un évêque sur les abus sexuels*, 86.
[279] Ibid., 84.

Abuses in the Religious Life and the Path to Healing

Corrupted spiritual authority is connected with clericalism, but it clearly goes far beyond this. Moreover, this authority has to be misdirected to the point where it is exploited for the sake of the perpetrator's ego. This, indeed, is what the Swiss bishops called *exploitation*.

The commission SOS Abus, which was established by the Community of St. John to investigation abuse, notes that "80 percent of cases of abuse of adults occur between a spiritual father and the person he is accompanying," which emphasizes once again that cases of adult sexual abuse are nearly always preceded by a period of spiritual abuse. Pedophilia is obviously a different matter. Additionally, if 95 percent of cases involve priests, does this really stem from the fact that priests are particularly dangerous because they have a position of greater power, or does it stem from the fact that companionship is something that is essentially practiced by priests? Another observation by the Swiss bishops points in this direction:

> All of those who are engaged in pastoral work and those who have consecrated their lives to God in a particular way enjoy a special status; people seeking advice generally do not distinguish between a pastoral worker who is ordained and one who is not. Many pastoral workers and members of religious communities enjoy a particular prestige as representatives of the institution that is the Church, with its high principles, and people ask them for help and assistance.[280]

It would seem, then, that the chief characteristic here is *the representative of the institution that is the Church*, whether they are ordained or not, whether they are men or women; this is clearly not limited to priests, as people marked out by a special sacrament. Because such people are representatives of the Church, others imagine that they share its *high principles*, which is probably true, and that they put them into practice, which may not be true. This observation is worthy of reflection, since it could help prevent us going down the wrong track.

The idea that priests are the only people responsible for abuse, and all because of their consecrated status, is simply not confirmed by the experience of religious life. Heavily female in character, the religious life does not suffer

---

[280] *Abus sexuels dans le context écclésial, Directives de la Conférence des évêques suisses et de l'Union des supérieurs majeurs de Suisse*, 1.1.4.

from the same [gender] imbalance for which the government of the Church [as a whole] is so often criticized, and therefore this affords good grounds for reflection. Experience confirms that problems relating to power and abuse are just as prevalent among women as they are among men. The way such things manifest themselves is different and, indeed, sexual abuse is very much a majority masculine phenomenon,[281] but spiritual abuse is equally common across both genders. Likewise, there is no significant difference between religious life, properly so-called, and lay movements within the Church. Jacques Poujol's analysis demonstrates that the aberrant behaviors that are found in a Protestant context are identical with those encountered in a Catholic setting, despite the structural differences between these two and the absence of ordained ministers [in some Protestant contexts].[282] The story of the Family of Nazareth leads us to the same conclusions for new forms of committed life within the Church.

It is thus overly simplistic to accuse priests simply because they are priests. It is more shocking when a priest falls [from grace], of course, but it would be better to focus on the danger area where two different factors converge: a close relationship and a position where there is a significant imbalance of power. When these two elements come together, the person who possesses the greater moral authority has much power, which can do real good or real evil.

The problem comes when moral authority gets out of sync with moral values, a fact that is rightly emphasized by the commission SOS Abus. Can we reduce the gap between these two? Obviously, this is a huge question. Some people would like to reduce the moral authority of priests [to eliminate imbalances of power], or certainly to eliminate excesses in this area. Msgr. Ravel emphasizes that the sacralization of priests has been extended quite unduly so

---

[281] In its first report of November 2019, the independent commission concerning sexual abuse in the Church reported that it had received 2,500 testimonies. Ninety-eight percent of the perpetrators of abuse were men, either priests (70 percent) or religious (30 percent). The investigation only dealt with priests and religious, excluding other pastoral workers.

[282] J. Poujol, *Abus spirituel*, chap. 4, "Les systèmes chrétiens abusifs," 35. This text, which was only discovered after most of the present book had been written, provides a nine-page summary, which bears striking resemblance to what has been written here.

that it now covers the whole of a priest's life, almost like a kind of exemption from civil law. Priests and religious are not divine beings. They still have to pay their electricity bills, and keep the rules of the road,[283] just like everyone else. The sacred dimension of a priest's [life] is connected with the sacraments; it does not extend to his whole person or his every word.

> The truth of the priesthood, what we might call its mystery, is related not to a sacralization that is human in nature, but rather to a sacramentalization, which is divine.[284]

It is crucial that we return the mystery of the priesthood to its proper place and stress its very real limitations. Simply to attack the uneven nature of the priest's position of moral authority does not appear to be a viable solution, since it will simply be transferred to others, and the problems will continue. Positions of moral authority are a part of human life; what society could survive without them? Yet there must be a clear connection between moral authority and moral values, and it is crucial that moral authority should flow from a consonance with moral values rather than from a particular role. Of course, seeing abuse being perpetrated by superiors, founders, or those with responsibility for formation is discouraging; is there anything we can still trust in? Marie-Jo Thiel points out the sociological dimension of the increase in abuse cases, and the collapse in moral values, in a chapter she has written entitled "All Those Years of Wrongdoing."[285] We might object that this explanation is insufficient, since serious abuses have taken place in congregations that set great store by traditional moral values. But this apparent contradiction only serves to emphasize that religious are a product of the culture from which they come; simply putting on a habit is not enough to change that. The young people who join our communities bring with them the values of today's world, including its relativism. It is quite possible for them to be seized with enthusiasm at the prospect of rediscovering moral values, and to

---

[283] In his pastoral letter, Msgr. Ravel adds humorously that he has just gained a penalty point on his driver's license.

[284] L. Ravel, "Mieux vaux tard," Pastoral Letter on sexual abuse, August 9, 2018. Special edition of *L'église en Alsace*, September 2018. This pastoral letter contains the structure of the material that would become the book *Comme un cœur qui écoute*.

[285] M.-J. Thiel, *L'Église catholique face aux abus sexuels sur mineurs*, I, C, 62.

speak warmly about it, but their fundamental mindset has yet to be transformed. It seems clear that many tragedies have resulted from a formation that focused too exclusively on the intellectual dimension. Words may weave an illusion, even perhaps for the one who utters them, yet the passions may still need to be evangelized. In short, this is a complex question, and we would be wise not to seek to reduce everything to a single element — clericalism — important as this might be.

Homosexual Abuse in Religious Life

In a religious community, whether male or female, a novice director can exploit his position so as to groom a given novice for a relationship with homosexual overtones, or even for a relationship that is explicitly homosexual in nature. The same is true of a superior, or an older member of the community. In the present climate, where homosexuality is more and more considered a fundamental right, this kind of behavior will doubtless remain very much hidden, even though this, too, is a great violence. The novice has been manipulated, so that his conscience is anesthetized, and made to do things he would never have chosen had he understood what was happening. He entered to give his life to Christ, and the vow of chastity is a fundamental element of consecrating one's life to God alone. And yet here, another religious who has also committed himself by means of this vow is making use of him, effectively destroying in another what he was unable to preserve intact in himself. Someone who has taken the same vow nevertheless ought to realize just what it is he is wrecking and how sacred is that vow. When a victim recognizes [the reality of] what has happened, he will feel he has betrayed their consecration to Christ but also that he himself has been betrayed.

This area is (and will doubtless remain) less well characterized, particularly in the context of women's religious life, where it is the most common form of sexual abuse. And yet the words used by victims [in their testimonies] are far from weak. Having been pursued by an older sister at some length, one young sister reports:

> For a semester I was taking a course of moral, affective, and sexual theology, which covered subjects such as incest, emotionalism, and sexuality. I then became painfully aware that this was exactly what had happened with Sister. The course put words to what I had experienced: incest, violation, sexual aggression, sexual relations that should not occur in the heart of a religious

family. My feelings of guilt were immense, and Sr. Catherine insisted on this guilt. I am certain that Sr. Catherine bears the responsibility for my brokenness. I began to go to pieces; I was starting to lose a lot of weight. I stopped eating, I wasn't sleeping, I began to sink into depression.[286]

All the dynamics we have been explaining can be found here: inducing guilty feelings, the mystical vision, a sense of trust that stifles the critical senses. One night when Andrea had taken refuge beside the tabernacle, hoping to be there on her own, Sr. Catherine finds her there. "She later told me that this prayer together was an extraordinary moment for her, and that, during it, God had approved our relationship." Andrea's state of mental confusion is now complete: "I'm really lost, crushed, I feel that it's not right, but because she tells me the opposite ..." Here again, we have the case of the hypnotized bird.

This all calls for prudence, vigilance, and formation. Telling young people, still full of idealism, that such things can happen in a community is obviously a delicate matter. But on the other hand, they are not children, and there is no reason why learning a few basics of analysis or even of healthy self-defense should be extraordinary. The novice director remains the key figure here since, if he or she is implicated [in the abuse], the whole formation program will be rendered ineffectual. The example given in the following chapter, about a case where a warning was ignored, demonstrates that being aware of danger is an effective protection, since it allows us to read signs that are not necessarily all that visible, whereas the automatic instinct that says "*It's impossible*" leads to a situation where even the clearest signs are ignored.

In present-day culture, which has less and less time for the idea that true friendship is possible without having a physical expression, clear emotional formation should help people to discern and to identify things done in the name of fraternity that may be ambiguous in nature. Anyone who has come to understand that chastity concerns not just the sexual aspect but rather the quality of the whole relational dimension of life should be able to distinguish between what is appropriate and what is not. In the end, it always boils down to the same temptation: that of wanting to possess the other person.

[286] B. de Dinechin and X. Léger, *Abus spirituel et dérive sectaire dans l'Église,* (Paris: Mediaspaul, 2019), 146–147, 166.

11

Victims

Putting Victims — Past, Present, and Future — in the Center

The fact that awareness of the challenge posed by pedophilia has been so slow to develop shows how long the journey is toward open acknowledgement of the harm done, of the responsibility we might have for this, and of the courageous decisions we might have to take. This process can be impeded by various powerful forces. On this subject, Fr. Klaus Mertes gives us a reflection drawn from lived experience.[287] As a school principal from 2008 to 2011, he became aware of abuse perpetrated against children that took place from 1970 to 1980. Because the witness testimonies corroborated each other, he sent a letter to the six hundred pupils from this period. When this was given to the press, it caused an immense media storm.

> Dear former pupils,
>
> In the last few years, several of you have contacted me to inform me that you were victims of sexual abuse perpetrated by certain Jesuits at School X. The abuse seems to have taken place throughout the 1970s and into the 1980s. I have been shaken to the core and filled with shame to learn of these horrific and brutal acts, which seem not to have been isolated, but repeated occurrences. Moreover, some of the victims felt that certain people preferred to avert their gaze, rather than fulfill their

---

[287] K. Mertes, *Verlorenes Vertrauen. Katholisch sein in der Krise* (Frankfurt, Herder, 2013).

duty to protect the victims. For this reason, as the school's representative, above all I ask pardon of all former students for what the school has inflicted upon them.

As I have spoken with some of the victims, I have come to understand better what deep wounds sexual abuse can leave in the lives of young people, and how a person's whole life can be overshadowed and damaged for decades. At the same time, some victims noted how liberating it had been to be able to begin speaking about what they had experienced, even though this happened in the distant past. It seems some wounds cannot be healed by time alone.[288]

The analysis set out by Fr. Mertes in the first part of his book is of great interest. It shows how widespread is the temptation to give up listening to victims, even among those who — with the best of intentions — vociferously denounce abuse and throw themselves headlong into the work of prevention. From that first press conference, one question was repeatedly put to Fr. Mertes: *What have you done in the way of prevention?* The letter had been sent ten days earlier and had been published the same day!

In the context of a discussion with the father of one of the students, it became clear to me how a hasty activism in relation to prevention could begin to look like evasion. The father protested that he was not concerned about victims of former times, but about the young people of today. Quite apart from the fact that this is, of course, an artificial distinction, this observation helped me realize that, because of its emotional import, the whole question of prevention could lead to a certain detachment from the victims.... This is why, in the very first months, I took the decision not to put prevention at the center of everything, but to emphasize instead the need to listen to the testimonies of victims.[289]

A personal encounter with victims matters enormously to them.

---

[288] See www.tagesspiegel.de/berlin (abbreviated text).
[289] K. Mertes, *La confiance perdue. Être catholique en temps de crise,* I, II, 2.2, 33.

What victims need is to be heard in their suffering, to be recognized as innocent, not guilty, and to be validated by realizing just how much they are valued by those who are seeking to accompany them.[290]

This personal encounter is also of great importance for our own understanding. In various recent meetings, those present have indicated that what impressed them most were the testimonies of victims. We might ask: why has this been so long coming? Probably because a little alarm bell sounds somewhere deep down inside our minds: "Be careful; if you meet them, you won't emerge unscathed." This is perfectly true, as long as the words "meet" and "listen" actually mean something in the context of such meetings; for if our approach — conscious or unconscious — is that the victims are basically ill-intentioned, we will never become capable of empathizing with them.

Msgr. Ravel shares the same perspective.

Real people: these are the way forward for the Church. Indeed, this is precisely what those in positions of responsibility had in mind when they were dealing with [allegations of] abuse that came to them, only they were thinking of priests first and foremost. Eventually, very much later, they turned to the victims, largely to ensure they kept quiet. The second conversion, to which we are being invited, reverses this approach. Its goal is to ensure the victims take first place in all our hearts. This is precisely what was lacking previously. This reversal of perspective is crucial in the work the Church is undertaking on itself. If this doesn't happen, we will inevitably slip back into the same old ways of doing things.[291]

The last observation ought to be underlined, since it is not only true for cases of sexual abuse but for all forms of deviance in the religious life. Wanting to reform an institute, even after an apostolic visitation, without wanting to walk the painful but necessary path of really listening to victims, exposes an enormous weakness in the process, and it leaves us with the fear that at some point we will go back to the same old ways of doing things.

[290] J. Poujol, *Abus spirituel, S'affranchir de l'emprise*, 9.
[291] L. Ravel, *Comme un cœur qui écoute*, p. 44, text abbreviated.

There is yet another reaction that involves a kind of role-reversal, with the accused taking on the role of the victim.

> Feeling that we ourselves have been wronged, we can lose sight of who the real victims are. A feeling of self-pity asserts itself: "We are the victims of a press campaign, a campaign intended to persecute the Church."[292]

This instinct to concentrate on the perpetrators and forget the victims has even manifested in the press when it reported abuse, since it has more often put the abusers at the center of the story, rather than the victims. Often the victim's key characteristic [in the eyes of the press] is that they were victims of a priest, whereas, if they had been victims of a teacher in gym class, they would have been of much less interest. Even if the situation has been in some sense reversed — formerly, the victims were forgotten so as to protect the priest; more recently, people can be so caught up with the business of accusing the priest that they, too, lose sight of the victims — the dynamic remains the same: the abuser is more important than the victim. This can even be seen in various proposals aimed at prevention, such as reducing abusers to the lay state. This is not a meaningless thing to do, of course, but who is going to show concern for the victims that this man could go on to abuse, now that he has been stripped of all supervision? Isn't this a bit like washing our hands of the problem? Too bad for future victims once [abusers] are no longer members of the Church. Msgr. Ravel has had sufficient courage to emphasize this point:

> We often hear, "The only solution is to defrock them! They should be 'reduced' to the lay state" ... For a bishop, it would no doubt be a great comfort to find himself relieved [of such a problem], and to set these people loose with no further barriers or checks. But is this reasonable or responsible?[293]

A conversion is thus required, and this is never an easy process. We would prefer to dodge the painful process of listening to the raw stories of those who

---

[292] K. Mertes, *La confiance perdue. Être catholique en temps de crise,* I, II, 2.2, p.30.
[293] L. Ravel, *Comme un cœur qui écoute,* 89.

have suffered at the hands of institutions or people that we love and respect: the Church, the community, the school, a priest, a religious. Much suffering could have been avoided if listening to victims had been placed at the center of things from the very start. Here is a text written by one victim following a meeting with the apostolic visitors conducting a visitation in her former community:

> I met the two of them in Paris. How carefully they listened; what fine judgment they had; how human they were, and full of fraternity. To be listened to at long last, heard, believed. All of a sudden to be rid of the stigma of being the "odious" little sister who had the temerity to leave, report what was happening, and finally to feel liberated, rehabilitated — recognized. Today, thirty-five years since I left, I still feel the pain of it — it is an invisible pain — a wound still there in my innermost self, hidden away, but that still brings me to tears. Who can understand this wounded love? "Set me as a seal upon your heart." And I say to him: "Set yourself as a seal upon my heart." I will die with this unspeakable suffering.

In the experience of Fr. Mertes, this real listening, a listening that is ready to believe, can bring peace.

> With respect to those former students [who had borne witness to the violence to which they had been subjected], I felt above all an enormous gratitude. Even today, I am still touched by the trust that was placed in me when meeting these pupils on January 14, 2010.[294] And that includes those times where there were differing points of view or conflicts. As well as grief, deception, and anger, I discovered, through this trust, a strong feeling of affection toward the school, and even toward us — the Jesuits — an affection of which we were unworthy, as the errors of the past have demonstrated. *Mutatis mutandis* the same has been true of many conversations, in which people who suffered violence at the heart of the Church confided in me. It is all the more painful for such people

---

[294] Three former students had come to tell their story, and this is what convinced Fr. K. Mertes of the gravity of the situation. Some days later (on January 20), he sent the letter.

to confide in someone [about what happened to them], because they still attach importance to the Church or to their old school.[295]

And yet it is true that we must not imagine that everything will be idyllic.

When they at last feel able to speak, victims are filled with unpleasant feelings — in this case directed at those who represent the system, since they happen to be within reach. I had of course prepared myself for that in theory, but the violence of the mistrust being aimed at me was disconcerting.[296]

The provincial had also adopted a clear position with respect to the victims.

During the press conference on February 1, 2010, Stefan Dartmann declared: "We are grateful to the victims for having spoken out." This goes for all the brothers, sisters, children, and parents of victims whom I have met in the course of many meetings. Heavy burdens were offloaded, people's life stories were brought out into the light once more, a mutual trust was discovered, healing and reconciliation took place in various respects — sometimes after weeks or even months.[297]

However painful their experiences may have been, the fact of finally being believed represents an enormous relief for victims, since they can at last let the weight of guilty feelings fall away.

Believing Victims

Fr. Klaus Mertes astutely explains why it is difficult to believe victims: it is because it involves *believing in the unbelievable*. In his reflection on "Complicity and Responsibility,"[298] he writes:

Discovering abuse involves, in principle, having to recognize that, in retrospect, there were various signs that we didn't recognize as clear signs of abuse, though these were recognizable as such.

[295] K. Mertes *La confiance perdue. Être Catholique en temps de crise,* I, II, 2.2, 36.
[296] Ibid.
[297] Ibid.
[298] Ibid., I, II, 5, 47.

Referring to things that took place in the school where he had himself studied, he writes these lines, with impressive clarity:

> We didn't want to believe our gut feeling, which seemed far too serious
> to us.... Despite everything, since the revelations of 2010 it is clear that
> I was already an accomplice, first as a fellow pupil and then as a Jesuit;
> I had "gut feelings" that I didn't follow.
>
> For as long as I don't know what I know, I don't yet have to assume
> any responsibility. Once I discover my own complicity, even in retro-
> spect, I must take up this responsibility. I can't simply take myself out of
> the equation, by asserting that "I didn't know," unless this is really true.[299]

The difficulty comes from the fact that victims shake the very world in which we live.

> At the end of the eighties, I was confronted by an experience of abuse
> in a family context. I witnessed a young person who had been rejected
> by his [extended] family, because he had begun to complain about the
> violence taking place within the family.... Why is an adolescent, or even a
> child, exposed to so much violence, when he is seeking to defend himself
> from it? The answer is: because people are afraid of victims. Victims have
> a story to tell, a story that is going to disturb the "normality" of a group,
> a family, a school, a society. Listening to a victim — not as an observer,
> or as someone accompanying or caring for [the victim], but rather as
> someone implicated and very much part of the equation — means
> opening oneself to a point of view different from one's own, letting go of
> one's misconceptions or "myths," of a sense of what is "normal"; it means
> ridding ourselves of the pride that comes from a sense of belonging. It
> is a painful process. Of course, deciding to reduce victims to silence is
> a possible alternative approach, one that avoids the pain altogether.[300]

There is nothing simple about believing victims, especially if we have no real understanding of the kind of abuse they are talking about, abuse that

[299] Ibid.
[300] Ibid., I, II. 1, 20.

seems in itself *impossible*. Thankfully, this situation has changed greatly in recent decades because of the revelations [of abuse]. It is simply no longer possible not to know that abuse exists, and this should make it easier to give proper attention to disclosures we receive. We must hope that we have seen the last of the instinct to reject disclosures, as happened in the following two examples.

- This is the official response of one congregation, relating to victims whose testimony had become public: "What does it mean for them today, before God and before human society, to hold to such deceitful and defamatory statements, relating to situations that, though they have an element of factual accuracy, are divorced from reality, due to the malicious intent behind them?"
- Two former novices of another congregation had complained about the actions of a novice master. An investigation was mounted, and they received this response: "While I accept that your letters were inspired by a feeling of suffering after you left X, it was clear that they had been written in a spirit of protest and revenge. Anyone coming to the case fresh could easily tell that many of the things mentioned had been viewed through the lens of malicious interpretation. These facts were incorrect, or given disproportionate importance, or taken out of their real context." Some years later, a new and more serious allegation came to light, and this time it was beyond doubt. The problem reported by the two former novices was real, and further victims could have been spared had their testimony been taken seriously.

Given that these are two very different situations, the similarity in the use of terms is striking:

- Deceitful ideas/incorrect facts
- Detached from reality/taken out of their real context
- Ill intent/malicious interpretation

One sentence in particular should be emphasized: *Anyone coming to the case fresh could easily tell that many of the things mentioned had been viewed through the lens of malicious interpretation.* This is a good example of the instinctive response to an accusation, even though it is very measured in its expression. Rereading the texts of the disclosures today, we see no protest, no spirit of vengeance, no malice, just two people who are trying to alert someone to a danger. It is only the defensive interpretation that imparts a negative character to them.

An important detail supports [the interpretation] that people can have a fear of seeing [what is really going on]. In the second case quoted above, the disclosures were followed by an investigation. But the only people to be interviewed were the local superior and the novice master concerning whom the allegation had been made, and their response was deemed conclusive. Those leading the investigation did not contact the complainants personally.

Really listening to victims, then, is hard, and anyone listening needs to be aware that he won't fully understand. Unless he has himself experienced the same thing, he will always fall short of grasping just how deep certain wounds can be, whether we are talking about sexual violence or spiritual violence, which is perhaps even more difficult to understand. One religious who left his congregation (which had been placed under the care of assistants appointed by Rome) writes:

> How could we make the apostolic assistants understand that it was not possible simply to boil everything down to "dysfunctionalities," which after all left only the tiniest wounds in the souls and spirits of those who had suffered because of them, wounds that in any event were easily healed?
>
> What happened was much more serious. We lived trapped in this situation for years, particularly me, because I was very close to X and left to his mercy.
>
> The assistants don't know what it's about, they can't even imagine; they have no idea of the trauma caused by living under someone else's control for long years ... It simply doesn't fit into their intellectual or spiritual categories; it is beyond their usual realm of thought. When it comes down to it, that's only to be expected: this is the business of specialists. Today, there have been enormous advances in the field of trauma psychology. If they want to help those who have been harmed by the religious life, they should accept help from those who have the experience necessary to treat this sort of violence. Otherwise, they will simply add isolation to loneliness.

Abuses in the Religious Life and the Path to Healing

The last observation is correct. When there have been instances of controlling behavior, there is no doubt that a multidisciplinary approach and specialist help can be indispensable for the victim — and also for those in the community who are accompanying him. Nobody can be competent in every field — that is why the more psychological aspects have not been covered in this book, except for one or two commonsense observations. It would call for further skills, at the same time more technical (trauma psychology) and more focused on accompanying communities and victims.

Superiors and bishops who may receive disclosures need to be trained in learning how to read them, or we might say how to decipher them. The example given above shows that the superior reading them was rather like the person he described: an *uninitiate*. That the violence that had been suffered should be reflected in the feelings expressed and the words used is hardly surprising. How are we supposed to speak the unspeakable? Indeed, when those who have attempted to speak out have for years met with a brick wall, the sense of indignation only becomes more pronounced. Are we surprised that many victims no longer believe in the institutional Church?

The Long Calvary of Victims

In her book *Étouffée, récit d'un abus spirituel et sexuel*, Sophie Ducrey describes the endless battles she underwent in order to get people to recognize that she had suffered abuse and to have the predator removed from situations where he could cause more harm. It is a poignant book, where a horror of denial and an underlying love for the Church mingle together, like a quiet undertone that nonetheless occasionally bursts to prominence with words full of emotion:

> O Church, my Church, I beg you: learn how to recognize deviants, corrupt priests, so as to avoid becoming a complete object of derision with no credibility left.[301]

And then, more obviously, the anguish of thinking that while there are young girls in danger, no one seems to want to lift a finger to do anything. There is something terrifying about this "doing nothing," when one has oneself endured

---

[301] S. Ducrey, *Étouffee; récit d'un abus spirituel et sexuel* (Paris: Tallandier, 2019), 147.

the horror. The book was written in 2012, but no publisher could be found. "There were different anxieties: my story was not credible;[302] they were running the risk of being accused of wanting to harm the Church; Catholic bookshops will boycott the book, and so on."[303] When the taboo was finally beginning to lift seven years later, all six publishers to whom she offered the book accepted it. Without setting out to do so, the text functions as a school of listening for those in positions of responsibility, and one they will find more effective than theoretical advice.

Sophie Ducrey describes her journey briefly in the testimony quoted in the appendix, from which the following passage is taken:

When someone decides to speak out, the different forms of pressure can be suffocating. At times, they plunged me into a distress I had never before known. They made use, by turns, of:

- Time; they pray and discern until the victim is exhausted.
- The totally hypocritical faking of a feeling of horror, of understanding, of compassion.
- Contrition and asking forgiveness (so as to be able to have peace [themselves], and then get on with their lives).
- If the victim carries on complaining, there is relativizing and doubt.
- Then the inducement of guilty feelings. "How can you want to do such harm to the community, and the whole Church?" or "You are doing the devil's work of dividing people!"
- Lastly, threats, or perverse thinking: "He didn't rape you, to the best of my knowledge, so there must have been some failing on your part. Have you asked his forgiveness for that?"
- And when it's not manipulation, it's fear: "If I do anything, they will finish me off."
- If the victim has the extraordinary courage needed to go and speak to bishops (and so to betray her community), she is stunned to

---

[302] What harm this reaction must cause when someone has actually experienced something in their very body! This is yet another example of the reaction "what is not possible does not exist."
[303] S. Ducrey, *Étouffée*, 209.

find things are no better here. And if one of them does stand up to tell it like it is and condemn [the behavior], the Vatican settles matters, in my own case at least, where my abuser's first victim had dared to go to Rome twenty years previously.

This sad story has, alas, been too often repeated. What must we do, then, if we are to learn how to hear? Amidst all the consideration, at present, of prevention or zero tolerance, is this question given enough attention? And yet it is of crucial importance when we see, in Sophie Ducrey's account, numerous examples of an attentiveness that does not really seem to involve paying attention. Had she not been supported by a loving husband, by family and friends, would she have been able to see the thing through? Why do so many churchmen not know how to listen to [accounts of] suffering? Shouldn't the Church be an expert in this area?

Learning how to listen to victims' stories, to build relationships with them, to accompany them, and to react correctly of course requires a specific formation, and we might well wish it featured more prominently on the agenda in the current situation. Sophie Ducrey had to wait thirty-five years to be heard; thirty-five years ... that is a long time.

Also long is the fifty-year period during which Marcial Maciel[304] managed to dupe everybody, though not without the connivance of others, whose guilt or innocence it is not our business to determine. Xavier Léger gives a detailed account in his thesis.[305] Only fifteen years after the foundation [of the Legionaries of Christ], two Legionaries (including the Vicar General of the Congregation) sent letters to the Mexican religious authorities, warning them about the situation. Sensing that the wind was beginning to turn, Maciel promulgated the *vow of charity*.[306] In 1956, he was suspended from his duties. The visitor wrote a damning report. The Congregation for Religious produced an overview, which was also damning. After various twists and turns, Fr. Mozicarelli, responsible for apostolic visitations, ignored these two official reports and suggested a

---

[304] Who in fact combines the roles of sexual and spiritual abuser.

[305] X. Léger, *Le statut épistémologique des concepts d'emprise, de manipulation mentale et de secte*, 56-66.

[306] See page 86.

solution that basically exonerated Maciel. From now on, he presented himself as a "victim of persecution," and he was able to pass unscathed through all the accusations made, and this for more than forty years.

What conclusions should we draw from this for the religious life? It is very difficult for someone from outside a community to understand what goes on within it. The façade may be carefully maintained, and dysfunctionalities may be difficult to pick up if we have no knowledge of these mechanisms and lack the means necessary to interpret various symptoms. But these days we can no longer say, "I didn't know such a thing could happen." A Dominican Father writes:

> There are those for whom such testimonies are largely inventions, the fruit of various resentments, destined purely to do damage to a particular community; and then there are those for whom the consistency of such testimonies, all coming from different backgrounds, shows them to be true.
>
> As for me, I confess quite openly that I am one of those who believe the witnesses, firstly because I know some of them, and secondly (and perhaps above all) because I know how much it costs them to report [what happened]; they know that they run the risk of being rejected, held in contempt, challenged. Referring to them, I speak of a "double hurt": the hurt of having suffered in the community they left, and the hurt of continuing to suffer (sometimes even more so) when they are not heard, or even subjected to vile judgments. Real courage is needed to give evidence in such circumstances, even under an assumed name! Anyone who thinks or says the opposite can never have met a victim.

We are no longer able to take these testimonies lightly and thus to rub salt into the wound. Please God, perhaps the journey — though far too long — that the Church has made from covering up sexual abuse to recognizing it will bear fruit in religious life with reference to the non-sexual abuse that is also committed at the heart of the Church.

A few pieces of practical advice may be useful, though the list is clearly not exhaustive:

- *The consistency of such testimonies, coming from different backgrounds, shows them to be true.* Coherence between testimonies of different sources or styles is a convincing sign. If there is some sort of manipulation, the different testimonies will be too alike for them to be honest.

• *Different views.* Do not keep it to yourself when a letter comes in making an accusation concerning a member of the congregation or the community. Ask advice from people who have suitable wisdom about, independence from, and experience of this sort of problem. A superior who receives such a letter may feel he himself is in the firing line in a sense, at least because of the implicit criticism that he has allowed such things to happen. This can give rise to a defensive reaction, which kills all sense of objectivity. And this reaction will be the stronger if the superior, even unconsciously, feels slightly guilty. Beware of the response that "what is impossible cannot exist."

• *Listen to the person who has been accused*, of course, but not only to him; listen as well to the one who is making the accusation, alongside someone else if you can, so that you can compare impressions afterward. You might think that this goes without saying, but it is precisely what did not happen in the example given above. Also, the quality of the listening is the most important thing. A suspicious kind of listening is bound to lead nowhere and may even cause harm.

From the victim's point of view, it is advisable that she get some help in putting her text together, so that it is not only comprehensible but readable. When pain and anger are strong, if this passes wholesale into the text, it runs the risk of being very difficult for an uninitiated person to interpret. After all, if we write something, it is so that we can be understood, so we might as well give it our best shot. It can also require prior self-discernment, a discernment that we cannot undertake on our own.

A Heart That Is Sympathetic toward Victims

When a community or a congregation becomes aware of complaints, the initial reaction to people coming forward can be to treat them as a threat to be warded off. So, the inner response is defensive by nature as a result. Even when the situation has moved on, and a process of redress is in place, a change in the way people coming forward are viewed — these can now be called victims — is only gradual. The instinct not to trust does not give way that easily.

Welcoming criticism continues to go hand in hand with a concern to protect the community. At this stage, the situation resembles the one we discussed in the context of sexual abuse. It is not the victims who are at the center of things but the perpetrator, even if the concern is to heal. And because the remedy is a somewhat bitter one, as soon as those coming forward have quieted down, and external interventions are over, it can begin all over again because the real problem hasn't even been touched upon. The heart of the problem is not that there are people coming forward *per se* — people that continue to be regarded by some as having been malicious enough to speak out — it is rather that there are people who have suffered, who are suffering, or who will continue to suffer. Those coming forward are a part of this, but they are not the only ones. So long as we remain at this stage, we may try to fix things up a bit, but we run the risk of merely papering over the cracks without actually putting things right.

We need a real path of conversion, and we should expect it to be arduous. Conversion means an "about-turn," a complete about-turn in the way we look at victims, not as a threat, but rather as people who have suffered because of members of the institute or because of the institute itself. The day when our heart is touched by the unjust sufferings of these wounded members, the day when the twofold intention to repair what can be repaired and to change what must be changed is real and active, the day when a true compassion for victims comes to birth (this *com-passion, suffering-with* that involves caring to the point of anguish), will be the day that marks the point of no return, and healing will really have begun. That day — not before.

One of the ways in which this conversion will be manifest will be showing gratitude toward those who have spoken out and who have pointed out a serious sickness that, without their intervention, would have continued to get worse — provided, of course, that it is a real gratitude that comes from the depths of the heart. This is the path traced out by Msgr. de Moulins-Beaufort, president of the Conference of French Bishops, in his speech at the end of the annual meeting of the French bishops at Lourdes in November 2019.

> The process of upheaval, which is what conversion is, must begin with ourselves. We undertake it thanks to those who have been victims. What they have revealed, concerning those acts that certain priests committed,

has brought to light, in the words of one bishop, an infection that was secretly sapping the life out of the body of the Church.

We have come to understand the victims are not asking for compassion, nor for compensation for their sufferings. They want the truth. Their stories help us to understand this: they have suffered and, often, they are still suffering because of the acts they endured, but they also suffer because of silence, because of blindness, a blindness that was sometimes even voluntary on the part of people around them, including within the Church and among church authorities. We commit ourselves, each one of us, to re-establishing contact with those victims we know, to showing them concretely that we recognize the double cause of this suffering.... We are aware that no process can make up for what happened or what they have lived through. We ask, with humility, to be allowed to start rebuilding our relationship.

Chastity, Justice, and Mercy

All of our research has brought us back to the question of chastity, in the strongest sense: the refusal to take possession of another person for one's own ends, and the refusal to practice the idolatry that is taking possession of God for one's own ends. There is no doubt that work needs to continue along the lines sketched out here.

This passage, which concludes the introduction of the document *Dérives sectaires dans des communautés catholiques,*[307] is all the more striking because it is not about sexual abuse as such.[308] *Using someone else for my own ends:* this is what sits at the very heart of abuse; it is diametrically opposed to the path Christ showed us, the path of self-giving, out of love.

The text goes on: "Likewise, we must continue to reflect on the remarkable dialogue between justice and mercy, the initial basis of which the reader can find here." Msgr. Ravel's book was published three months after the publication of this document. In the book, he offers a lengthy and commendable treatment of this question. Since we cannot reproduce the full text here in all its richness, we

---

[307] Sect-like tendencies in Catholic communities.
[308] *Documents épiscopat,* 2018, no. 11.

will at least try to give some idea of its overall structure. The following paragraph is a series of quotations from chapters 5 and 6 of the book.[309]

> The human channel of justice is our only access to the divine ocean of mercy. Justice allows us to give victims their dignity back, despite their wounds, and to reform perpetrators, despite the judgment against them. If there is a great risk of silencing justice in order to be merciful, then the risk of ignoring mercy in order to content ourselves with justice is no less significant. Some are terrified by justice, but there are also those who are irritated by mercy. Chronologically speaking, mercy follows justice. For all that, unlike other processes, where the second stage absorbs and destroys the first, simply by happening after it, mercy never abolishes justice. Mercy is not a kind of recompense arising from a justice that is slipshod, equivocal or imperfect. There is a way of talking about mercy that wrecks justice. Unlike the first criminal, the good thief does not insist that the demands of justice should be set aside, nor does he mock God's salvation ("Save yourself and us too"). He implores mercy and receives it precisely because he recognizes that his condemnation is just. There is no difference between the crimes of the two thieves. But one of them, by accepting justice and recognizing that he is in the presence of Christ on the Cross, turns "naturally" toward mercy, whereas the other, holding justice in contempt and mocking Christ, "naturally" shuts himself off from mercy.
>
> To be effective, the mercy granted to the sinner has to be preceded by justice imposed upon the criminal. Justice is about actions, whereas mercy is more about the person. Justice is bound up with actions (and proven facts), even if it condemns the person responsible for those actions. Mercy concentrates on the person, even if it purifies that person of the actions for which he is responsible. These purposes are not the same, but they are not opposed.

Of course, we must not forget to show mercy to the victims; they are the ones who have the clear right to it. "A man went down from Jerusalem to Jericho." This

---

[309] L. Ravel, *Comme un cœur qui écoute, la parole vraie d'un évêque sur les abus sexuels*, 103, 104, 150, 153–157.

man's neighbor is "the one who showed him mercy."[310] Bandaging wounds, as far as possible, is the first duty of mercy. In the realm of sexual abuse, we must hope that the necessary process of conversion has taken place, since there was a time when people spoke of mercy toward the aggressor, suggesting even that the victim ought to forgive him, though in practice this amounted to leaving the victim half-dead at the side of the road. It is less clear that this conversion has occurred in the domain of spiritual abuse; of course, every case is unique. One of the best signs of the [Church] community's healing will be the mercy it shows victims, a mercy that is not content simply with words but which takes the trouble to pour out oil and wine on the wounds, taking care of the injured person and being concerned for her future, a mercy in the image of Christ's mercy.[311]

Of course, we must not apply more generally what only relates to a minority. We need also to be careful to remember the countless communities that live their life quietly, following a path of conversion, service, and love with a clear awareness of their limitations. But when one member of the body is seriously ill, the whole body is sick, and we cannot simply remain indifferent if young people who had placed their trust in the Church and in religious life end up with their trust betrayed and their life in pieces. By the same token, even if we have had no active part in the tragedy, we still need to try to put things right, show compassion, and start rebuilding.

---

[310] Luke 10:30–37. The Greek term *eleos* is the same one used in the *Magnificat*, Luke 1:50–54, and about Elizabeth, Luke 1:58.

[311] Various Fathers of the Church read the parable in this way: the Samaritan is Christ, the injured person is sinful humanity, the inn is the Church, and the expression *when I pass by again* stands for the Parousia.

12

Some Elements of Reform and Prevention

A Clear View

Even communities are allowed to hope. In recent years, the Community of St. John has given a remarkable example of clear-sightedness and has worked courageously at reform. The first report of the SOS Abus commission, set up by the community itself, bears witness to this clear-sightedness; it gives us a clear view of the situation, allowing us to contemplate, in a practical way, the remedial measures that had to be provided, as well as the preventative measures that needed to be put in place.[312] [In the report,] the causes [of abuse] are analyzed uncompromisingly. There was a lack of definition in the relationship of spiritual companionship, which had become confused with that of friendship, whose boundaries are somewhat blurry. There was a lack of supervision, or if there was supervision, it was seriously incompetent. There was insufficient human formation and such a lack of affective maturity that the brothers were not able to live the demands of their vow of chastity. An accent was placed upon intellectual formation, to the detriment of self-knowledge, or of spirituality, which became detached from its proper roots in the human person. There was insufficient preparation for the exercise of authority and clericalism; both of these led to abuses of power, whether in the form of intruding on people's consciences, or in terms of an abusive understanding of obedience.

There then follows a reflection on the structures present in abusive situations, since indeed it is possible to observe, in the relationship between different

---

[312] *Premier rapport d'activité de la Commission SOS abus* at the General Chapter [of the Community of St. John], May 2019.

cases of abuse, a kind of "abusive system" at work, which can be present either in a diffuse way or in a rather focused and serious way, depending on the individual cases.

> In a more diffuse form, it is possible to find a lack of formation in spiritual companionship; particularly, there is evidence of a lack of formation in psychology and self-knowledge, especially acceptance of one's sexuality.
>
> Speaking more precisely, there is also a positive causality where abuse leads to abuse. In several cases, someone providing spiritual companionship who had himself committed abuse was unable to give appropriate guidance to the person being accompanied, when he was close to committing abuse himself. In some cases, a brother who had been abused himself became an abuser, repeating the usual acts and the justifications for them.[313]

This analysis is worth quoting, both because of the quality of its content and the example that it gives of the capacity for reform that a community can find, if it allows itself to be examined and guided by the Church.

A certain abusive system. The word "system" often crops up in testimonies describing aberrant behavior in communities. Most often, the process of arriving at this sort of clear thinking does not happen overnight; at first, the most natural thing is to accuse just a few guilty parties. The recognition [that an abusive system might be at work] is therefore a sign that the process of diagnosis has matured, which is significant in light of the previously quoted observation made by Jacques Poujol: "In the context of an abusive system, even someone who is not an abuser but finds himself in such a group is not immune from operating like an abuser."[314] The fact that such an unconscious tendency to drift toward abuse exists calls for a clear, public analysis of the abusive system, if it is to be prevented. This is why it was both courageous and clear-headed on the community's part to place this report on its website, demonstrating the clear will to get out of this situation and to provide themselves with the means to do so.

---

[313] Ibid.

[314] Chap. 1, *Les systèmes chrétiens abusifs.*

The first public recognition of the abuse by Fr. Marie-Dominique Philippe[315] occurred in the general chapter of 2013. Six years later, the general chapter of 2019 agreed that there needed to be a real process of refoundation [of the community].

> It is important to establish a distinction between the charism of the founder and the charism of the institute itself, which is the only thing approved by the Church.... If a charism is a way of life according to the Holy Spirit, Fr. M.-D. Philippe cannot be a model for this way of life because of the serious abuse he has committed. Consequently, the brothers no longer refer to him as a norm for the purposes of living out their charism today.[316]

It took only six years to succeed in finding the right stance with respect to a founder who, until that point, had been almost the only point of reference; that is impressive. Calling a founder into question is always a difficult process, and the brothers of the Community of St. John provide us with a good example, showing us that it can be done, without the community collapsing. They have been working with the Church for years — they invited Msgr. José Rodriguez Carballo[317] to their last chapter. There is still a long journey ahead of them, but the direction of travel has been mapped out as a result of some bold decisions:

> We no longer wish to make Fr. M.-D. Philippe the point of reference for our formation. In the light of the spiritual experience of the brethren and the teaching of the Church, the Rule of Life and our proper law will be revised. Within our priories, any photographs of Fr. M.-D. Philippe will be removed from public areas, and from common areas within the enclosure. Likewise, for the time being, his books will not be sold in

---

[315] Translator's note. Marie-Dominique Philippe (1912–2006) was a French Dominican friar who founded the Community of St. John in 1975. Complaints of sexual abuses perpetrated by Philippe began to emerge in 2013.

[316] Final message of the second session of the General Chapter, November 1, 2019.

[317] Secretary of the Roman Congregation for Institutes of Consecrated Life and Societies of Apostolic Life (CICLSAL).

our monasteries, and his audio teachings will no longer be circulated outside the community, pending a process of discernment.

We have permission to hope, then; with the express condition that we accept the help that the Church can offer, a way of truth and reform can be found.

How Can We Escape This Imprisonment?

An abbot has reflected on this question.

It is a very delicate matter, and of course no two communities function in quite the same way, nor will they have the same response to injunctions from the Church. But I would venture to suggest a twofold conviction: we need to be both astute and firm.

We need to be *astute* and wait for the appropriate moment before intervening, since if we move too early, while there still seems to be a perfect uniformity among the members of the community, the community will not be able to hear criticisms as something constructive. Trapped in their own little bubble, they will interpret the least attempt to question things as persecution by the Church, which is tormenting its most faithful children. They are only following their master, they will think. But they will not be dismayed by the prospect of such a fate; on the contrary, this idea will simply reinforce them in thinking that they are on the right path. There is a risk that such an inopportune intervention will result in a strengthening of the notion of enclosure in a way that conceals things from the eyes of those outside the community and protects the life inside.

We need to be *firm* once objective failings come to light. Here, it is indispensable that an authoritative statement should be made, clearly condemning this or that aberrant practice. This will bring comfort to victims, allowing them to find new confidence in their own ability to interpret what is going on and begin to rebuild themselves. Without such a clear pronouncement, it is very difficult for anyone living in a closed environment to believe he may be right, against all the other members of the community, who seem so united. But if a certain aspect [of the community's life] is authoritatively condemned, it is possible that the light offered by this will find its way into souls and minds, so allowing other negative aspects to come to light too. And so a turning point may be reached.

We need to keep in mind that it is not a question of rejecting every aspect of the way the community is currently living its life; there is certainly some good, perhaps a lot of good, but there are also some defects, which can prove to have a very damaging effect on some people. These are the things that have to be identified and eradicated. Often in this situation, healing can only come from outside, from the Church, as Mother and Teacher. Within the community, some may have surrendered their freedom of judgment under pressure of one kind or another, or lost the ability to see clearly as a result of authoritarianism, whether on the part of certain individuals or within the community as a whole, and bad habits may have suffocated the desire for a different sort of life. Only external intervention can reconfigure the life into something that can form free people who are seeking to follow Christ.

A great difficulty arises in that the Church, observing these communities from outside, sees only what people want to show it — most often, the positive things. Such communities appear radiant, young, dynamic, demanding in holiness. In today's world, it is reassuring to know that spiritual places like this exist, and nobody wants to find out that all is not as beautiful as we thought, that this community (which seemed to be a model) is not as good as it would like people to believe. A protective psychological mechanism kicks in, preventing us from accepting the unvarnished reality that is beginning to show itself. This is denial, of course, a common reaction when faced with something that is too much for us to cope with, too brutal, so much that we have difficulty understanding it. It may take a long time for old attitudes to fade away and give us the space we need to accept reality in all its ugliness. So we may tend to soften the facts, look for excuses; truth is too painful, disappointing, we need time to be able to hear it.

But truth demands that steps must follow in terms of sanctions and reform. Those in positions of responsibility may be afraid to press too hard here, for fear of breaking everything and ending up doing more harm than good, so they prevaricate. Is this cowardice? Realistic prudence? Pastoral wisdom?

It is difficult to know if we are always doing the right thing. We need to be careful not to judge people who do not react the way we would. Some people will recall that Jesus recommends that we let the darnel grow in the wheat field, only distinguishing between wheat and darnel later on. This is true at the level of individuals, but if we are thinking of institutions, can we allow a deeply flawed system to go on existing, a system that will lead to some people being crushed? The need sometimes arises for clear thinking and courageous determination, to condemn what is unacceptable and take steps to ensure that no more people will be destroyed by a broken system: clear condemnation [of aberrant behavior], the removal of manipulative people, changes in the leadership of the community, adjustments to the constitutions, and so on.

In some cases where the influence of the founder has been particularly significant, it may be that measures such as these prove insufficient. They will have to be supported by the presence in the very heart of the community (or congregation) of some strong personalities, appointed by the Church, to get a sense of the ethos as it is really lived within the community and to help each person to embrace the changes put into effect. Without this radical step, there is a risk that the defective way of doing things is so ingrained in people's mentality that it will keep drawing people back to the way things were before. They will not be able to disengage from it completely.

When people leave a community that has begun to function in this aberrant way, we often observe that they need many years to re-establish themselves fully. They maintain crooked patterns of behavior, all the old reflexes, for a long time. The same will be true of those who remain in the community, even when it is in the process of reforming itself. How could it be otherwise? A founder has brought them to accept a false value system. They have absorbed this teaching and identified with it. Even if the whole community has come to understand there was something wrong, still the old ways of thinking remain. For example, we may welcome the Church telling us that something is not really working, but in concrete terms, we might go on acting as we did before. Indeed, it can even happen that for some years we really do enter into what the Church is asking, only to find that, little by little, the old instincts return!

The phenomenon of controlling behavior [on the part of such influential people] has far-reaching effects, and the Church must be conscious of this in the way it accompanies communities.

Setting Speech Free

These reflections call for discernment. What is going on at the moment [in a particular context] will have to be evaluated both in terms of its seriousness and its extent. Maybe it is a whole congregation that is affected, or just one community, or a part of the community (for example, the novitiate, if the novice master is the problem).

Once the pathologies have been recognized and identified, remedies arise almost spontaneously. Many of these have been alluded to in previous chapters or flow naturally from them, so there is no need to list them here. Is there a particular order that needs to be respected? Not really, except there are a few things that ought to be given special priority.

The first is restoring freedom of speech, and thus re-establishing the horizontal links that have been severed in the star-shaped structure, so as to allow the community to come to a clear, common view of itself. A community cannot be reformed despite itself; this would amount to reconstructing an identical structure, with changes that are merely cosmetic in nature. If there is a structure in place that is preventing the members of the community from communicating with each other, the most important task must be to get rid of it. In practical terms, this shouldn't really be complicated; the obstacles will only arise at a psychological level. Perhaps it would be good to apply Vittoz's three questions concerning voluntary acts here:

- What do I want?
- Is it possible?
- Am I sincere in wanting it?

If the answer to the first question is not clear, nothing can change.
The second question brings us back to good sense and to wisdom.
The third question is sometimes the most important one. Here is an example that is very relevant when the alarm goes off in the morning:

- What do I want? To get up.
- Is it possible? Yes.
- Am I sincere in wanting it? No.

The fact is that I have no desire to get up, and so I don't really will it. I would like to, if it came without cost. Consequently, I stay in bed. We should note, by the way, the difference between desiring something and willing it. I can will something that I don't desire at all, like undergoing surgery.

Abuses in the Religious Life and the Path to Healing

We can come up against such situations, at least some of the time, in a process of reform. It is good to clarify what is going on, since it doesn't necessarily arise from ill will. If what is going on in a given situation is not made clear, it can become very crippling. Someone may appear to be very enthusiastic about reform yet be a real millstone in practice.

Thinking about these three questions in concrete terms as a community can be a good way of broaching the subject.

Of course, before we get to *What do I want*, we have to analyze the situation, to determine what things are preventing legitimate and truly free communication between community members. The difficulty is that, if this process of reflection is to occur, then there has to be free speech; it is the dilemma of the chicken and the egg! It will be indispensable to have someone from outside, preferably someone neutral, and this person will need to know how to take his time with things. When speech has been stifled for years, it does not become free after a few sessions; there are many fears and conditioned responses to be overcome. Patience and time will do more good than force or anger — provided they are accompanied by perseverance.

At the Service of Truth

As long as a culture of lying prevails, it will be impossible to achieve anything serious, since, though it starts from the head, this culture tends to pervade the whole body. This will be the second priority. Emerging from lies calls for courage, and coming to a better understanding of just how noxious lying is will underpin the effort required to correct what needs correcting. The goal of the following reflection is to provide some assistance in this direction.

White Lies

Whenever we look at the subject of lying, a question immediately springs to mind: Is it sometimes okay to lie? The examples most often advanced come from very real situations: the Gestapo knocks at the door of a member of the resistance and asks him where are the Jews he is hiding. Is he bound to tell the truth? It seems clear the answer is no, but when we look for a way to justify this response, it quickly becomes apparent that it is more difficult than we may have imagined.

St. Augustine addresses the question in two works.[318] He makes the case for a strict answer: it is never permitted to lie. St. Thomas follows him in this: "All lying is thus sinful, as St. Augustine affirms."[319] Fr. Luc-Thomas Somme looks at the question in an article whose title sets the scene well: "The Truth about Lying."[320] He, with others, manages to qualify St. Augustine's rigorous position in serious cases. On this point, almost every author seems to give the same examples: that of the case of people seeking someone out to inflict a great evil upon them, and that of sick people, when others hesitate to tell them the truth about their condition.

We don't need to go into the debate on the first example (which could be interesting for formation), since dysfunctions in the community are not usually about anything so serious; they are more to do with the multiplication (and in particular the justification) of smaller lies, which end up eating away at the people's sense of what the truth is. And on the subject of these small lies, it is worth asking whether they might sometimes be justified, whether it is permissible, for example, to lie "for charity's sake," so as not to cause pain, or trouble a person in danger of death.

THE CIRCUMSTANCES

We must beware, first of all, of adopting a movable principle, which would provide a good answer in some circumstances but not at all in others. Faced with a patient suffering from terminal cancer who will not survive beyond a week, doctors might ask themselves whether they must tell the patient the truth and, if so, to what extent. It is no longer a medical question, as there is no longer any possible treatment. It is an ethical question and, in the final analysis, a religious one. To what extent will the patient be able to accept the reality? Ought they to avoid causing him distress and reassure him instead? These are legitimate questions; they would not be legitimate in the case of a doctor who had just discovered an already advanced cancer in a patient. A doctor in this position

---

[318] The *De Mendacio* of 396, and the *Contra Medacium* of 420.

[319] Thomas Aquinas, *Summa theologiæ*, IIa-IIae, q. 110, a. 3, c.

[320] L.-T. Somme, *La verité du mensonge*, Revue d'éthique et de théologie morale, 2005/HS no. 236, 33–54.

can ask how to inform the patient in as kind a way as possible, but we cannot imagine there would be a doctor who would keep it from the patient "so as not to cause him any distress."

The example of someone close to death comes up regularly in the debate about lying, although the question here is different, since it is not necessarily a matter of telling a lie; it may be a case of applying the principle that some truths are better unsaid. We need discernment to know how much we should say and what might be better left unsaid. Failing to tell a terminally ill patient who was capable of bearing it the news that his death was near would be to rob him of something that belongs to his death, which would be regrettable. But in the case of a different patient, who might be totally panicked by the knowledge, is it really a good thing to tell him? Here it is not a question of lying, just of not saying everything.

But more discernment is needed here, since not saying everything may be a way of tacitly lying, as in the case of the penitent who accuses himself in confession of having stolen a rope. The parish priest, knowing this man, asks him a few questions and discovers that at the end of that rope there was a cow … clearly, not a totally irrelevant detail.

ONE LIE CAN CONCEAL ANOTHER

If a half-truth may, in certain situations, represent a half-lie, one lie may also conceal another, and the most visible lie is not always the most serious. A young sister leaves the community. The prioress announces: *Sister N. has been sent to another house.* She explains to one or two sisters who know the truth: *I'm saying this to avoid causing the community any distress.*

The first assertion, which is clean contrary to the truth, perfectly fulfills the definition of a lie: saying something false, knowing it to be false. Here we have a spoken lie, which can be easily identified.

The second assertion — *I'm saying this to avoid causing the community any distress* — introduces us to something more serious: the justification of a lie. Isn't this assertion just a new lie, only more hidden? Is the intention really not to cause the community distress? This intention is in a sense real. It is like our thief with his rope, since the notion of not wanting to distress the community is not untrue, but is that really all that is going on? Isn't the aim of the lie to hide from the community an embarrassing turn of events that would tarnish the impeccable façade we would like to maintain? In short, is it not the case that the sister is afraid, above all, that the community might begin to ask questions? Since this is unpalatable, a more plausible excuse is found. Or maybe it's not an excuse at all but a sort of denial of reality, leading to unconscious blindness. This second part shows a habitual intention to lie, in the sense of concealing things that the community has a right to know. We are back to the case of the doctor who discovers a tumor in his patient but says nothing about it, *so as not to trouble him*. In this way, what is inconceivable in the doctor's case may actually happen in a community context.

JUSTIFICATION FOR LYING

Everyone is capable of slipping into a lie when caught off guard. As long as we are aware that it is a lie, the evil is not irreparable, because so long as we acknowledge that something bad is an "evil," conversion is still possible and we can ask forgiveness, thereby re-establishing the truth. But as soon as we seek to justify the lie — which basically means no longer considering it to be evil but something good instead — the conscience becomes darkened, and the sense of truth is at risk. This sets off a chain reaction, with one lie leading to another, and once we begin to lie habitually, the boundary of what is considered acceptable is constantly extended; as the saying goes, "He who will steal an egg will steal an ox."[321] The "culture of lying" is now established, and it is considered a normal means to a particular end.

The disputes between Jeremiah and the false prophets offer us a dramatic depiction of this situation. In chapter 28, the prophet Hananiah prophesies:

> Thus says the Lord of hosts, the God of Israel: I have broken the yoke of the king of Babylon. Within two years I will bring back to this place all the vessels of the Lord's house, which Nebuchadnezzar king of Babylon took away from this place and carried to Babylon. (Jer. 28:2–3)

---

[321] Translator's note. In the French, this is *Qui vole un œuf, vole un bœuf.* In the original, the proverb has the advantage that there is only one letter different between the two objects, emphasizing the small step from the one to the other. This seems impossible to render in English.

And He breaks the yoke that Jeremiah had placed on his neck. Jeremiah answers Him on two occasions:

> Amen! May the Lord do so; may the Lord make the words which you have prophesied come true and bring back to this place from Babylon the vessels of the house of the Lord, and all the exiles. (Jer. 28:6)

Jeremiah wanted nothing more than for all of that to happen and did not prophesy misfortune with any joy in his heart. As he bitterly complains to the Lord: "The word of the Lord has become for me a reproach and derision all day long" (Jer. 20:8). But he perceives that Hananiah does not want what is good for the people and that it is only out of self-interest that he tells the people what they want to hear. This is why Jeremiah then says:

> "Listen, Hananiah, the Lord has not sent you, and you have made this people trust in a lie. Therefore thus says the Lord: 'Behold, I will remove you from the face of the earth. This very year you shall die, because you have uttered rebellion against the Lord.'"
>
> In that same year, in the seventh month, the prophet Hananiah died. (Jer. 28:15–17)

Hananiah's lie is trying to reassure the people so that they can carry on their lives as before, whereas Jeremiah does not cease preaching about the need for conversion, without which disaster is certain. Lies intended to conceal the community's failings play the same role. They are like the whitewash that Ezekiel speaks of: "They have misled my people, saying, 'Peace,' when there is no peace; and because, when the people build a wall, these prophets daub it with whitewash" (Ezek. 13:10).[322] The whole book of Jeremiah is shot through with a recurring lament on the part of the Lord: "I have spoken, and you have not listened."[323] Indeed, the whitewashers do all they can to ensure that the people cannot hear Jeremiah's troubling message, and so they bear the responsibility for the disaster according to the words of Ezekiel about the watchman (Ezek. 33:1–9).

Suddenly, we are a long way from the "small" lie, since something as troubling as exile now lurks on the horizon. Is there such a thing, then, as a "small

---

[322] This passage was directly translated from the French to maintain original emphasis.
[323] E.g., Jer. 7:13: "When I spoke to you persistently you did not listen."

lie?" In our example, the law of consequences comes powerfully into effect, because once this lie is told publicly, it becomes essential that the community never discovers the truth. So there is a need for dissimulation, which poisons relationships. And when the truth finally does come out, people's trust will be shaken to the foundations. Why go through all that?

It is so much easier simply to tell the truth. Sister has left; the community will be able to understand this if it is accustomed to being spoken to honestly, if it is accustomed to not being treated like a child. Any community that couldn't cope with the news that someone had left would be worryingly immature.

Lies Destroy Relationships Because They Destroy Trust

Are there such things as small lies that are acceptable because they have no serious consequences? The one kind of lie that people consider acceptable is lying for charity's sake, to avoid causing distress. Saying that love comes before all else [in order to justify lying] is too facile a shortcut here. If our Christian faith does not permit us to lie, it is not because of some divine *diktat*, issued for no reason. We can't develop all the implications of this vast subject here; they can be found in Fr. Luc-Thomas Somme's article. Here, we will look at the question through the lens of the consequences.

I am going to tell a small lie, so as not to cause someone distress. Perhaps the intention is charitable, but the risk is much more serious. Let's suppose that a friend has given me a book, and after reading three pages, I got bored of the book, so much so that I didn't go on reading it. Later on, I meet this friend, who asks whether I liked the book. Because I don't want to hurt him, I tell him I thought it was very interesting. But if this friend discovers later on that I didn't really read it, he will be much more deeply hurt. Why am I so distrustful of him that I would lie to him? I say that he is my friend, but is that true in the final analysis? Can he count on my word? He will have his doubts from now on.

Being truthful, quite simply, is certainly more demanding, but it is also more profitable: *Thanks! I was really touched by your gift and by the fact that you thought about me. I had a flick through and, sorry — I don't want to offend you — but it's not really a subject that interests me, so I didn't get very far.* Of course, that would be a bit unpleasant for the friend, but he would go away with the deeper satisfaction that he has a real relationship and even increased confidence that he can count on what I tell him because it is reliable.

The question would be slightly more delicate if the friend was the one who wrote the book. In this case, sensitivity might demand that I read the book, even if it didn't interest me.

Witnesses of God

The promises God makes to us human beings are so extraordinary that our reason finds it very difficult to believe they are true. When we see what we are, does it seem credible that we might be called to a divine life we can't even imagine? Is it reasonable to commit our whole life to a reality we have never touched? Doubt is always waiting at the door of faith. The young will be prepared to take the risk, particularly when they encounter the witness of older people, who will show them the way. But if, one day, it appears that those who, in the eyes of these young people, bear witness to the truth of God in fact allow themselves to lie, even in little things, the resulting shock will extend far beyond those particular witnesses and may even call into question the truthfulness of God Himself. This shock will be all the more painful where emphasis is placed on the idea that the superior is God's representative and the community has received the high calling to defend in all its purity the unadulterated truth, of which the community itself is thought to be the incarnation. For anyone who has obediently followed this ideal, the collapse may be serious and may take everything with it, including his vocation and maybe even his faith. "If those who call themselves God's representatives lie like this, what respect can we accord to the God they represent?" The caution of the prioress in our example will come back to bite her. She wanted to avoid distressing the community, but the result of her lie creates an even greater distress. This is very like what has happened in the wider Church, where the protective silence, which sought to avoid scandal, has only produced scandals worse than the abuse itself.

Happily, the opposite is also true. Coming back to the truth and accepting the need to regard dysfunctional behaviors in a clear-headed way can restore trust in a new way, if not among those people who have been betrayed too seriously, at least among those who may come after them.

In the course of normal life, religious (particularly the older members of the community) have a particular mission to bear witness to the truth of God, by their words and by their lives. And precisely because the word of God is so incredible, it is of great importance for the young that their witness should be faultless and become flesh in the reality of day-to-day life. If God is Truth, every lie bears witness against our faith.

If a community has managed to hold on to a sense of the truth, can it run the risk of sliding into aberrant behavior? It seems improbable. Consequently, a sense of the truth is an excellent sign of health, and returning to it, if it has been lost, is a very important step.

The Immune System

Like any living thing, a human community contains within itself elements of disintegration. Very soon after death, the body manifests this tendency to corruption, which had been present [within it] since the moment of birth but had been kept in check by the immune system. A community is born, grows, becomes weak, and disappears. Except for the Church itself, no community has received the promise of eternal existence. What help can a religious community seek to ensure it retains its integrity over a lifetime that may be centuries long? A religious community, just like a body, needs a kind of immune system, which has two aspects: the first is institutional, consisting of the rule, canon law, chapters, visitations, councils, and so on. The other is more interior, and we should mention particularly the gifts of the Holy Spirit, then humility, a sense of service, and an attentiveness to those other virtues that resist the natural tendency to egocentricity, which eats away at any social body from within.

THE RULE OF THE INSTITUTE AND THE LAW OF THE CHURCH

The institutional aspect has been discussed by Fr. Loïc-Marie Lebot, O.P., in "Religious Life and Freedom."[324] Looking at the phenomenon of aberrant [community] behavior from the perspective of a canonist, he sees in it, above all, "a serious misunderstanding of the notion of religious vocation, arising from a denial of the rights and freedoms of community members."[325] Taking that in

---

[324] Conférence Monastique de France, *Vie religieuse et liberté, approche canonique, pastorale, spirituelle et psychologique* (Paris: CORREF, 2018).
[325] Ibid., 27.

reverse, this assertion tells us why we should adhere to canon law: to protect the freedom and rights of religious, as legitimately recognized by the Church. Canon 630, quoted above, is a notable example of this. The law also includes prescriptions designed to prevent the superior from becoming an autocrat.

> For me, there are three principal canonical conditions that can allow an institution consciously to avoid sliding into aberrant behavior patterns or attacks on the personal rights of religious: clearly written constitutions that conform to the principles of religious life, institutions that work as envisaged by those constitutions, and effective checks — both internal and external — carried out by the Church.[326]

On the first point, it is important to have "a book of the constitutions that is well put together and easily accessible."[327] Clarity and concision are recommended. A text that is overly precise about every last detail becomes rather heavy and may be a source of rigidity. On the other hand,

> The Proper Law must be as precise as possible in determining the respective competences of the community, the various councils, those who are responsible for different areas of the life, and the superior. Lack of clarity in this area is a source of confusion and an occasion of conflict.[328]

The constitutional documents must establish institutions that together form an organic unity and that are capable of functioning without constant or arbitrary changes: the chapter, the superior, the council, those responsible for formation, the bursar. There must be a system of checks and balances, so that if one day the wrong person ends up in the wrong position, the community will not end up trapped in a situation from which there is no escape.

Concerning the superior, canon 618 was quoted above. Canon 619 is along the same lines:

---

[326] Ibid., 29.

[327] Ibid.

[328] CICLSAL, Instruction *Congregavit nos in unum Christi amor*, of February 2, 1994, no. 51. This text, which is both important and of high quality, deserves to be better known. The number quoted is reused in the same Congregation's Instruction *The service of authority and obedience* of May 11, 2008, no. 20.

Superiors are to devote themselves to their office with diligence. To-gether with the members entrusted to them, they are to strive to build in Christ a fraternal community in which God is sought and loved above all. They are therefore frequently to nourish their members with the food of God's word and lead them to the celebration of the liturgy. They are to be an example to the members in cultivating virtue and in observing the laws and traditions proper to the institute. They are to give the members opportune assistance in their personal needs. They are to be solicitous in caring for and visiting the sick; they are to chide the restless, console the fainthearted, and be patient with all.

Canon 650 § 2 establishes a clear distinction between the superior and the novice director. In a more general sense, the *Code of Canon Law* seeks to avoid a situation where one person holds multiple offices, for reasons that should be obvious; if this happens, there is a greater risk that someone will be controlling everything. In a monastic community, experience shows that things will go well if it rests on the three pillars of abbot, cellarer, and novice master, provided these communicate with one another harmoniously. We might add to that the prior; four pillars are as good as three.

CANONICAL AND APOSTOLIC VISITATIONS

Since no community is totally immune from sickness, it is necessary that the Church exercise a certain vigilance, principally by means of the canonical visita-tions provided for in the rule. The term "canonical visitation" designates a visit from an authority from outside the community: the bishop for communities of diocesan right or the religious superior in other cases. There is both a frater-nal and a juridical aspect to this. The role of the visitation is multifaceted: [to examine] the life of the community, the quality of the liturgy, fidelity to the constitutions and to the spiritual patrimony of the institute, the way the superiors govern the community, formation, the temporal goods of the community, and so on. The visitors must listen to all the members of the community to get a picture of the strong and weak points of the community's life. If a more serious situation demands it, Rome can ask directly for a visitation to be conducted, and this is called an apostolic visitation.

Abuses in the Religious Life and the Path to Healing

Within an order or congregation that has its own system of canonical visitations, if a community is afflicted by some kind of dysfunction, the higher authorities should be able to realize this and act. Canonical visitations never bring about revolutions, and the process may take years. It is also necessary for the visitors to have appropriate powers if their visitation is to be anything more than a "tourist trip," as one sister put it, describing the manifest ineffectiveness of the visitations she had experienced. In cases where the whole body of the institute is called into question, visitations from within the institute will no longer be able to rectify matters. An apostolic visitation will need to be called for, even if this is always a painful experience.

A canonical visitation comes at things from a different angle, which may be best suited to pick up on small failings that have become established but which the community has lost sight of. The fruits of the visitation will depend largely on the way it is conducted and received. Although it should generally be fraternal in character and conducted in a way that shows solicitude for the whole community, it must nonetheless have the necessary powers to respond to situations where things have gone more seriously off the rails. In the Carthusian Order, the visitors have the power, in the most serious cases, to remove the prior. This occurs only rarely,[329] and such a decision would never be taken by visitors acting alone, but the simple fact that they have this power lends real weight to their authority.

For its part, the community can either impede the work of the visitors, actively or passively, or ensure that the visitation is a fruitful experience.

> The community, desiring to ensure that the visitation is a favorable time where God gives His grace, should receive the visitors or commissioners in a spirit of faith, vested as they are with the authority of the general chapter or the Reverend Father. Everyone should be at pains to help them in the fulfillment of their duty. Hence the visitors and the monks should do all in their power to establish a climate of mutual trust.[330]

[329] Except in those cases where the prior himself asks to be relieved of his responsibilities because of age or health.
[330] *Carthusian Statutes*, 32.4.

"A favorable time, where God gives His grace," and not an implicit threat that we have to strive to defend ourselves against. In the end, one question is asked of everybody: is our attitude disposed to conversion, in the spirit of our third vow,[331] or, on the contrary, do we imagine everything is fine and nobody has anything to say to us?

During a visitation, each person has a responsibility, and everyone has to know that a gag order is null and void and might even, in fact, be a strong reason for speaking out. Each member of the community, in his own conscience, needs to discern what he should say, keeping his gaze fixed on the common good.

An apostolic visitation tests whether our trust in the Church is real or not. It will always be a challenge for those called into question in this way, but wasn't it precisely to learn conversion of heart that we entered religious life?

The View from Outside

The immune system is composed not only of active elements but also of elements whose function is to raise the alarm and draw attention. A community's relationship with the view of people outside is one such element [in the religious life]. If a community is living normally, what does it have to hide? Communities need to demonstrate that they can respond calmly when, as inevitably happens, outsiders don't altogether understand them; however, experience shows that this is rarely the case. Families in particular, even though they may suffer a little because of a degree of separation that religious life entails, will often enough accept (sometimes with great generosity) a choice that involves a real cost on their part but which they can see has meaning, so long as the one choosing the religious life is at peace and feels they are both in the right place and at ease in a community they love (despite its limitations) — in short, so long as they are happy.

We should consider it a positive sign when a community feels free to be seen as it really is, without seeking to impose special limits on communication between members of the community and their families. Being told to keep things secret, on the other hand, is a warning sign: what is going so badly that people feel the need to hide it? The whole area of relations with the family ought to be guided

---

[331] In monastic profession, the third vow is that of *conversatio morum*.

by a healthy freedom and a bit of common sense. If this is not the case, we need to start asking questions. *Mutatis mutandis*, the same is true of other relationships with the outside world, in particular confessors, as we discussed above.

AT THE BOUNDARIES OF RELIGIOUS LIFE

The Swiss bishops have emphasized that imbalances of power do not only crop up in relation to ordained ministers, but they can also occur in relation to those who "represent the institutional Church, with its high principles." In this respect, the newer forms of consecrated or "committed" life[332] are just as much in danger of abuse as [more established] religious communities, but are they as well protected? There are fairly new community structures in the Church that have often grown quite rapidly, but have they had the time to put in place the necessary checks and balances and an effective immune system? Some recent examples of serious situations may lead us to doubt this. If an abusive situation is recognized, there is a risk that the local bishop may find he is powerless, especially when the organization in question is international. In the case of a religious congregation or a society of apostolic life, the Roman Congregation can intervene, and it does — regularly. But when a group does not fall under the jurisdiction of that Congregation, who is going to act? It is hard to see the Dicastery for the Laity, Family and Life taking part in this complicated exercise. The statutes, published on May 8, 2018,[333] speak of this in article 7:

> Within the sphere of its competence, the Dicastery accompanies the life and development of the aggregations of the faithful and of lay movements; it then erects those of an international character and approves or recognizes statutes, without prejudice to the competence of the Secretariat of State; it also deals with possible administrative appeals relating to the matters under the jurisdiction of the Dicastery.
>
> Concerning the Secular Third Orders and the associations of consecrated life, it is occupied only with matters relating to their apostolic activity.

[332] This term is used so as to include groups like the Family of Nazareth, where there was a commitment, eventually for life, but no canonical vows.
[333] They came into force on May 13, 2018.

"Administrative appeals" is a bit thin. An association or movement whose statutes have been recognized by the Church acquires from the Church a certain prestige, but this comes with a certain responsibility: that of offering something that truly represents a gospel way of life. Lay people will commit themselves to institutions like these, believing that they are benefitting from the Church's wisdom and the security that that gives them, whereas in practice this wisdom seems limited to granting official recognition to the statutes. That is all well and good, but woefully insufficient in a crisis. The reader will recall that O. Braconnier complained that the Church didn't intervene to ensure that the statutes of the Family of Nazareth were respected.[334] The stories of communities that have now disappeared show that a leader's aberrant behavior can result in catastrophic situations, in the course of which lay people, who have given everything, suddenly find themselves with nothing, left to their own devices, defenseless, without any kind of support. Before the catastrophe takes place, we may know of serious situations where those concerned do not know who to turn to, since the local bishop is too far removed from the situation and does not really know enough about life inside the institute.[335] Most of the time, he will only see what people let him see. There is a gap in the law here that urgently needs sorting out, but this won't be easy since the Church lacks perspective and experience in dealing with difficulties within such movements or associations and, moreover, finds itself in a difficult position, running the risk of being accused of clericalism when it intervenes in structures that are essentially lay. The problem is that these structures represent the Church, and so become its responsibility, since those who commit themselves to them generally imagine they are entering into a Church organization, as we said earlier. Meanwhile, people are suffering and do not know where to turn. We may well fear that nothing will change until a few disasters have occurred.

---

[334] See page 25.

[335] We should observe that this is the major difference between a visitation conducted by the bishop, or his delegate, and one conducted by members of the institute. These latter will be able to understand dysfunctionalities much more easily. On the other hand, this is only an asset if the structure as a whole is healthy and the dysfunctionality is quite localized. If the whole system is affected, only an external visitation (generally an apostolic visitation) will be able to have any effect.

Abuses in the Religious Life and the Path to Healing

"Given the reputation the movement had, none of us dared open our mouth, as we knew that the Church hierarchy would NEVER believe us," writes one witness.[336] There is something quite striking about this *never*.

Formation, Companionship

It goes without saying that the quality of formation, both initial and ongoing, is a key foundation stone for the human and spiritual health of a community, and these days the Church insists upon it.

A spiritual and theological formation that embraces Christian thought through the centuries, in all its breadth and diversity, is a great antidote to uniform thinking.

The formation of those in positions of responsibility will help them realize the dangers that may lie in store and help them to choose the right way forward.

An understanding of the way aberrant behavior works and of its symptoms will prevent people from being overly naïve and will also provide them with a source of personal protection.

> Thanks to the solid formation I had received in my first community, I was able to keep my inner freedom, and did not become a victim of the aberrant behavior or the spiritual abuse. But this framework was in place. Even if it is not a source of great danger for those people who do not become actual victims, this aberrant behavior nevertheless demands an enormous amount of their time and energy, as they have to keep asking themselves the question: Am I crazy or not? Am I wrong or not?

Understanding aberrant behavior and the way it works allows us to call out evil when we see it. Doing this in an appropriate way is a service to the community.

Nor should we forget that the community itself needs to be formed; living together is not something that just happens automatically. We can learn, for example, how to talk about contentious subjects in community, which can help to defuse ticking time bombs before they explode. We can learn how to get the community to participate in decision making without denying legitimate authority. We can learn how to listen, learn how to express ourselves in a truly

---

[336] The capitals are in the original text.

personal way, learn that forgiveness calls for an inner journey that can take quite some time, and so on.

The Riches of the Christian Tradition

There is always more to learn about the mystery of God in His infinite diversity. Our intellect was given to us precisely for this purpose, and the richness of two thousand years of Christian life should be a great help to us. From the letters of St. Ignatius of Antioch to the writings of Mother Teresa of Calcutta or Fr. André Louf, we are offered an immense panorama of spiritual teachings. No two saints are totally alike; each one has incarnated a particular aspect of the unfathomable richness of Christ in his or her life. St. Francis of Assisi is not St. Antony of Egypt; St. Ignatius of Loyola is not like St. Thérèse of the Child Jesus. The Eastern Church is also available to us, in recent authors such as Fr. Matthew the Poor. Discovering this entire universe ought to be a source of enchantment in the first years of the religious life. Theology, too, offers us a world of variety, since the richness of Christ is too great for any one theologian to be able to grasp in its entirety. Generally, different theologians tend to concentrate on different aspects of Christ. A vast expanse opens out before us, stretching from the Fathers of the Church, both East and West, to St. John Paul II and Pope Benedict XVI, from the great Trinitarian and Christological councils to the two Vatican councils.

Nothing is more desirable (we might even say more indispensable) for a religious than a broad knowledge of the history of theology and spirituality. People need this so they can situate their own institute's particular spirituality in its proper place; after all, it didn't emerge from nowhere. Every spirituality, every theology is a facet allowing us to approach the boundless diamond that is God from a particular angle. These different facets are not in competition with one another; rather, they complement one another. A proper understanding of them will help us avoid the temptation to regard the special teaching of our own institute as superior to all the rest. Everyone will be able to see it for what it is; a beautiful facet, but one that is by no means unique and which, in fact, only fully reveals its own beauty when integrated into the whole.

13

An Understated Beauty

We've spoken a lot about sicknesses and a little about the remedies for these; shouldn't we perhaps conclude by speaking a little about health? Health is much more difficult to define — perhaps even impossible — precisely because it is such a rich phenomenon. Situations where aberrant behavior has arisen should not cause us to forget the countless communities that are quietly living out their love for the Lord in the simplicity and weakness of our human condition, in the daily, purifying trials of community life, and in the self-giving for which community life provides an opportunity. Jesus went down to Nazareth without anyone knowing who He was. The vast majority of religious communities share in this hiddenness. Some figures emerge [more prominently], but are these necessarily greater than the others, whom nobody knows about? Everyone has heard about Sr. Emmanuelle and how much she put into her work with the trash collectors of Cairo, with great results. And no doubt the Church needed this flaming torch. But who ever thinks about the thousands of Little Sisters of Jesus (the congregation that Sr. Emmanuelle had thought of joining) who live out the same ideal in places that nobody ever speaks of? The same love is given to the poor in the name of the same Jesus, just with less fame, and that is good. In the thousands of different forms of the religious life, the burdens and difficulties of everyday life notwithstanding,[337] people quietly live out their path

---

[337] We might think of the humor of St. Mark (in Mark 10:30) who promises the hundredfold, "but with persecutions."

toward God in peace and joy, and it is a path whose understated beauty should at least be sketched out.

Religious life will exist for as long as the Church exists, since the call to give oneself totally will always strike the hearts of people that are open to the totality of God's love for us. We are offered holiness; this is the essential call of every Christian, and fundamentally of every human person. Among the different forms of this mysterious love, one possesses the distinguishing feature of being exclusive. It can be experienced in the love of a man and a woman, but it has also found its place in the Church under the form of this love for God that excludes the possibility of experiencing another's life in marriage. "Let anyone accept this who can!" says Jesus (Matt. 19:12).[338] Those who have understood this would not give up this treasure for anything in the world, because for anyone who has received the call, the love of God is so deep that it really deserves the gift of our whole life.

In Praise of Simplicity

Anyone looking for differences between normal communities and those that tend to drift off course will probably not find significant disparities in the virtue or generosity of community members. On the other hand, where aberrant behavior thrives, we will probably find a pronounced appetite for the extraordinary, which is itself fairly characteristic of contemporary society. Jesus of Nazareth is calling us to another way, a way that involves evangelizing human life in all its breadth, a way that allows God to break into the everyday reality of life, which made Paul Verlaine say:

> Humble life, with its dull and facile tasks,
> Is a work of choice, that demands much love.[339]

Jesus practiced this "work of choice" for thirty of His thirty-three years on earth, and it is precisely here that most of those who love Him will find Him. Married life and religious life commit us to a long-term path of fidelity, fidelity that comes about as we accomplish modest tasks, or by the regular participation

---

[338] This passage was directly translated from the French to maintain original emphasis.
[339] From the collection "Sagesse."

in the liturgy, where nothing extraordinary seems to happen. We are men and women who are in it for the long haul.

Above all, we are disciples of Christ, who renounced the glory that was His and strongly rejected the Evil One's temptations to a power that was more visible and sensational. Rereading the temptations that crop up in aberrant communities in the light of the temptations of Jesus in the desert gives food for thought. He could have changed the stones into bread, He could have lived like a prince in the desert, He had the power to do all of that; but as a human being, He had received that power for the service of a particular mission, and He did not want to divert it for His own personal profit. He could have thrown Himself from the top of the Temple to enthrall the crowds; walking on the air wouldn't have been a problem for someone who walked on water. But He didn't want to impress the crowds by being the superficial object of people's fascination; had He done so, the followers He gained would have been like the seed sown on the rocky ground, which dries out before it can grow. What the demon is suggesting seems to be a cheap way of making up the numbers. As for the temptation to power, purchased at the cost of submission to the prince of pride and lies, isn't this what we have encountered in the culture of lies and in pretentions to superiority?

Contemplation of the life of Christ leads us [to follow] in the same direction [as He did], by applying to our everyday lives what Jesus showed us in the desert. Thirty years living in Nazareth, without the Nazarenes even noticing who He was: this means that Jesus didn't do anything extraordinary. With a word, He could have done all the washing for the house or squared off the beams for St. Joseph; He showed that at Cana. He could have justified it by saying He was helping His parents. But He had come for a higher mission than that: the mission of entering fully into our life, just as it is, with all its sweat, fatigue, and suffering. During His public life, He tells those for whom He works miracles over and over again not to say anything about it, so that His miracles are not misinterpreted; they are all signs of this higher reality: the salvation of God that has come into the world. During His public life, He has nowhere to lay His head, even though He could have had a crowd of followers that would have idolized Him. But when the crowd wants to make Him king in a fit of enthusiasm, He withdraws to the mountain, alone (see John 6:14), and the next day, when they seek Him out because He gave them bread, He tells them directly that they haven't understood anything (see John 6:26–27). And when He explains to them the miracle's meaning, this higher understanding is lost on those who simply wanted some earthly bread, and most of them leave Him. He could have enticed them back to Him; a few words or some concessions to their way of seeing things would have been enough. But He had come for the Truth; even if it was too elevated for His listeners, He could not dumb down the Father's gift, simply to hold on to a spurious popularity.

Our life of following Christ can only be understood in the light of Christ Himself and His life. It is characteristic of Him to be hidden, simple, on the same level as the majority of other people. And yet His life contains an unimaginable mystery: the mystery of eternal life, which needs to be protected by poverty and humility. St. Francis of Assisi, gripped with love for the poor and humble Christ, is a great teacher for us in this. So is St. Paul, when He tells us that we carry this treasure in earthen vessels (2 Cor. 4:7). Extraordinary things don't really fit well with religious life. True, they happen sometimes, but just as is true in the life of Jesus, they need to keep to their role of being signs of something more. Indeed, the great sign in the life of Jesus is His humanity, a testimony of the Father's infinite love; the most extraordinary thing in the life of the Incarnate Word is that His life is so ordinary, so human; who could have imagined such love on the part of our Creator?

Conversion of heart is the work of a goldsmith; it happens through patience, the divine patience that accompanies us through our resistance, day after day, year after year. The horizons of our inner world surpass all our understanding, not because they are extraordinary but because of the greatness they bestow on the narrow limitations of our human life. They do not destroy our human life, just as the divinity of Jesus remained at peace in the limitations of His human body. His divinity doesn't replace what is ordinary with what is extraordinary; rather, it leads us to discover to what extent the divine and extraordinary inhabit our ordinary human existence, without needing to change it externally. The din of human greatness obscures this vision, and anyone who seeks God will generally make their own the saying: *If we want a happy life, let us live a hidden life.*[340]

---

[340] The last section of the poem *Le grillon* of H.-P. Claris de Florian (1755–1794).

"You have passed through death, and your life is hidden with Christ in God," St. Paul says, with greater depth (Col. 3:3).[341] Such is His greatness, a greatness that is present at all times, that a living faith can perceive in every encounter, in every action, and in every silence too. The secret love that the soul in love with God experiences in the depths of the heart leaves all that glitters in the world far behind in the distance.

> What benefits and divine exultation the silence and solitude of the desert hold in store for those who love it, only those who have experienced it can know. For here strong men can enter into themselves and remain there as much as they like, diligently cultivating the seeds of virtue, and eating the fruits of Paradise with joy. Here, they can acquire the eye that wounds the Bridegroom with love by the clearness of its gaze, and whose purity allows them to see God Himself. Here they can observe a busy leisure, and rest in quiet activity. Here also, God crowns His athletes for their stern struggle with the hoped-for reward: a peace unknown to the world, and joy in the Holy Spirit.[342]

These words of St. Bruno, shot through with scriptural allusions, are speaking of the solitary contemplative life, but each form of religious life can adapt them to its own concrete reality, knowing that God is offering to it this "peace unknown to the world, and joy in the Holy Spirit."

The Fruits of the Spirit

The fruits of the Spirit that St. Paul lists in the letter to the Galatians are without a doubt the best proofs of the health of a community and its members. "Love, joy, peace, patience, kindness, goodness, faithfulness, gentleness, self-control" (Gal. 5:22–23).

We spoke above about the connectedness of the different virtues. We can observe that they often seem to come in pairs, even if these associations are rather free. One virtue on its own is perhaps more dubious than a virtue that is linked with another, that completes it or serves as a counterbalance.

---

[341] This passage was directly translated from the French to maintain original emphasis.
[342] St. Bruno, Letter to Raoul le Verd, 6. Online at www.chartreux.org.

Abuses in the Religious Life and the Path to Healing

Joy and peace: when this fragrance is found in a community, it is on the right path. Joy alone is not enough, at least external joy, which can be the fruit of a kind of self-control and a carefully maintained appearance. We need, then, to pay attention to the quality of this joy, as well as its depth. Peace is more spontaneously true. There are different degrees of depth to this too, and a real peace can go hand in hand with great trials.

Love and patience: we should note that it is easier to fabricate love than patience. Patient love, with its way of showing respect to people, is thus a very good sign.

Goodness and kindness: here again are tangible signs of God's action. These signs are more at the level of individual persons than of whole communities, for someone who suffers in an unhealthy environment can demonstrate great riches of goodness, like Fr. Kolbe in the concentration camp. But goodness and gentleness in superiors remains an excellent gauge of the quality of a community's life because they radiate naturally upon the whole community.

Didn't Jesus even make a beatitude out of gentleness? But it is good for gentleness to be linked to uprightness, for example. Another inseparable pair.

These virtues harmonize naturally with one another. But it can also sometimes be more a question of the contrasts between them. Broadly speaking, life is made up of different balances, without which it cannot continue to exist. The slightest gesture we make sets in motion two sets of muscles that work against each other, the one having some control over the other. Without this, our gestures would be totally erratic. In *The Need for Roots*, Simone Weil describes, in a loose way, these contrasts between the different *needs of the soul:* order and freedom, obedience and responsibility, equality and difference, as well as hierarchy, honor, and chastisement, safety and risk, private property and common property. Almost all social and political disorder comes from one of these elements becoming unbalanced with respect to another. It could be very profitable to apply this reflection to the religious life.

HUMILITY AND TRUTH

These two virtues, which go together, deserve special mention. Having a sense of the truth is an incomparable quality for anyone but especially for superiors. It can hardly ever blossom outside the fertile ground of humility. The capacity of everyone (but especially superiors) to say, "Yes, we got it wrong; we are in error" and to take the necessary steps to get out of [the unfortunate situation] is an excellent sign of health. This last point should be emphasized because we have only truly recognized error when we have decided to make our way out of it. Until we have arrived at that point, there is really only a truth that we reluctantly accept, but it doesn't affect us at depth.

This truth we are talking about is not a dogmatic truth but a truth of everyday life, which popular wisdom has summed up in a dictum: *calling a spade a spade*. This means that if a sister has decided to leave the community, we explain to the community that the sister has decided to leave.

This everyday truth — which makes us able to trust what people say (precisely because we know that it is true), which allows us to say we have done something stupid when we have done something stupid, and also to say that we have had success when we have had success (there is nothing true about false humility) — this truth, made up of many smaller everyday truths, provides us with fertile ground, where trust and true relationships between all members of the community can flourish, whatever their responsibilities or tasks. This trust is worth its weight in gold. It creates unity among all in the community, a solid unity that is founded on rock, the rock of the place where one's word is one's bond; it is solid because it is true.

Fervor and Freedom

A fervent community attracts people. Don't we all want to become fervent? Yet fervor on its own is not a sign of health. It only becomes one when it is associated with a real inner freedom. Outside the liturgy (which is more strictly regulated), prayer is the soul's freedom. Remember the glider, free from everything, carried by the wind, without any need for effort, but not without skill. The freedom to choose one's own inner path, and thus one's own guide (at least after the years of formation, which are usually a bit more well defined) [is important]. Formators must lead people to freedom. They need to remember that one day they will have to release the glider.

As for spiritual fathers, one of their tasks is to free the soul from the bonds that hold it back, so that the fervor of its love for God can be set free in its own personal form, which is unlike anyone else's.

Abuses in the Religious Life and the Path to Healing

Anyone who is being accompanied needs to feel that he is respected with regard to the spiritual path that he finds attractive and as a person. The confidentiality of what he shares also needs to be respected.

Trust

The experience of trust in a community — of the religious toward their superiors but in particular of the superiors toward their religious — radiates health and allows each person to give of his best. Trust is diametrically opposed to control. Trust says to the other person: *you can do it*. And perhaps even more: *I want you to be able to show that you can do it*. Just as total control is anxious when it sees someone emerging that could overshadow the leader's prestige, so trust desires to see people's talents blossom. And if someone should end up showing that they are worthy to be the superior, isn't that great news? Trust makes people grow, helps them to find a healthy independence, rejoices to see that they are more and more in control of their lives. Have things been done not quite as the superior might have wanted? Well, that is a little renunciation that must be accepted, which will very much be compensated for (if the superior knows how to see it) by the good that has been done to the person who was the recipient of his trust. Initiative — even if it is bad — is much better than passivity. For the superior's part, this does not mean letting people muddle on, without really being interested in what they are doing but rather encouraging and supporting initiatives, helping when necessary (but not more than necessary!), which is an art in itself.

Trust gives a certain lightness to the exercise of authority, because authority is not jealously guarded but distributed, as far as possible. It helps it to remain authority *for* other people and not *over* other people.

Fraternal Love

Why put the thing that should occupy the first place last? Because "it is not those who say to me, 'Lord, Lord,' who will enter the Kingdom of Heaven, but those who do the will of my Father, who is in Heaven" (Matt. 6:21).[343] We can go on talking forever about freedom, charity, and fraternal love, but concrete

---

[343] This passage was directly translated from the French to maintain original emphasis.

reality sometimes reveals something quite different. Fraternal love is proven on the ground, and everything we have said up to now can, for the most part, be considered as concrete proof of a lived experience of fraternal love.

"A righteous man has regard for the life of his beast, but the mercy of the wicked is cruel" (Prov. 12:10). This saying from Proverbs tells us everything we need to know. Situations where a community's behavior has become aberrant are sources of suffering that can sometimes be strangely ignored. When superiors are aware of the difficulties, sufferings, and needs of the people in their communities, if they are taking care to supply a remedy for these insofar as they can — at least by offering the comfort that comes from a real understanding of these problems — an authentic charity radiates over the community members themselves, who will learn quite spontaneously to act in the same way.

The ability to rejoice at the good of other people is one of the most beautiful signs of a fraternal love that is real and deep, a sign that cannot usually be fabricated. Although it is above all a testimony to the spiritual quality of an individual person, it can also become an atmosphere in the community, if it is shared enough.

One abbot said: "Whenever two monks are talking together, within five minutes they are bad-mouthing someone." This little perversity of human nature shows that this is a long task. Those who give themselves to it will be the first to benefit from it, since their own inner light will become all the brighter, and all those around will benefit. It is so nice to live with someone who never says a bad word about other people.

Happiness

"I am happy." Which superior would not rejoice to hear one of his monks says these three words? They are one of the best signs of spiritual health, as long as they are true and not just an empty form of words, of course (but this is easy to pick up on). We might also say: as long as the source of this happiness is well and truly rooted in one's vocation and not in various compensations. A monk who is happy in his vocation, and who shows it by being faithful to it with great joy (even in the midst of trials) — what a joy this is, especially if his happiness spreads to others.

Abuses in the Religious Life and the Path to Healing

These three words will carry more weight if they come after many years in the religious life. And yet the formator who hears them at the end of the period of formation can say to themselves: *Mission accomplished.* There will be all the more reason when we hear them on the lips of an old monk. And, thanks be to God, that is not as rare an occurrence as all that.

Conclusion

A passionate text, which discretion does not allow us to cite here, demonstrates how a tree that has been battered but not totally uprooted can come back to life. The shattered trunk and branches remain on the ground, since the past suffering is not erased and the memory of the trauma remains very much alive, but the love of God is stronger than all of that. What the person was hoping for when he entered religious life, what seemed to have been lost forever at the moment when it became necessary to leave the life in difficult (or even dramatic) circumstances, when God seemed far off, absent, or lost, springs back to life years later with a new shoot. It will be different from the first experience forevermore, but it can still lead, by means of a mysterious shortcut, to closeness with God, a closeness once dreamed of, seemingly wrecked, but found at last where it was least expected.

> Re-found, or found for the first time? I wonder. For fourteen years I have felt drawn by God, I have wanted to pray, to love Him, to live for Him, but what I am experiencing now is so, so different.
>
> I really *believe* that He is there; that He hears me, and so on. The psalms I used to love to sing are becoming a living word for me. Despite the difficulties, the loneliness, and sometimes the sadness, I really believe, deep down, that I can say I am happy, because I have found him … or rather, the other way around.

We thought it was a fir tree, but behold, from the same stump grows a cedar. This is the mystery of [dark] paths marked by failure and suffering, on which grace can cause light to spring forth. The religious life is not a goal; it is merely a means. The goal is a person, Jesus Christ, or better, three divine Persons who are One. What was not granted in the religious life may be granted some other way; nothing will be lost. The face of God, discovered at the end of the journey, will be different, and probably more beautiful, more profound, more radiant, above all truer, than the one that might have been discovered by the normal route. Even the religious life has its illusions, but now these will all have been swept away. We would like to think that Jesus and His Spirit, observing such journeys, might say: *Mission accomplished.*

But we mustn't dream too much. Not all journeys involving abuse end in such an encounter, and the consequences linger on. Just because a disabled person can lead a very beautiful life doesn't take away the difficulties of disability. Msgr. Ravel, who has been bishop for the armed forces, is well acquainted with the permanent effects of certain forms of violence, which can even get worse over time rather than better:

> Fifty years after the events, their emotional force is still intact, perhaps even more intense. As we get older, our physical and psychological strength diminishes, and with them our ability to keep those acts at one remove from our life. The consequences of the trauma resurface, with no inner defense. They come back up from the cellar where we had tried to keep them contained, to occupy a place on the upper floors, where normal life goes on. This is why we talk of the permanent nature of such crimes.

It may therefore be really painful for a victim when people encourage them to move on. And yet we may be hopeful for every victim, even for those who have lost, or seem to have lost, their faith. In every case of abuse, we can say the victim has rejected something evil, not something good. They have not rejected the face of God, only a mask. God alone is the judge; He alone knows people's hearts.

"Lord, you have made us for yourself, and our heart remains restless until it finds its rest in you." This call, which You address to everyone because You created everyone in Your image, You address in a particular way to those whom You are inviting to a special communion with You. How is it that those whose job it is to guide them can be so imperfect, and in certain cases so dishonest? We know that You take care of everyone because they all belong to You, but how difficult it can be, sometimes, to understand or even accept things that happen in the course of our lives.

For years, You have been expelling from Your Temple the cattle, the sheep, and the money changers. Your whip inflicts pain on Your Church, humiliated as it has been, and some of its children abandon it. Take care of them, because You understand them, but do not stop until all that needs to be thrown out is gone, and help us to cleanse what remains, so that Your Church may once more find the beauty it has lost. Give us the courage to speak when we need to, regardless of the consequences. And if we need shaking up a little — or even a lot — because we are too timid, then do it, so that others do not suffer. Give us the courage never to accept what is unacceptable and not to close our eyes and ears when You are suffering, lest we one day hear You say: *I am Jesus, whom you allowed to be abused, while you said nothing.* The deep night of guilty silence is drawing to its close, and dawn is approaching; help us not to give up, because there is still an enormous amount of work, still so much listening to be done, so many wounds to be bandaged, so much that still needs protecting. Make us Good Samaritans for those who have been wounded by religious life.

What will You do with those whose sufferings only You know about? In Your goodness, hold on to their desire, their longing to love You, their gift of themselves, like a treasure. Have You not Yourself transformed it and made it even more beautiful through their years of suffering? We would like them to be able to see You at work in this life. It won't always be possible, but what does that matter? As for those who have apparently abandoned You, will it not be enough for them simply to cry out, *It's You!* on the day they meet You face to face? You who continued all along to dwell silently within them, because You could not forget that day when they chose to give You their life.

This is a crucial moment. Help us not to fail or do only half the job. We have grave responsibilities for those who still choose to join us, without hesitation, despite all they have heard, because it is You that they seek. Keep us humble, so that our ancient pride, buried under the rubble, never grows back; and let us not cause them any harm.

Abuses in the Religious Life and the Path to Healing

We love You, Lord, because You have loved us so much. Do not allow our searching for Your face to be twisted into a search for ourselves. Guide us all, the young, the old, superiors, the sick; stay with us on the path of poverty and hope. Amen; come, Lord Jesus.

Appendix

Testimony of a Young Woman
Attracted by the Religious Life

It is difficult to understand abuse when one has never met a survivor. There are many who say that an encounter with such a person has opened their eyes. For those who have not had the opportunity to do this, it seems important to quote a witness testimony, which illustrates in a most vivid way the formidable manner in which abuse mechanisms work and the difficulty that people often have later in making others recognize what they have experienced. The following text may seem hard, but it is only an attempt to put into words a reality that is even more terrible.

A silent cry in the night of faith,
The shut-in screams of a woman,
And yet...
I was sixteen years old when I met you all,
And without you, I don't think I would have been able
to get up again.
A painful shipwreck on the shores of my childhood,
Your light has given meaning back to my existence.

I've received from you the most precious pearls of light.

Why cast them before swine?
Why betray so great a Gift
And why, afterward, allow silence and shame to reign?

Abuses in the Religious Life and the Path to Healing

You have taught me to love the truth,
To draw from there the source of my freedom.
Today, allow me to be your disciple, all the way to the end.
I do not want, through my silence, to be an accomplice of the thing that
destroys you from the inside, coming right from the roots.

Here is how it happened with me:

"Do you want to offer yourself? That is a very great thing. I had already
understood in prayer that the contemplative life was made for you."

"The contemplative life? Wow!"

"Yes, I think that God has chosen you for the royal road, that of the religious
life, the life that gives the greatest happiness. You'll see, you will go from peak
to peak, to the highest peaks.

"It is good for you now to choose a spiritual father. It is a bond of loyalty
like no other that is made with a priest who is particularly close to you, so that
he can guide you on your way, with the gentle firmness of a father."

"There is only you that I am really close to, Father. You have been a real
father to me for the last two years."

"Very good. Let me guide you then. Make sure you enter into a real docility
to the Holy Spirit, so you can allow yourself to be transformed into a daughter
of light. Begin right now to make your life a life of adoration, so that you can
place everything in God's hands. We'll see each other once a week, and you will
come to the Mass that I celebrate every morning in the chapel."

"Yes, Father; thank you, Father."

I was already soaring through the air.

In the days that followed, my spiritual father began to reveal to me secrets
in the spirit of St. John, which plunged us into the closest friendship with God.

"When two contemplative souls are united in a bond of love, of friendship, they experience the greatest love that can be experienced on earth. It is
greater than the love between spouses, whose love is only natural. The love
between two people who give their all in the religious life is a divine love. In
the context of that love, one can experience a certain tenderness. The founder
has written some very beautiful texts about this. We are united in a secret.
It is not good to share it, because other people won't understand. It is a gift

of God, a most exquisite gift," he said to me, taking me by the hand, with incredible tenderness.

> I have never been treated so gently by a man.
> I am bowled over. All shaken up.
> Everything [we live] is experienced in God.
> Taste of His Goodness and be thankful.

Our bond becomes stronger with each day. Father takes me to see a place that is particularly dear to him. He takes me in his arms. He begins to speak to me about himself, sharing confidences with me. He takes me home, then stays for a meal. Then — the supreme privilege — he invites me to be present at Mass, just me and him.

Little by little, he becomes the center of my life. I am fulfilled by the bond between us. I just can't understand why this man, who is so busy and held in such great esteem, can give all this time to little me. I feel deeply valued. Because I have reached the depths, God is bestowing upon me the extraordinary grace of reaching the peaks in an instant!

I begin to imagine that it is too good to be true. Ah! If only I had understood how true that intuition was!

He asks me to do things. I realize that I am ready to accept anything he might ask of me, and even more. So I give over an afternoon to sorting files for him. That day, he comes really close to me, kisses my cheek, then approaches to kiss me on the mouth. I refuse.

He tells me that this rejection will be difficult for him.

Everything in my head is all mixed up. The different truths are colliding with one another. The knots tighten with all the effort I am putting in to untying them. Then nothing works any more. As though, all of a sudden, I had become stupid. The system crashes.

> What is impossible cannot be. It can't. Nothing happened.
> Nothing.
> And I come back to see him. Regularly.
> He holds in his hands my mind, my heart, my soul, my spirit, and my
> body.

Abuses in the Religious Life and the Path to Healing

Again and again, he takes my hands, which I draw back too timidly, to slide them under his habit, then onto his buttocks. He strokes himself.

"We should talk, Father."

He whispers in my ear: "No. Not us. We don't need words anymore."

"But I don't know if I want to ..."

"Shh! In the love of friendship, we have the same desires."

All the founder's teachings. Truth. Who am I to resist? I must want it. Docility. Letting oneself be guided by something bigger than oneself, in a kind of dependence that sets one free. Not becoming critical; that would be doing the work of the Evil One, who wants to divide people; love surpasses the understanding. We don't need anything other than the founder's teaching; everything comes from his mouth.

One day, when I am speaking to my spiritual father about a young man who loves me with a beautiful love, saying that I think I am falling in love with him, he warns me off. I am being tempted. This human relationship is maybe a sort of springboard that I need at the moment to lead me to Heaven, but that's all it is. According to my spiritual father, I have to tell this man, gently but firmly, to keep his distance from me, so as not to get in the way of God's plan for me.

I become an oblate. On my own, without my friends or family, who just can't understand all this fanaticism.

Shortly after the oblation ceremony, I start to have to strip more and more; and then all the things I had to do with his genitals.

"What about chastity?"

"You haven't understood yet, then? The love of friendship demands to be made flesh, to be demonstrated by actions. As long as there is no penetration, the spirit of virginity remains intact. Don't worry. Trust me. The founder knows. He knows how much I have suffered and still suffer because of celibacy. You are allowing me to live my priestly life in happiness and sanctity. I owe something of all my apostolic fruitfulness to our relationship!"

"But there are other girls that you do these things with, aren't there?"

"Don't tell me you have been gripped by the spirit of jealousy?!"

One day, I ask him all the same to reassure me that there is no sin in what we are doing. He answers:

"Haven't you noticed how I celebrate Mass just after? Do you know that everything is forgiven us in the Mass? I wash my hands of all sin before I touch the Body of Christ. And you know very well that the sins of the flesh are not very serious in God's eyes. It is the sins of the spirit that wound our Lord. Our love is pure because it is lived in God. Read the Gospel again: Jesus loved the prostitute Mary Magdalene in particular, precisely because she can receive His forgiveness fully."

My holiness, what am I saying, my *raison d'être* depends on my ability to allow myself to be prostituted by my spiritual father. The system crashes.

It has taken me fifteen years to sort out this crashing of the system. Fifteen years to accept the pain of recognizing that this person — once a hero in my life — was actually a very sick man. To understand, also, that it hadn't been a case of stupidity on my part but of manipulation, of control, of brainwashing. Even today, more than a quarter of a century later, I am sometimes plunged back into the nightmare, and I feel even more keenly the depth of the betrayal. Other young girls from my time are still held under his sway.

Fifteen years to understand the rage of Jesus, when He was chasing the people selling things out of the Temple, shouting: "Do not make my Father's house into a marketplace!" Then He says that even if people destroy this Temple, He can build it up again in three days, because He is speaking of the temple of *His body*, adding later, through the mouth of St. Paul: "Your body is the Temple of the Holy Spirit." [The body] is thus the primary sacred space in our lives. It is not just our casing; it is the heart of our being. Respect for God begins with respect for the body.

A corrupt priest. When love is transformed insidiously into a relationship of power, without the person who is being destroyed even knowing about it. When the total gift [of self] becomes an open door to being held in someone's sway, by a narcissistic need that is blind and insatiable. When secrecy is used to entomb a body that is still all too alive. He squashed the flower that was my body, a flower that had scarcely begun to open, causing it to wither before it even had a chance. And my heart became smaller because of mistrust; it anesthetized itself so as not to feel much anymore. Sexual abuse is like invisible murder.

Why wait until girls are eighteen, and why avoid penetration, unless it is to try to slip through loopholes in the law, and that alone? Many of the people in

Abuses in the Religious Life and the Path to Healing

the community are healthy, no doubt. I had many significant and real friendships there. But abuse, unfortunately, has very great ramifications. Because [the unhealthy sap] had already reached the root, and from there it had flowed into the whole of the rest of the tree.

Most victims are convinced that they are doing the right thing by not speaking out. After all, we are asked to forgive unfailingly, and to be totally discrete, supposedly so as to live in the spirit of St. John. Our rule of life requires us to keep all the business of the community confidential. We are given to understand that priests, by their ordination, are for all eternity above the common level of mortals. He has been renewed in Jesus in his very being. In other words, he is already like Jesus. He has His thoughts, His words, His behavior. And it is drummed into us that the community is above the rest of the Church because the deepest mysteries have been committed to the community, and to it alone.

Other victims shut themselves away in panic. A third sort have come to understand that by fighting, they end up suffering even more than they would by simply trying to live with the physical and psychological damage that they already bear within themselves. "Don't add evil to evil!" And in the meantime, the tree continues to rot from the inside, sweeping still more victims along with it. Not more than a few weeks ago, if that, a young girl ended up in the hands of a major predator, who had been at it for the last twenty years. But the parents just want to move on; it's too difficult for their daughter and for them. They don't know what they are doing, and yet, at the same time, it is so easy to understand it.

When someone decides to speak out, the different forms of pressure can be suffocating. At times, they plunged me into a distress I had never before known. They made use, by turns, of:

- Time; they pray and discern until the victim is exhausted.
- The totally hypocritical faking of a feeling of horror, of understanding, of compassion.
- Contrition and asking forgiveness (so as to be able to have peace [themselves], and then get on with their lives).
- If the victim carries on complaining, there is relativizing and doubt.
- Then the inducement of guilty feelings. "How can you want to do such harm to the community, and the whole Church?" or "You are doing the devil's work of dividing people!"

• Lastly, threats, or perverse thinking: "He didn't rape you, to the best of my knowledge! So there must have been some failing on your part. Have you asked his forgiveness for that?"
• And when it's not manipulation, it's fear: "If I do anything, they will finish me off."

If the victim has the extraordinary courage needed to go and speak to bishops (and so to betray her community), she is stunned to find things are no better here. And if one of them does stand up to tell it like it is and condemn [the behavior], the Vatican settles matters, in my own case at least, where my abuser's first victim had dared to go to Rome twenty years previously.

In other words, the only power victims have is to complain in the civil courts, before the statute of limitations sets in. But all the indoctrination that has come before is so extensive that they basically can't do it. For too long, many years even, they remain convinced that, if they went forward with it, they would be entering into a pact with the devil, which would make them real monsters. In this way, the infernal spiral of perversity closes in on their annihilation.

About the Author

Dom Dysmas (Michel) de Lassus entered the Carthusians when he was twenty years old and has resided at the Grande Chartreuse since then. He served as master of novices until 2012 and as prior of the Charterhouse of Portes from that time to the present. In 2014, he was elected superior general of the Carthusians, the sixty-fourth successor to St. Bruno.

Sophia Institute

Sophia Institute is a nonprofit institution that seeks to nurture the spiritual, moral, and cultural life of souls and to spread the gospel of Christ in conformity with the authentic teachings of the Roman Catholic Church.

Sophia Institute Press fulfills this mission by offering translations, reprints, and new publications that afford readers a rich source of the enduring wisdom of mankind.

Sophia Institute also operates the popular online resource CatholicExchange.com. *Catholic Exchange* provides world news from a Catholic perspective as well as daily devotionals and articles that will help readers to grow in holiness and live a life consistent with the teachings of the Church.

In 2013, Sophia Institute launched Sophia Institute for Teachers to renew and rebuild Catholic culture through service to Catholic education. With the goal of nurturing the spiritual, moral, and cultural life of souls, and an abiding respect for the role and work of teachers, we strive to provide materials and programs that are at once enlightening to the mind and ennobling to the heart; faithful and complete, as well as useful and practical.

Sophia Institute gratefully recognizes the Solidarity Association for preserving and encouraging the growth of our apostolate over the course of many years. Without their generous and timely support, this book would not be in your hands.

www.SophiaInstitute.com
www.CatholicExchange.com
www.SophiaInstituteforTeachers.org

Sophia Institute Press is a registered trademark of Sophia Institute.
Sophia Institute is a tax-exempt institution as defined by the
Internal Revenue Code, Section 501(c)(3). Tax ID 22-2548708.